tion Data

omed WWII mission to save

ndex.

915–1944. 2. World
rican. 3. World War,
ilots, Military—United
—Biography. 6. World War,

                    2014034776

LOST DESTINY
Copyright © Alan Axelrod, 2015.
All rights reserved.

First published in 2015 by PALGRAVE M*
in the United States—a division of St. Mar*
Avenue, New York, NY 10010.

Palgrave® and Macmillan® are registered
States, the United Kingdom, Europe and o*

ISBN: 978-1-137-27904-0

Library of Congress Cataloging-in-Publica*

Axelrod, Alan, 1952-
    Lost destiny : Joe Kennedy Jr. and the d*
London / Alan Axelrod.
        pages   cm
    Includes bibliographical references and *
    ISBN 978-1-137-27904-0 (alk. paper)
    1. Kennedy, Joseph P. (Joseph Patrick), *
War, 1939–1945—Aerial operations, Ame*
1939–1945—Campaigns—France. 4. Air
States—Biography. 5. United States. Navy*
1939–1945—Biography. I. Title.
E843.K44A94   2015
940.54'4973—dc23

Design by Letra Libre, Inc.

First edition: May 2015

10 9 8 7 6 5 4 3 2 1

Printed in the United States of America.

For Anita and Ian

CONTENTS

PROLOGUE   1
TWO VIEWS FROM LONDON

CHAPTER 1   35
CHOSEN SON

CHAPTER 2   71
MOST DANGEROUS

CHAPTER 3   83
THE BITTER FRUIT OF PEENEMÜNDE

CHAPTER 4   103
NEVER SO LUCKY AGAIN

CHAPTER 5   123
WAR-WEARY

CHAPTER 6   145
FOGGED IN

CHAPTER 7   181
THE DRONES OF AUGUST

CHAPTER 8   219
A BASKETFUL OF RATTLESNAKES

CHAPTER 9   251
"I DON'T WANT TO HAVE TO
TELL HIM THE TRUTH"

Notes   271
Index   285

PROLOGUE

TWO VIEWS FROM LONDON

A BIRDCAGE, STILL HANGING IN A WINDOW
WITH A LITTLE DEAD CANARY IN IT

Everyone knew—the world knew, the Germans certainly knew—that four in the afternoon was teatime in London and throughout England. At almost precisely that hour, on September 7, 1940, 348 Luftwaffe bombers escorted by 617 fighters began raining bombs on London. They left at six—the end of teatime—having reduced a portion of the British capital to rubble and flame.

The fires were of great tactical significance for the raid: Two hours later, at about eight, a second wave of bombers swept in, guided by flame through the deepening autumn dark. This part of the raid lasted until 4:30 on the morning of September 8. As daylight returned, Doris Louisa Scott emerged from a shelter in an East London park. She made her way to her house—"those all around were bomb blasted, and I saw this woman cleaning the front doorstep of her demolished house as if it were business as usual."[1]

This was day one of what Londoners would call the Blitz, short for *Blitzkrieg*, a German compound word meaning "lightning war." For the next fifty-seven days, daily or nightly or both, London was bombed.

During the rest of 1940 and through the spring of 1941, London and other cities—most horrifically Coventry, on November 14, 1940— would be pounded sporadically. In some families, parents responded by sending their children away, either into the English countryside or abroad, across the Atlantic, far from England. This wasn't necessarily safe. That September, a Welsh lad named Colin Ryder-Richardson was put aboard the British-flagged City Line Ltd. steamer *City of Benares,* bound for New York. Four days after leaving Liverpool, the ship was torpedoed in the middle of the night.

> There was a loud bang, a very loud bang, and almost immediately a smell of, presumably cordite—it was an unmistakable smell. . . . I was in my pyjamas—and I hadn't got my lifejacket, but I immediately put it on as I got out of bed. I put on my slippers. . . . There was a Force 10 gale. The ship's nurse held my hand and got me on to a lifeboat. It was freezing cold and the boat was waterlogged. I clung to the nurse, then as the night went on, lots of people were dying. This man on the boat gently suggested to me that I should release the ship's nurse, as in his view she was dead . . . [but] I didn't really want to let go of her because I felt that I would then lose whatever resource that I had in my arms.[2]

Day after day, night after night, the bombs fell. December 29, 1940, "was a night," American war correspondent Ernie Pyle reported,

> when London was ringed and stabbed with fire. . . . Flames seemed to whip hundreds of feet into the air. Pinkish-white smoke ballooned upward in a great cloud, and out of this cloud there gradually took shape—so faintly at first that we weren't sure we saw correctly—the gigantic dome of St. Paul's Cathedral. St. Paul's was surrounded by fire, but it came through. It stood there in its enormous proportions— growing slowly clearer and clearer, the way objects take shape at dawn. It was like a picture of some miraculous figure that appears before peace-hungry soldiers on a battlefield.[3]

Journalist Pyle found a "monstrous loveliness" in his view of London, "stabbed with great fires, shaken by explosions, its dark regions along the Thames sparkling with the pin points of white-hot bombs, all of it roofed over with a ceiling of pink that held bursting shells, balloons, flares and the grind of vicious engines."[4]

The Londoners Pyle encountered were stoic and heroic. Bad as the "St. Paul's Blitz" was, even worse was to come. May 10, 1941, Ellen Harris, a Reuters reporter in the Houses of Parliament, recalled, "was the night that London was set afire." German bombers dropped a combination of high-explosive and incendiary bombs, which created massive firestorms throughout entire stretches of the city. Harris emerged from a shelter the next morning and picked her way over the smoldering rubble to get home and change her clothes. Along the way, a middle-aged man stopped her.

"What are we going to do?" he asked her. "We can't go on like this. We've got to seek peace." He was practically in tears.

"Do you realize," Harris asked him, "that you're playing right into Hitler's hands? This is just what he's setting out to do. If he can do this to you, to get you into this state, and you start on me, and I join in—and go up the road and tell somebody and you do the same to somebody else—now, you'd get people in the state of mind and their morale goes. What you've got to do is remember what I'm telling myself—this is my war effort. And this is your war effort. Buck up. . . . We've got to keep going."

"Thank you," he told her. "Thank you very much."

And, with that, Harris continued toward her home, wondering all the while if her home still existed. She passed "people moving children's prams which they'd filled with little things they'd rescued from their homes. There were no tears—nothing whatsoever—just firmness— 'We'll rescue what we can.' They were all right—but what got me into tears was a birdcage, still hanging in a window with a little dead canary in it."[5]

DEMOCRACY IS FINISHED IN ENGLAND . . .

All four grandparents of Joseph P. Kennedy Sr. came to Massachusetts dirt poor, in flight from the famine that devastated Ireland in the 1840s. His father, Patrick Joseph "P. J." Kennedy, set up in Boston as a saloonkeeper, investor, and local politician, earning a level of prosperity that propelled his elder son through Boston Latin School and Harvard

College. In 1914, P. J. married Rose Elizabeth Fitzgerald, daughter of Boston mayor John Francis "Honey Fitz" Fitzgerald. Uniting two rival Irish American political families, the marriage positioned Joe Sr. for a powerful life in politics, but he chose instead to continue the business career he had begun after graduating from Harvard. His first job, in 1912, was as a state bank examiner, and he used it as a kind of post-graduate course in banking. In 1913, he borrowed from family and friends the equivalent of a million dollars in today's money to purchase the controlling shares of Columbia Trust Bank, thereby becoming, at age twenty-five, the country's youngest bank president.

He went on to profit in real estate and, when the United States entered World War I in 1917, he secured himself from conscription by becoming assistant general manager of Bethlehem Steel's Quincy, Massachusetts, shipyard—a civilian position deemed vital to the war effort. Not only did the new job honorably keep him out of uniform and allow him to continue pursuing his investments, it brought him face-to-face with a young Franklin Delano Roosevelt, at the time assistant secretary of the navy.

Leaving the shipyard in 1919, after war's end, Joe Sr. became a stockbroker, riding the Roaring Twenties bull to a multimillion-dollar fortune, then making even more money when, acting on insider information (not illegal at the time), he anticipated the crash of 1929 by shorting a large portfolio of stocks. During the 1920s, Kennedy became a movie studio head and the owner of the Keith-Albee-Orpheum chain of more than seven hundred vaudeville theaters, which had just begun to replace live shows with movies. In 1928, he founded the Radio-Keith-Orpheum film studio, RKO, and had a torrid three-year affair with movie star Gloria Swanson. In the meantime, he managed to buy the sixty-three highly profitable Pantages theaters at a fire-sale price during the spectacular rape trial of theatrical mogul Alexander Pantages. Eventually acquitted, Pantages later claimed Kennedy had framed him just to drive down his asking price.

A still-enduring urban myth adds "Prohibition-era bootlegger" to the varied Kennedy resume. Despite decades of digging by enemies and scholars alike, no evidence of this vocation exists—although Kennedy certainly invested in legal liquor importation and was so quick to get into the liquor business after the repeal of Prohibition following ratification of the Twenty-first Amendment on December 5, 1933, that many believe he had deliberately used the Volstead Act, which locked out competitors, to amass a huge liquor inventory to meet what he knew would be pent-up demand. In any event, Kennedy partnered with Franklin Roosevelt's son James to found Somerset Importers immediately after repeal and the installation of FDR in the White House. Kennedy's introduction to James Roosevelt had come via James's father, to whom Joe Sr. variously donated or loaned campaign funds in 1932. As president, FDR rewarded Kennedy by naming him the first chairman of the New Deal's Securities and Exchange Commission (SEC).

It was not what Joseph P. Kennedy Sr. really wanted. Ultimately, the presidency was his desire—but, for now, his minimum expectation was a cabinet post, preferably secretary of the treasury. In fact, FDR came under harsh criticism for the appointment he did make. The wily Kennedy had an unsavory reputation, especially among Boston Brahmins and the Wall Street old guard. Asked how he could appoint a "crook" to oversee the new regulatory agency, President Roosevelt offhandedly replied, "It takes one to catch one."[6]

In fact, Kennedy proved highly effective as the SEC's inaugural head, and when he left the SEC in 1935 to accept a presidential appointment as the first chair of the Maritime Commission, he efficiently applied his brief wartime shipyard experience to the new post. But his eyes were on 1936 and FDR's bid for reelection. Once again, he both raised and supplied campaign funding while also organizing support for the sweeping economic programs of the New Deal from among the recalcitrant business community. It was yeoman's work, and, this time (according to James Roosevelt), he "hinted broadly that the reward he had in mind was the post of secretary of the treasury." The president was hardly inclined to make way for Kennedy by moving the brilliant New Dealer Henry Morgenthau out of the treasury, but he never directly told Kennedy that he was out of the running. By late 1937, the president acknowledged to his son that the time had come "to do something for old Joe."[7]

The problem, FDR said, was that Kennedy "wants what he can't have." In search of "something we can give him he'll be happy with," the president commissioned James to feel him out. At length, Joe Sr. allowed that, if he couldn't be secretary of the treasury, there was one other job he'd consider: "I'd like to be ambassador to England." When son reported to father, President Roosevelt "laughed so hard he almost toppled from his wheelchair."[8]

Kennedy proved himself skilled at many things, but never—ever—did he so much as mention foreign affairs. Worse, he was, if anything, the anti-diplomat: plainspoken, prone to argument, hotheaded, and, when provoked, foul-mouthed. Besides, he was a proud Irishman and, despite his multiple infidelities, a devout Irish Catholic. The idea of sending *him* to represent the United States to a nation that had oppressed Irishmen and Catholics for seven centuries seemed like something of a sick joke.

And yet, as FDR saw it, there was actually a good case to be made for the appointment. For one thing, with war clouds gathering both in Europe and the Pacific, the president believed that a hard-nosed, even ruthless businessman might be able to provide a better understanding of the motives of Hitler, Mussolini, and even the Japanese government than a more conventional diplomat could. Certainly, Kennedy was tuned in to economics and finance as well as the concerns of bankers, entrepreneurs, and industrialists. He was also, FDR believed, a keen observer and had no partisan axes to grind. James Roosevelt felt sufficiently emboldened in December 1937 to tell Kennedy that his father was going to send him to London. No sooner had he conveyed this news, however, than FDR vacillated, telling James to tell Kennedy that he wanted to appoint him secretary of commerce instead.

Kennedy exploded at news of this shift. FDR had "promised me London," and he told James "to tell his father that's the job, and the only one, I'll accept."[9] Then Kennedy took another step, leaking news of the impending appointment to Arthur Krock, known at the time as the dean of Washington newsmen. Krock ran with the scoop he'd been given, infuriating the president, who not only hated to have his hand forced but had not even told the current ambassador that he had talked to *anyone* about his job.

Earlier, appointing Kennedy had begun to seem like a good idea to FDR. Now that the leak had boxed him in, however, the president reviewed in his mind the numerous times Kennedy had criticized him behind his back and had made no bones about declaring himself the smartest man in the room, even when he shared the room with the president of the United States. Any support Kennedy had given the New Deal and the president himself, FDR began to reflect, was almost certainly entirely self-serving—and subject to withdrawal at a moment's notice. Henry Morgenthau, whose job Kennedy had so wanted, warned the president that Kennedy was "a very dangerous man"—and now Roosevelt openly agreed. He suddenly assured Morgenthau that the appointment to London was for six months and, with that, "any obligation he had to Kennedy was paid out."[10]

Morgenthau did not feel assured. "Don't you think you are taking considerable risks by sending Kennedy who has talked so freely and so critically against your Administration?"

To this, the president responded that he had taken measures "to have Joe Kennedy watched hourly and the first time he opens his mouth and criticizes me, I will fire him." Then he told Morgenthau—repeating it "two or three times"—"Kennedy is too dangerous to have around here."[11]

* * *

WHEN THE OFFER WAS MADE OFFICIAL, objections came from many quarters—with some of the most insistent from Kennedy's own friends. The popular anti–New Deal radio commentator Boake Carter, for example, warned Kennedy that FDR would give him no real power, would reduce him to a servant, and might cost him the ability to position himself for higher office. Then Carter hit Kennedy with both barrels: "You are an honest man. But the job of Ambassador to London needs not only honesty, sincerity, faith and an abounding courage—it needs skill brought by years of training. And that, Joe, you simply don't possess."[12]

Another friend, South Carolina senator James Byrnes (future secretary of state in the Truman administration and, at the time, among the most powerful men in Congress), counseled Kennedy to stay put in the Maritime Commission. Kennedy responded that doing so would be a "waste of whatever talents I possess." He vehemently denied any "political ambitions," protesting that he was "only vitally concerned with where we are headed."[13] However, Kennedy was well aware that *five* American presidents had been ambassadors to the Court of St. James's.

The newly appointed ambassador set off across the Atlantic in February 1938 to be welcomed warmly by a British press that was generally enthusiastic about his appointment. Almost immediately, he found himself occupying a front-row seat to the first crisis in the overture to world war—the prospect of Adolf Hitler's invasion of Austria. Ambassador Kennedy's response, first to British foreign secretary Lord Halifax and then to Prime Minister Neville Chamberlain, was that the prevailing American attitude was isolationist. He told both men bluntly that they should not count on the United States to back Britain should it become involved in a war. Immediately after telling this to Chamberlain, Kennedy left 10 Downing Street, returned to the embassy, and summoned the press. He declared to the assembled reporters that the average American was "more interested in how he's going to eat and whether his insurance is good, than in foreign politics." In fact, he continued, clearly intending to be provocative as all Europe stood in fear and trembling, some are even "more interested in how Casey Stengel's Boston Bees are going to do next season."[14] While he may have sincerely believed he was speaking for most of America, the sentiments he expressed were by no means authorized by President Roosevelt.

As it turned out, the German annexation of Austria—the *Anschluss* of March 13, 1938—was accomplished with bloodless efficiency. This, however, put Czechoslovakia next up on the block. The nation, created after World War I, was now bordered by the German Reich on three sides. Its richly industrialized Sudetenland contained some 3 million German-speaking ethnic Germans. While many Austrians actually had welcomed annexation, the fiercely nationalist ethnic Czech majority would surely do no such thing. Moreover, Britain was obligated by the Covenant of the League of Nations, which it had signed in June 1919 as part of its agreement to the Treaty of Versailles ending World War I, to defend the sovereignty of Czechoslovakia. Winston Churchill—in 1938, nothing more than an eloquent member of Parliament—spoke of "unflinching adherence" to the treaty and the covenant and counseled the House of Commons to move the nation to the center of a "Grand Alliance . . . against aggression," but Prime Minister Chamberlain urged calm, assuring Parliament as well as the British people that neither the *Anschluss* nor an impending invasion of Czechoslovakia was any reason to go to war against Germany.

In fact, the latter was a very good reason—and history has judged Chamberlain harshly for his infamous policy of "appeasement," buying off Hitler at the expense of a nation Britain was sworn to defend.

At the time, however, there was a practical case to be made against going to war. Germany and its ally Italy had been vigorously rearming themselves, whereas Britain and its ally France had been assiduously disarming themselves. Chamberlain had actually reversed the post-1918 disarmament policy, but he believed that the nation's army and air force were not yet in any shape to fight both Germany and Italy—and win.

As the ambassador of a neutral country, Kennedy should have remained resolutely noncommittal with respect to both the Churchill and the Chamberlain factions. Instead, without presidential authorization, he openly embraced Chamberlain's policy of appeasement, deeming it the path to peace. Just as openly, he rejected Churchill's call to defiance and honor, condemning it as the quickest way to start the *second* world war in fewer than twenty years. In taking this position, he was not thinking—as Chamberlain was—of Britain's military unpreparedness. The ambassador was considering two things: War would be bad for business, including and most importantly *his* business. And, even worse, war would endanger his sons. His eldest two boys, Joe Jr., twenty-three years old in 1938, and John (called Jack), two years younger, were both old enough to fight. Robert ("Bobby") was only ten, and Edward ("Teddy") six.

* * *

AMBASSADOR KENNEDY HAD ALREADY deeply ingratiated himself with the trinity of appeasement—Chamberlain, his foreign secretary Lord Halifax, and Sir Alexander Cadogan, undersecretary of state— when, on March 18, 1938, he observed the tradition of introducing himself to the British government and its people by way of a speech at the Pilgrims Society banquet. Fellow diners included the trinity and King George VI. Kennedy spoke of the innate neutrality of the American people and their overwhelming opposition to what he characterized as "entangling alliances." Although he allowed that "circumstances, short of actual invasion" *might* move Americans to fight, he warned against assuming that the United States "could never remain neutral in the event of a general war."[15]

Six days after this speech, the ambassador sat in the House of Commons to hear Prime Minister Chamberlain disclaim any "prior pledge" of military assistance to Czechoslovakia should Germany invade, though he did not rule out going to war if driven by the "inexorable pressure of facts." Hitler almost certainly received the speech as it was intended to be interpreted—ambiguously—but Kennedy chose to take it as a guarantee that "there will be no war if Chamberlain stays in power. . . . Germany will get whatever it wants in Czechoslovakia without sending a single soldier across the border. The Czechs will go, hat in hand, to Berlin and ask the Fuhrer what he wants done, and it will be done. . . . The Germano-Czech situation will solve itself without interference."[16]

From association with Chamberlain and his immediate circle, it was inevitable that the ambassador would be drawn into the so-called Cliveden group, the moneyed Tories who gathered in Taplow, Buckinghamshire, at Cliveden, the Italianate mansion and estate of Lord and Lady Astor. Here was a center not only of appeasement policy but of outright admiration for Hitler and Mussolini. Lady Astor's very public criticism of "anti-German propaganda," which she attributed to "the Jews," did not discourage the ambassador from accepting her increasingly numerous invitations. Kennedy likewise believed that "the Jews" had brought German persecution on themselves.[17] Thanks to a column written by the enormously popular and influential Washington-based columnist and radio commentator Drew Pearson, Kennedy's connection with Astor and the Cliveden set quickly became global news.

In June 1938, Ambassador Kennedy took a brief leave of absence and returned to America to attend the graduation of Joe Jr. from Harvard. Of course, he also called on President Roosevelt, whom he lectured condescendingly on foreign affairs. He was particularly critical of the president's vocal opposition to fascism. Nazism, Kennedy conceded, was fair game for criticism, but, as for fascism, he told Roosevelt that the United States itself would probably "have to come to some form of fascism." As Secretary of the Interior Harold Ickes recorded in his diary, the "President thinks that Joe Kennedy, if he were in power, would give us a Fascist form of government" run by "a small powerful committee under himself as chairman . . . without much reference to Congress."[18]

The ambassador was back in London during the run-up to the Czech crisis and, on September 14, was summoned to 10 Downing Street, where Prime Minister Chamberlain told him that he was off to Munich the next day to meet with Hitler. On the evening of the 16th, the prime minister briefed Kennedy, conveying to him Hitler's warning that he would "chance a world war if necessary" to secure the transfer of the Czech Sudetenland to Germany. Hitler promised, however, to refrain from ordering military action pending Britain's decision on whether it would accept "self-determination" for the "Sudeten Germans" or support Czechoslovakia. To Kennedy's immense relief, Chamberlain told him that he was prepared to give Adolf Hitler what he wanted.

The ambassador's relief would have been short lived, had he been privy to the step President Roosevelt was taking in Washington. Telling Secretary of the Treasury Henry Morgenthau that he believed the Czechs would surely resist invasion, the president was eager to advise the French government to mobilize its army but to keep its troops behind the Maginot Line and, along with other countries surrounding Germany—including Czechoslovakia—wage a defensive campaign that would cut Germany off from all sources of supply. When Morgenthau brought him back to earth by asking how he intended to convey his message to France without abrogating neutrality, FDR asked, "What about Kennedy?" Morgenthau responded that the ambassador could not be trusted, and so President Roosevelt immediately summoned Sir Ronald Lindsay, the British ambassador, conveyed his proposed blockade to him, and asked that he communicate it to the French government. To America's own ambassador to Britain, FDR never revealed the plan.

In the end, it was all moot. On September 21, a fearful Czech government agreed to negotiate the cession of territory in exchange for Germany's international guarantee to refrain from aggression. On the 22nd, Chamberlain made a second flight to Germany, presenting Hitler with a proposal to create an international commission to redraw the borders of Czechoslovakia. Hitler rejected the proposal, demanding instead the *immediate* cession of the Sudetenland. If the Czech government failed to agree to this by October 1, Hitler warned, he would take the Sudetenland by force of arms. Chamberlain objected—but, before he left the Führer's presence, caved in, agreeing to present the demand to the Czechs.

Returned to 10 Downing Street, Chamberlain summoned Kennedy and told him that Hitler's demands were "preposterous." Kennedy made no response, but, once back at his desk in the embassy, immediately requisitioned a thousand gas masks in addition to those the embassy had already laid in. Subsequently, Chamberlain told Kennedy that he had decided to make a radio broadcast plea to Hitler. Instead of judging this as desperate, if not abject, Ambassador Kennedy saw the broadcast as a very good idea, and he asked U.S. Secretary of State Cordell Hull to arrange for it to be carried over U.S. radio as well. When Hull flatly refused, Kennedy pressed. Unwilling to make the U.S. government a party to pleading with a dictator, Hull stood firm.[19]

With each passing hour war seemed more certain when, on the afternoon of September 28, Chamberlain was handed a note just as he concluded a speech to Parliament on the crisis. Kennedy was present in the gallery to hear Chamberlain turn to the House and announce that "Herr Hitler" had agreed to postpone mobilization for twenty-four hours pending a conference with him, "Signor Mussolini and Signor Daladier at Munich."[20]

At this, the House burst into cheers—"terrific cheers," Kennedy euphorically cabled to Secretary Hull—and no one seemed to notice that Chamberlain had granted *Herr* Hitler and *Signor* Mussolini their national identities, while (presumably inadvertently) robbing "Monsieur" Daladier of his. The ambassador returned to the embassy and announced to his staff, "Well, boys, the war is off."[21]

Chamberlain, as the world well knows, did fly to Germany a third time—to Munich on September 29—and returned to London the next day to declare that he brought back from Hitler "peace for our time." The Führer promised to cease aggression in exchange for most of Czechoslovakia. Three weeks later, Ambassador Kennedy delivered a speech at the annual Trafalgar Day dinner of the Navy League, in which he lightheartedly advised the leaders of the Western democracies to "attempt to reestablish good relations" with the leaders of Nazism and fascism. "After all, we have to live together in the same world, whether we like it or not."[22] The *New York Times* headlined its report of the remark this way:

KENNEDY FOR AMITY WITH FASCIST BLOC:
URGES THAT DEMOCRACIES AND DICTATORSHIPS
FORGET THEIR DIFFERENCES IN OUTLOOK.
CALLS FOR DISARMAMENT.[23]

A furious Cordell Hull held a press conference to disavow Kennedy's remarks as reflecting the ambassador's personal opinion, not the policy of the U.S. government. Nevertheless, the public uproar against Kennedy only gathered intensity, and a week after the Trafalgar Day speech, President Roosevelt broadcast a speech of his own, from the White House, in which he categorically repudiated every word of his ambassador—albeit without mentioning Kennedy by name. If Ambassador Kennedy had hoped to position the United States for appeasement, he ended up goading the administration into taking a more aggressive and public anti-Nazi stance. If FDR thought *his* speech would defuse the furor, he, too, was mistaken. Public condemnation of Joseph P. Kennedy as an "appeaser," a "defeatist," and even a coward intensified. Yet, far from coaxing Kennedy into contrition, the criticism made him more defiant. "You fellows in Washington should know one thing," he wrote to J. P. Moffat, the State Department's chief of the Western European section, "that if I am to get results here I can only do it by staying on the right side of the men in power"—and by that he meant continuing his advocacy of Neville Chamberlain's appeasement policy.[24]

As he, Ambassador Joseph P. Kennedy, saw it, the United States was facing a choice: make war against Hitler and Mussolini or make peace with Hitler and Mussolini. And, to him, the choice was simple and obvious: Hitler and Mussolini were powerful and motivated, whereas the British and French were weak and dispirited. He wrote to Tom White, of the Hearst news organization, that "unless England and France are prepared to fight and endanger civilization, then there is no point in staying on the side lines and sticking your tongue out at somebody who is a good deal bigger than you are. As far as the United States goes, we ought to mind our own business."[25] It was simple common sense, and Kennedy was not merely outraged over the controversy his position had stirred, he actually could not understand it. Failing to understand, he fell back on the belief that the turmoil was being created by the Jews, who (he *did* understand) had a motive for going to war against Hitler. The dictator was (he wrote in an unpublished "Diplomatic Memoir") destroying "the lives and futures of their compatriots."[26] Yet, as he saw it, the misfortune of the Jews was hardly a sufficient reason to antagonize the Third Reich.

Jack Kennedy, still at Harvard, wrote to his father that the Trafalgar Day speech did seem "to be unpopular with the Jews, etc." However, he assured the ambassador, it "was considered to be very good by everyone who wasn't bitterly anti-Fascist."[27] In the weeks to come, Jack would change his views and turn against his father's support of appeasement. Joe Jr. would never really break with his father. While in law school, he would form and lead an isolationist antiwar club at Harvard, and he eagerly corroborated his father's assessment of Jewish agitation against Hitler.

The view of "the Jews" the Kennedys shared as a family was common among many, perhaps most, American gentiles. Indeed, the ambassador lobbied both the Roosevelt administration and the Chamberlain government to push negotiations with Germany for the "resettlement" of its Jews in a variety of countries, including the United States, Palestine, and British Guiana. He got nowhere, and his unauthorized initiative served only to increase tensions between him and the State Department. Instead of seeking to understand the position of the Roosevelt administration and subordinate himself to it, however, Kennedy blamed those tensions on what he persisted on characterizing as the "Jewish media." More to the point, he saw "the Jews" as directly menacing his sons. In a November 25, 1938, letter to Harvard classmate Robert Fisher, he wrote how "disturbed" he became "reading about what's taking place in America on the Jewish question." What *he* claimed to hear was that "America wants to be an isolationist country," and yet, he complained to Fisher, "people get themselves into such a dither over this question." When they do, he concluded, "I wonder how safe your sons and mine are from war."[28]

Ultimately, for *this* ambassador, tyranny, terror, persecution, and the prospect of genocide did not come down to geopolitics and diplomacy. All of it was personal, and all of it paled in comparison to the future of *his* legacy, *his* family, *his* sons. "Of course," he admitted to Fisher, "frightful things are happening in the world and we all feel terribly sorry about it, but we have a country of our own with problems that require all of our ingenuity and sympathy."[29]

* * *

THROUGH THE GLOOMY AUTUMN of 1938, Ambassador Kennedy dug in deeper, shaking off the ceaseless blows of British and American newspaper attacks against him. These increased in intensity at the end of November after it was reported that Sir John Simon, Chancellor of the Exchequer, told the House of Commons that Kennedy had actively aided the Chamberlain government in censoring Paramount newsreel interviews with anti-appeasement journalists. The *Chicago Daily Tribune* now accused Kennedy of "playing the role of office boy of empire."[30]

The end of 1938 was the beginning of the end of Kennedy's career as a United States ambassador. He himself began talking of quitting, and, even in the midst of the growing crisis in Europe, he took a leave for the Christmas holidays. Savvy reporters believed this was also his last-ditch attempt to repair relations with Washington and position himself for a run at the vice-presidency—some even speculated on a presidential run, against FDR—in 1940. Whatever motivated his leave, Kennedy stretched it out as long as possible. He took time in January 1939 to testify to the House and Senate Committees on Military Affairs in support of FDR's request for a spectacular $2 billion "peacetime" national defense budget supplement. Kennedy's isolationism did not extend to rendering the nation defenseless. He was genuinely intimidated by the military might of Germany and Italy. In the end, however, it was not Roosevelt who sent him back to London but Chamberlain who asked for him back. Kennedy sailed on February 23, 1939.

The London to which he returned buzzed with talk of imminent war. That was disturbing enough, but even worse was Kennedy's growing realization—based on briefings in Washington with Secretary of State Hull—that his hero, Neville Chamberlain, was actually in denial and wildly out of touch with the latest developments in Germany. Chamberlain told Kennedy that the German economy was near collapse and that, therefore, Hitler would have no choice but to turn from threats of war to overtures of trade. Kennedy the businessman could see only signs of growing economic strength in Germany. Now doubting Chamberlain, he cabled President Roosevelt early in March that "Great Britain and France are no longer able to maintain the old world order. They are on the defensive; the totalitarian states are on the offensive with the rise of air power. The preeminence of Great Britain has disappeared, for obviously a country so vulnerable to air attack cannot be the center of a really stable world system." He predicted that Britain would lose its empire, which would impact the United States by cutting in half the demand for American exports. As Kennedy saw it, the danger to America in Britain's decline and fall was not a direct military threat

to the United States but an economic one, and, in order to survive—
economically—the American people would have to accept "a regi-
mented industrial order under Government control. Such centralization
would tend to reproduce, possibly under other names, the basic features
of the Fascist state: to fight totalitarianism, we would have to adopt
totalitarian methods."[31]

The president did not respond to his ambassador. He read the memorandum and forwarded it to his chief of naval operations with the stern
warning that it be "kept confidential."[32] Clearly, FDR did not want it
leaked that his ambassador to Britain had moved from neutrality, to
appeasement, to defeatism, to surrender, to the exchange of democracy
for fascism—and all before a single shot had been fired.

* * *

"PEACE FOR OUR TIME," Neville Chamberlain had promised back in
September 1938, when he returned from Munich. Handed the Sudetenland, the Führer professed himself satisfied. On March 16, 1939, however, he sent German army units to occupy Prague. The entire Czech
nation suddenly ceased to exist, and Kennedy, like most everyone else,
now believed that war was imminent. What he did not admit to others
or himself was that the appeasement policy he had cheered on was not
only failing to avert war, it was making war inevitable by encouraging
Hitler in his program of territorial aggression.

No matter. Ambassador Kennedy left London on July 21, 1939, to
vacation at Cannes in the south of France. Astoundingly, he wrote to
President Roosevelt from that playground of the rich and idle that "cad-
dies, waiters and residents" in this part of the world all exhibit "a very
strong anti-Semitic feeling," adding, "Beyond that . . . I can contribute
nothing to an understanding of the international state of affairs."[33]

His sojourn in the sun was interrupted on August 21 by an announcement on German radio that Germany and the Soviet Union had
concluded a "non-aggression pact." Kennedy flew back to London, well
aware what the pact meant. The Soviet Union, implacable Marxist foe
of fascism, now promised not to stand in the way of a German invasion
of Poland. And the ambassador also knew that the treaties binding Britain and France to defend Poland against invasion could not be so casually broken as those pledging them to the defense of Czechoslovakia.

Britain and France had surrendered the Sudetenland in exchange for Hitler's pledge that he would seek no further conquest. They could not give in on Poland after Hitler had so blatantly broken his word.

Yet, remarkably, Kennedy had not given up on appeasement. Close to midnight on August 24, he put in a call to President Roosevelt. It was picked up by Under Secretary of State Sumner Welles. Kennedy pleaded with Welles to convey to Roosevelt the urgency of pressing Poland to negotiate with Germany. Although Welles did not hand the receiver to FDR, Kennedy heard the president's voice. "Something," the voice said, would be done that very night.

Doubtless feeling a modicum of relief, Ambassador Kennedy went to bed. The next morning, he discovered that President Roosevelt had done nothing more than advise both Hitler and the Polish president to find a nonviolent way of settling their dispute. Further than this the administration would not go.

It was not until 10 pm on August 25 that Kennedy was invited to 10 Downing Street. There he was told that Hitler had demanded an immediate settlement of the "Polish question"—by which he meant satisfaction of Germany's claim to the Free City of Danzig and the "Polish Corridor" separating East Prussia from the rest of the Reich—in return for a new promise of peace. If his demands were not immediately met, he would go to war.

What Kennedy said in response to this news must have stunned Chamberlain. He "felt strongly" that the prime minister "could not quit on Poland no matter what else happened." To do so would "jeopardize not only the honor of Britain, but would completely break his political party."[34] But then the ambassador continued, far truer to isolationist form, by advising Chamberlain to include in his response to Hitler's demand "a suggestion that if [Hitler] accepted a reasonable Polish settlement perhaps he could get the U.S. and other countries together on an economic plan that certainly would be more important to Germany than what he [Hitler] could possibly get out of getting anything in Poland."[35] Pausing, Kennedy added, "You must pass the hat before the corpse gets cold."

Chamberlain confessed that he did not understand, so the ambassador laid it out: "Propose a general settlement that will bring Germany economic benefits more important than territorial annexation of

Danzig. Get the United States now to say what they would be willing to do in the cause of international peace and prosperity. After all, the United States will be the largest beneficiary of such a move. To put in a billion or two now will be worth it, for if it works we will get it back and more."[36]

Chamberlain and his cabinet listened politely but rejected the proposal as soon as Kennedy left the meeting. The idea of treating the dictator like a rational businessman willing to trade conquest for a couple of billion dollars and the promise of trade struck even the apostle of appeasement as absurd.

While awaiting Hitler's reply to whatever Chamberlain would propose, Kennedy worked the phones, trying to persuade U.S. and European steamship companies to evacuate the thousands of Americans now clamoring to escape from Britain. At this point, Ambassador Kennedy had all of his family living with him in the official London residence. But for now, he resisted immediately sending his wife and children packing, explaining in a letter to theatrical manager and longtime friend Arthur Houghton that this restraint was "[a]nother one of those great moral gestures that the American people expect you to make; that is, get your own family killed, but be sure and get Miss Smith of Peoria on the boat."[37]

*   *   *

ON SEPTEMBER 1, Kennedy put in a call to Ambassador William Bullitt in the U.S. Embassy in Paris. The two diplomats agreed that things were actually looking up. Bullitt told Kennedy that Hitler "didn't have the guts to fight."[38] Doubtless relieved, Kennedy hung up—and, just then, received the news that Germany had launched a massive invasion of Poland.

There would be a brief pause before England and France declared war as the two countries delivered pro forma diplomatic notes demanding Germany's withdrawal from Poland and awaited replies. Kennedy used the interval to arrange for his family's return to America, and on September 3, he and his staff gathered around the small radio in his office to hear Neville Chamberlain's announcement: "This country is at war with Germany." The prime minister pronounced it a "sad day for all of us" but judged that "to none is it sadder than to me. Everything that I have worked for, everything that I have hoped for, everything that I believed in during my public life, has crashed into ruins."[39]

Kennedy later wrote that he was near tears himself. "I had participated in this struggle and I saw my hope crash too."[40]

*   *   *

ON THAT SEPTEMBER SUNDAY, it seemed as if the war would come to London very, very quickly. Chamberlain made his announcement at 11:15, and air raid sirens screamed across the city less than a quarter of an hour later, at 11:27. The ambassador was aware that the U.S. Embassy lacked an adequate cellar, let alone an underground air raid shelter. By prearrangement, the elite British fashion designer Edward Molyneux agreed to allow the embassy staff to shelter in the basement of his famed shop, which was located around the corner from the embassy. Kennedy now sent his staff to Molyneux's. Joe Jr. and his brother Jack, along with their mother, Rose, were standing outside the embassy, intending to go with their father to the House of Commons to hear the prime minister's formal request for a declaration of war. Instead, Kennedy met them outside and ushered them into the tony dressmaker's basement. So World War II began for the ambassador, his wife, and their two eldest sons.

It soon became apparent that there was no air raid and that there would be none. Kennedy returned to the embassy and called President Roosevelt to report the substance of Chamberlain's broadcast. In fact, he went far beyond it. He told the president that Britain would surely soon be invaded and overrun, that the democracies, in their fight against fascism, would have to forsake democracy and act as Fascist states themselves, that economies would dissolve, that the well-fed would go hungry, and that the hungry would starve. He predicted that a new "dark age" was even now descending upon Europe and concluded by declaring "It's the end of the world, the end of everything."[41]

In the days, weeks, and months that followed, virtually all of the war news was bad, very bad, yet the war also remained strangely distant from London and the rest of Britain. From October 1939 through April 1940, neither England nor France launched any meaningful offensive operation. The press took to calling it "the phoney war," using the British spelling. Yet Ambassador Kennedy continued to see it as the end of the world. Worse, he made no attempt to disguise his despair, and he never hesitated to act on the basis of it.

The focus of his immediate attention was the evacuation of U.S. nationals from London and what he seems to have considered certain and imminent death. When the State Department refused his demands for the redirection of all U.S.-flagged ships to pick up Americans at British ports—an authority the government lacked—he excoriated the department in the international press. One department official complained that Kennedy "seems to think that the only people needing repatriation are in the lobby of the American Embassy in London."[42] This interpretation of Kennedy's narrow field of vision was actually quite accurate. Moreover, Kennedy made certain that his efforts to get Americans out of London were highly publicized. In part, it was to portray himself as a man of action. In part, it was to provide an apparently selfless context for his successful efforts to finally get his family back home. Kathleen, Eunice, Bobby, and Rose Kennedy sailed together on the *Washington* on September 14, Joe Jr. set off on the *Mauretania* four days later, and Jack flew out on a Pan Am Clipper the day after that. On September 20, Patricia, Teddy, and Jean were put aboard the *Manhattan*. Rosemary Kennedy, who was developmentally disabled, remained with her father, who wanted to keep her at the local Montessori school where she was making good progress.

With his family safe, the ambassador now set about personally trying to end the two-week-old war. His discovery that Secretary of State Hull had cut him out of the loop by routinely contacting members of the British government directly rather than through him prompted Kennedy to retaliate by including President Roosevelt in all of his communications rather than relying on Hull or his staff to convey them. Among these cablegrams was a report of King George VI's estimate that Poland would be defeated within three weeks, at which time Hitler would offer to commence peace talks with England and France. Kennedy reasoned that this would put Prime Minister Chamberlain in a tight spot. Either he would agree to negotiate and thereby be voted out of office or he would refuse, thereby committing England to a war in which defeat was certain. Kennedy informed the president that he saw only one way out of this impossible situation. Chamberlain could not surrender, nor could he fight (and win), but the American president could negotiate an end to the war and, in so doing, "save the world."[43] Problem solved. World saved.

It requires no diplomatic experience to see the scheme as mad. In the first place, what could Roosevelt offer Hitler? Short of an alliance—which was, of course, impossible—the president had nothing. And what standing had he to bargain? For Hitler even to consider negotiating with the United States, the president would have to concede the legitimacy of the annexation of Austria and Czechoslovakia—two actions that went against everything America symbolized. President Roosevelt dismissed the Kennedy proposal as "the silliest message to me I have ever received" and stated that he believed Kennedy was "frantic."[44]

* * *

ON THE VERY DAY that he received the "frantic" Kennedy cable, President Roosevelt quietly began a correspondence with Winston Churchill, at the time no more than a member of Parliament and a longtime lonely voice against appeasement. The correspondence would prove momentous. Was its commencement precisely at this juncture a coincidence? Or did the ambassador's reckless recommendations, born in the extremity of his defeatism, have the unintended consequence of helping to forge what would prove a historic bond between the president and the soon-to-be prime minister?

In any case, President Roosevelt told Kennedy nothing of the messages that began to pass between him and Churchill. Kennedy learned of the correspondence only because Churchill casually revealed it to him. The revelation made him furious on two counts. He was both enraged and embarrassed at being ignored by the very man who sent him to London. Even more, he was genuinely appalled by Roosevelt's trust in Churchill, someone, Kennedy believed, who would "blow up the American Embassy and say it was the Germans if it would get the U.S. [into the war]."[45]

The more Roosevelt and Hull continued to ignore him, the more intensively Kennedy peppered them with dire cables. It was not just that he believed Britain's defeat inevitable—that estimate was, in fact, not unreasonable—it was that Joseph P. Kennedy Sr. could discern no

British motive for fighting other than a desire to preserve the empire. Freedom, justice, honor, the defense of civilization—all of these "motives" he dismissed as mere "idealism."[46]

And as the Roosevelt administration cut Kennedy loose, so Kennedy severed ties with the Chamberlain government. Now that the prime minister had abandoned appeasement and pursued war, it was as if Kennedy and he simply had nothing more to talk about. For its part, the British Foreign Office, hitherto so solicitous of the American ambassador, began to shadow Kennedy, meticulously accumulating a dossier in an effort to document a defeatism that, once used to bolster the appeasement policy, was now seen as a palpable menace to the war effort. In the end, no one in the British government thought the ambassador was deliberately attempting to sabotage morale. The evolving semiofficial "insider" interpretation of Kennedy's attitude was that, as the son of a self-made man and largely self-made himself, he could not see beyond the goal of preserving his wealth. This meant preserving the global status quo—or at least as much of it as was salvageable now—rather than pouring national treasure into what seemed to him an unwinnable war. Kennedy's hope, if he had much of a hope left, was for the democracies to survive as best they could until such time as, somehow, the German regime would simply change.

As the phoney war continued, a false calm settled over London and the embassy. Largely cut off from both his own government and that of his hosts, and with his family gone home, Joe Kennedy Sr. was plunged into an increasingly dark mood. He made a feeble effort to brighten it by reasoning that Germany was making such rapid gains and the French and English doing so little to reverse them that the war, of necessity, would at least be short. To anyone who expressed doubt about this judgment, Kennedy would simply reply with the non sequitur that the war *had* to be short—because the alternative to brevity was unthinkable.

Toward the end of November 1939, Kennedy applied for home leave. That it was instantly granted is testament to how little either government valued him at this point. He conducted a round of pre-leave meetings with members of the government, including Chamberlain, the cabinet, members of the royal family, and Winston Churchill, who was now first lord of the Admiralty. To each he delivered this advice: Appease Hitler—and appease him before the phoney war became a war of real bombardment and actual invasion of the British Isles. To do otherwise, he warned, would be an act of national suicide.

On his arrival back in the States, Kennedy offered to see the president immediately. Roosevelt insisted that he first spend time with his family instead. This obvious rebuff prompted Kennedy to push his offer harder, and Roosevelt gave in. The president greeted his ambassador with disarming warmth, which both surprised and gratified Kennedy—but did nothing to dilute his pessimism. FDR later confided in Harold Ickes that Kennedy "believes that Germany and Russia will win the war and that the end of the world is just down the road."[47]

Kennedy did not reserve his pessimism for the president, but (as popular columnists Joe Alsop and Bob Kintner reported), "To anyone who comes within hailing distance, our ambassador to England freely predicts the collapse of capitalism, the destruction of democracy and the onset of the dark ages." Worse, Alsop and Kintner explained, Kennedy believed "that only an early peace, at almost any price, can save the world."[48]

Kennedy returned to his post in London early in March 1940 and found that his absence had not made the English heart grow fonder of him. If anything, the Chamberlain government had been relieved to see Kennedy leave for a time, but, once he had gone, the government, press, and public began to resent his absence in such a period of crisis as a kind of insult. Kennedy wrote to his wife that Britain had turned decidedly anti-American and "anti-U.S. Ambassador Kennedy."[49]

* * *

IN APRIL, THE PHONEY WAR came to an abrupt end. German forces invaded Norway and Denmark—speedily, violently, and with relative ease. In May, they invaded Holland and Belgium. With the bombs and bullets came the resignation of Neville Chamberlain. He tapped Lord Halifax—his partner in appeasement—to succeed him, but Halifax declined. With that, Chamberlain turned to Churchill, who, of course, accepted. Kennedy was devastated.

For his part, in a letter marked "Most Secret and Personal," the new prime minister wrote to President Roosevelt on May 15:

As you are no doubt aware, the scene has darkened swiftly.... The small countries are simply smashed up, one by one, like matchwood. . . .

We expect to be attacked here ourselves, both from the air and by
parachute and air borne troops in the near future, and are getting
ready for them. If necessary, we shall continue the war alone and we
are not afraid of that. But I trust you realize, Mr. President, that the
voice and force of the United States may count for nothing if they are
withheld too long. You may have a completely subjugated, Nazified
Europe established with astonishing swiftness, and the weight may be
more than we can bear.[50]

On May 20, the tenth day of the Battle of France, Kennedy wrote to
Rose, "I think the jig is up" and that it would mean "a terrible finish for
the Allies." He let her know that he planned to send Rosemary either to
Ireland or Lisbon, because he expected London to "be in for a terrific
bombing pretty soon." He believed the "English will fight to the end
but I just don't think they can stand up to the bombing indefinitely." He
continued: "What will happen then is probably a dictated peace with
Hitler probably getting the British Navy, and we will find ourselves in
a terrible mess." Curiously, this was precisely the strongest argument—
and one that FDR would soon make—for relaxing U.S. neutrality laws
and providing to Britain materiel and other aid (including old destroyers): Germany's possession of the greatest naval fleet in the world would
certainly menace the United States across the Atlantic. But Kennedy
was oblivious. He closed his letter by saying that his ambassadorship
had "certainly been a great adventure," but "[i]t's getting near the finish."[51] His defeatism ran so deep that, for him, the war, barely begun,
was already as good as lost.

Seven days later, he cabled Washington that "only a miracle can
save the British expeditionary force from being wiped out" in France at
Dunkirk, the coastal town to which the advancing German armies had
pushed French and British forces, trapping them with their backs to the
English Channel. Facing certain annihilation of their ground troops on
the Continent, the Allies, Kennedy believed, had no alternative to immediate and total surrender.[52]

Kennedy would be proved right about needing a miracle, but he
did not anticipate that miracle actually arriving in the form of the spectacular cross-Channel evacuation of the cornered British and French
forces. To his credit, the ambassador was tremendously moved by Prime

Minister Churchill's speech on June 4, following the deliverance from Dunkirk:

> We shall fight in France, we shall fight on the seas and oceans, we shall fight with growing confidence and growing strength in the air, we shall defend our island, whatever the cost may be. We shall fight on the beaches, we shall fight on the landing grounds, we shall fight in the fields and in the streets, we shall fight in the hills; we shall never surrender . . .

Kennedy did not even criticize Churchill's obvious inference that America's entry into the war was a foregone conclusion: how the struggle would be continued "until, in God's good time, the new world, with all its power and might, steps forth to the rescue and liberation of the old."[53]

Yet, moved though he was, Kennedy remained convinced of the certainty of total defeat. He told son Joe that he would now send all of his staff away except for a skeleton crew of ten. As for himself, he intended "to try to keep this place operating as long as they leave the building standing up."[54] A defeatist, yes, but Joseph P. Kennedy wanted his son and the world to know that he was no coward.

As he awaited the German invasion everyone expected, Ambassador Kennedy had remarkably little to do. The normal business of an embassy was essentially suspended, and Roosevelt and Hull routinely bypassed him in their dealings with Churchill. Kennedy grudgingly accepted this situation until July, when, at the president's request, Secretary of the Navy Frank Knox asked retired army colonel William J. "Wild Bill" Donovan to travel to London on a mission to "unofficially" assess Britain's military prospects. Both Knox and Roosevelt believed that Donovan, who had been awarded the Medal of Honor for his service in World War I, could be trusted to provide the realistic evaluation that Kennedy's defeatism made impossible.

Told nothing about the Donovan mission, Kennedy instantly grasped its purpose when he accidentally heard about it. He cabled Hull and Roosevelt that he—the ambassador—was already gathering information and that sending "a new man in here at this time . . . is to me the height of nonsense."[55] Both Hull and the president brushed off the ambassador's complaint, and Donovan's low-key mission would prove history making. Yes, Donovan reported directly to the president, the situation in Britain was indeed dire, but Churchill was magnificent and the British were fully prepared and willing to fight. He advised Roosevelt to give them all possible assistance. Donovan gave the president all he needed to complete the write-off of Kennedy's assessment. From this point on, FDR became committed to an escalating program of material aid to the Churchill government.

*   *   *

DONOVAN'S MISSION CAME at the beginning of Germany's air attacks against Britain, which commenced on July 10, 1940. At its inception, Hitler's air war was not waged against civilian targets but against military objectives—Royal Air Force (RAF) bases, Royal Navy ships, ports, and facilities, and defense installations intended to repel invasion. The bombing was intense and highly destructive. Kennedy had expected that. But he had not expected the RAF to fight so effectively against the Luftwaffe. From 1936 to 1938, Charles A. Lindbergh had made several tours of Germany, in part to report to the U.S. military on the state of German military aviation. His assessment was that German air power was far in advance of anything in Britain or France or, for that matter, the United States. In 1938, Joe Jr. toured Europe, even spending two months as the attaché of William C. Bullitt, U.S. ambassador to France. On a diplomatic passport, Joe Jr. visited Prague, Warsaw, Leningrad, Copenhagen, and Berlin. He was impressed with "bustling" Germany and, like Lindbergh, was awed by the German military. To his father, Joe corroborated and even magnified Lindbergh's assessment of German airpower.

With aerial combat under way, however, British pilots were taking a heavy toll on the German bombers and fighters, and Kennedy's cables to Cordell Hull seem almost perverse. "If the British air force cannot be knocked out," he wrote on August 2, "then the war will drag out with the whole world continuously upset, with the final result the starvation of England and God knows what happening to the rest of Europe."[56] This was the Kennedy defeatism distilled. German victory over the RAF would bring destruction, to be sure. But, as Kennedy saw it, the *success* of the RAF would bring even worse. He seemed, quite frankly, to be cheering for the Luftwaffe.

At first thought, President Roosevelt's attitude toward his Cassandra in London might also seem perverse. Wasn't it long past time to recall and replace him? No, FDR phoned his ambassador to tell him that the Democratic Committee was going to ask him to come home to run the 1940 Democratic campaign. The president told Kennedy that "the general impression is that it would do the cause of England a great deal of harm if you left there at this time."[57] This, of course, was a lie, but FDR wanted Kennedy to remain far outside of the country until the election was over.

The decision to keep Kennedy in place was strategic election politics. No fool, Kennedy must have sensed this. He protested to the president that he was "not doing a damn thing here [in London] that amounts to anything and my services, if they are needed, could be used to much better advantage if I were home." No, no! FDR assured him. On the contrary, "constant reports of how valuable you are to them over there" keep pouring in, and "it helps the morale of the British to have you there and they would feel let down if you were to leave."[58] The insincerity was spectacular. Kennedy, however, allowed himself to believe—or to pretend to believe—it heartfelt.

On August 15, Kennedy heard the first air raid siren in London since the one that had sounded less than fifteen minutes after Chamberlain's broadcast on the first day of the war. It did not stop him from attending a London Symphony concert at Queens Hall. What was "remarkable" to him at the concert was "how well behaved and quiet whole audience was. A young man came on the platform to apolog saying, since some of the orchestra were missing due to air raid w ing did we mind waiting 4 or [5] minutes." Kennedy could not d whether the English, this "strange people," were "stupid, courag or complacent."[59]

As August drew to a close, Kennedy wearily sent anothe long series of complaining cables to President Roosevelt, this ti nouncing his humiliation at not having been informed of the a a high-level U.S. military delegation, come to discuss with (the particulars of the "destroyers-for-bases" deal, in which th States would give or lend some fifty obsolescent destroyers in for leases on British naval bases and facilities in the Caribbear and honestly," Kennedy complained, "I do not enjoy being

am very unhappy about the whole position and of course there is always the alternative of resigning."[60]

Ever anxious to keep Kennedy across the ocean, FDR appealed to his ambassador not to "forget that you are not only not a dummy but are essential to all of us both in the Government and in the Nation."[61] The sugared words probably did little to placate Kennedy, but the president's request that he personally "explain" certain aspects of the destroyer deal to Churchill did gratify him. He did as he was asked, then cabled Churchill's understanding to the president and secretary of state. He awaited a reply, received none, and wondered why—until he learned, unofficially, from one of the military delegation, that the agreement was to be signed on the next day. As usual, neither president nor secretary had informed him.

For Kennedy, the days passed in the emptiness of uselessness until September 7, 1940, when a terrific and prolonged air raid hit London. With his speechwriter Harvey Klemmer, he walked down Piccadilly that evening. "I'll bet you five to one any sum," he told Klemmer, "that Hitler will be in Buckingham Palace in two weeks."[62]

It would prove to be the first night of the Blitz, a campaign of air raids beginning with fifty-seven consecutive raids and continuing, with some intermissions, through May 21, 1941. Through day and night after day and night of bombing, where so many others saw the heroism of ordinary Londoners, Kennedy could only write to son Jack, "When I hear these mental midgets talking about my desire for appeasement and being critical of it, my blood fairly boils. What is this war going to prove? And what is it going to do to civilization? The answer to the first question is nothing; and to the second I shudder even to think about it."[63] In his eyes, Londoners had brought the air raids upon themselves— much as the Jews had brought the Nazi persecutions upon themselves.

Through each day and night of attack, the British Spitfires and Hurricanes met the incoming German bombers and fighters, exacting on the Luftwaffe a much heavier toll than the Luftwaffe took on the RAF. As a result, the anticipated German invasion did not materialize. "Never in the field of human conflict was so much owed by so many to so few," Churchill had said of the RAF's performance in the Battle of Britain in a speech on August 20. But Kennedy confined his Washington-bound cables to claims that wartime weapons production was

falling "regardless of what reports you may be getting." He did not substantiate his assertion but merely insisted on it: "I cannot impress upon you strongly enough my complete lack of confidence in the entire conduct of this war."[64]

*   *   *

ON OCTOBER 8, Joseph Alsop and Robert Kintner published in their North American Newspaper Alliance–syndicated column a story that presented a remarkable inside picture of the Kennedy-Roosevelt dynamic. They wrote that "an obscure but exciting little game" was under way, in which Kennedy's goal was "to come home as soon as he decently could" and Roosevelt's goal was "to keep Kennedy in London as long as possible." The president's fear, Alsop and Kintner wrote, was that Kennedy, once returned, would "reduce large numbers of leaders of opinion to such a state of hopeless blue funk that our foreign policy will be half-immobilized by fear."[65]

As soon as Kennedy read the article, he understood that the State Department had been leaking his gloomy dispatches to the columnists. By way of retaliation, he let it be known that, if he was not officially recalled to the United States immediately, he would come home anyway and tell the American people that the destroyer-for-bases deal was a terrible mistake. With the election around the corner, President Roosevelt finally gave in and instructed Under Secretary of State Sumner Welles to cable Kennedy that he was being recalled "for consultations." This was followed by a letter, drafted by Welles but signed by Roosevelt, in which Kennedy was effectively slapped with a gag order—"I am . . . asking you specifically not to make any statement to the press on your way over nor when you arrive in New York until you and I have had a chance to agree upon what should be said."[66] And so, on October 22, 1940, in the midst of the ongoing Blitz, Kennedy sailed for America and took daughter Rosemary with him.

Back home, the ambassador obligingly played the good Democrat and endorsed FDR's reelection in a radio speech. The Wednesday following the election, Kennedy paid a visit to the president in the White House. After congratulating Roosevelt on his election to an unprecedented third term, Kennedy told him he wanted to resign. The president asked only that he wait until his replacement could be named.

From the White House, Kennedy went to the State Department to call on Cordell Hull. Hull and others buzzed with news of the RAF's victories, the surprising and gratifying fact that Fascist Spain had chosen to remain neutral, and the apparent fact that Hitler had decided not to launch an invasion of England. Kennedy, however, spoke of the necessity of talking to Germany and Japan about a policy of economic cooperation and repeated his earlier prediction that the United States would have to adopt some form of fascism just to survive. Assistant Secretary of State Breckinridge Long listened and, in a friendly way, advised Kennedy "not to talk to the press or to talk in a way that would scare the American people."[67]

Kennedy promised Long that he would not repeat his grim opinions to the press. But the very next day, on November 7, he responded favorably to a request from the *Boston Globe*'s Louis Lyon for an interview. And he opened up, and he did not stop.

"People call me a pessimist," he told Lyon, who interviewed him in Washington. "I say, 'What is there to be gay about? Democracy is all done.'"

Lyon drilled down. "You mean in England or this country, too?"

"Well, I don't know. If we get into war it will be in this country, too. A bureaucracy would take over right off. Everything we hold dear would be gone. . . ."

Lyon pressed this, asking him about the effect of the new Labour Party influence in wartime Britain. Remarkably, Kennedy replied that it meant the coming of "national socialism," and he concluded: "Democracy is finished in England. It may be here." Then he announced his intention "to spend all I've got to keep us out of the war. There's no sense in our getting in. We'd just be holding the bag." The ambassador who had been bypassed by his president in the conduct of foreign relations for so long concluded: "I know more about the European situation than anybody else, and it's up to me to see that the country gets it."[68]

Three days later, on November 10, Kennedy was shocked to discover that Lyon had printed every word he had uttered. The *New York Herald Tribune* was not alone in demanding that the ambassador either explain himself or resign. About all he could manage by way of explanation, however, was the blatant falsehood that he had thought his remarks were off the record. But before the month ended, he told Joseph

Patterson of the New York *Daily News* that the British situation was "hopeless" and that the very best outcome now possible was a "negotiated peace."[69] On December 1, he formally presented his resignation to President Franklin D. Roosevelt.

A private citizen again, Joe Kennedy set out to crusade against U.S. entry into the war. It was to son Jack, not Joe Jr., that he turned for advice in this endeavor. The number-two son advised him to avoid personal attacks against the legion of newspaper columnists who were assaulting him daily and to instead calmly lay out his case. Above all, he counseled his father to make it crystal clear that he abhorred dictators and that he understood they could not be trusted. And—yes—one more thing: He was never, ever to use the words *appeaser* or *appeasement* in any public statement.

When he approached the microphones of New York's radio station WEAF on January 18, 1941, Kennedy defied his son's advice by almost immediately bringing up the appeaser "label." Acknowledging that he had been called an "appeaser," he said that if this meant he opposed "the entrance of this country into the present war," he would "cheerfully plead guilty. So must every one of you who want to keep America out of war."[70] Scenting red meat, anti-Roosevelt Republicans in Congress called on Kennedy to testify against the pending lend-lease legislation, which would give the president tremendous executive power to aid Britain and the other Allies with war materiel.

Those who opposed lend-lease expected from Kennedy blunt, authoritative support for their position. Instead, he navigated a course he thought was brilliantly fair and balanced. He opposed entry into the war, but, he explained, he did not believe President Roosevelt was making secret deals with the British, and he did believe the president should be empowered to provide Britain with immediate material and financial assistance. His only objection to the lend-lease bill as written was that it did not provide a "coordinating function" for Congress. Asked what he meant by "coordinating function," he just couldn't say.

The press attacked him—from both sides now, left and right. To some, Kennedy was an appeaser, a defeatist of the worst kind, even a pro-Fascist. To others, he had betrayed his promise to give everything he had to keep America out of the war. Either way, after his congressional testimony in February, any political future he may have had was ended.

*   *   *

HE DID STILL HAVE HIS SONS. His two eldest, Joe Jr. and Jack, had stuck by their father through the two and a half years of the ambassador's tenure. Joe Jr. had frankly emulated and even amplified his father's isolationist and then defeatist stance, contributing to it by reinforcing the prewar assessment Lindbergh had made of Germany's Luftwaffe as essentially invincible and establishing at Harvard an isolationist student association. He would not change his position until Pearl Harbor.

Jack was different. Early in his father's ambassadorship, he had echoed, albeit faintly, his arguments for appeasement. But soon his views began to diverge. In his senior year at Harvard, Jack Kennedy wrote a thesis titled "Appeasement at Munich: The Inevitable Result of the Slowness of Conversion of the British Democracy to Change from a Disarmament Policy to a Rearmament Policy." His father read it as a justification of his own support for appeasement, and he even used his considerable influence in the media and publishing industries to sell the manuscript to publishers in New York and London. It appeared in print on both sides of the Atlantic in 1940 as *Why England Slept*.

In fact, the central idea of both the senior thesis and the published book differed significantly from Ambassador Kennedy's position. JFK did not defend Chamberlain's appeasement policy so much as he refused to condemn it, arguing that the British people—not its politicians—had blindly demanded disarmament and refused to prepare for war. This left Chamberlain with no choice but to play for time to rearm, so he did what he could to delay war with Italy and Germany. For Ambassador Kennedy, appeasement was a desirable alternative to war and a tactic that might actually bring what Chamberlain claimed to have brought from Munich: "peace for our time." For his son Jack, however, appeasement was a legitimate alternative only to waging war prematurely. By no means a formula for sustained peace, it was merely a tactic to avoid immediate defeat by overwhelming forces. Well before Pearl Harbor forced the United States into the conflict, JFK would voice his support for Roosevelt's progressive dismantling of U.S. neutrality laws and his policy of providing material aid to Great Britain.

As Joseph Sr. feared, it would be the fate of both of his sons to be swallowed up in the war. Yet he also hoped that both would perform heroically. It turned out that the younger, Jack, would do so out of the very reserve of idealism and strength that Ambassador Kennedy saw during the Blitz but could never bring himself to recognize, much less understand. The oldest son, the ambassador's namesake, would—as the saying goes—make the supreme sacrifice. But he would do so less in service to an ideal than in defense and exoneration of his father.

Joe Jr. would give his life in a mission whose objective was to save London and the other cities of England from a new kind of airborne warfare. The Blitz ended on May 21, 1941, when Hitler called off the raids in order to move his bombers east in preparation for Germany's invasion of Russia. The new air war against the British, the onslaught of the pilotless *Vergeltungswaffen*—the V weapons, or vengeance weapons—commenced on June 13, 1944. By March 1945, 9,251 unmanned V-1 "buzz bombs" had been fired at targets in England, most of them directed against London, where they killed 6,184 civilians and injured another 17,981. The even more advanced V-2, a ballistic missile, would claim 2,754 civilian lives in London, injuring an additional 6,523. Because there was no effective defense against the V-2s, destroying the sites from which they were being launched became an urgent Allied priority. The daring and desperation of military leaders and pilots in the U.S. Army Air Forces and U.S. Navy—among them Lieutenant Joseph P. Kennedy Jr.—led to a series of missions that pushed the envelope of technology, courage, and selflessness.

CHAPTER 1

CHOSEN SON

PLACE—POSITION, DOMAIN—WAS ALWAYS IMPORTANT TO JOSEPH P. Kennedy Sr. When he took up his ambassadorship in London, he complained that the embassy at 1 Grosvenor Square was not only "badly laid out" but that the "beautiful blue silk room" he had for an office called for nothing more than the addition of "a Mother Hubbard dress and a wreath to make me Queen of the May."[1] While his official residence at 14 Prince's Gate, donated to the U.S. government years earlier by financier J. Pierpont Morgan, was more to his liking, he nevertheless found its fifty-two rooms insufficient for his family of eleven and immediately set about extensively refurbishing it—on his own dime.

The ambassadorship, the embassy, and the residence were the fruits of three generations' distance from the poverty that had driven his paternal grandfather from Ireland to America. Patrick Kennedy went to East Boston from County Wexford at the height of the potato famine and English oppression in 1848 or 1849. Ireland, which would figure so prominently in the ancestral memory of all the Kennedy clan, was, in the mid-nineteenth century, a place to leave, and East Boston was a resolutely working-class but relatively prosperous community. And work Patrick did, at a cooperage, making barrels twelve hours a day, seventy-two hours a week, until, at the age of thirty-five, he dropped dead. The cause was cholera complicated by soul-killing labor, and he left his widow, Bridget, to support four children, among whom was a

single male, Patrick Joseph "P. J." Kennedy. The widow labored as a
house cleaner and moonlighted as a hairdresser, managing to squirrel
away enough money to open up a small combination grocery-bakery-
liquor store and to get P. J. educated at Sacred Heart School. He went on
to earn a living as a stevedore and, later, a pipe fitter before buying into
several local saloons during his mid-twenties. From these enterprises, P.
J. branched out to local and state politics, retail liquor sales, banking,
real estate, and coal.

By the time P. J.'s first son, Joseph Patrick, was born in 1888, it was
into the fine house of a rather wealthy man. It was, that is, a fine house
in Irish Catholic East Boston, separated from Brahmin Protestant Boston proper by both the Inner Harbor and class prejudice. Of the two,
the harbor was far easier to cross, and, at the prompting of his wife,
Mary, P. J. saw to it that Joe was sent across that harbor to Boston Latin
School. Founded in 1635, the institution was widely regarded by 1901,
when Joe enrolled, as the most elite public school in the nation. The
academic quality of the education it offered mattered less to P. J. than
Boston Latin's function as a door to admission into the socioeconomic
realm reserved for "proper Bostonians."

Joe was far from a standout student—Ds and Cs abounded—but
he was an outstanding baseball player and sufficiently charismatic to
win election as class president. The mere fact of having graduated from
Boston Latin secured him a place at Harvard, and so, after commencement in 1908, he crossed the Charles River to Cambridge. He graduated
in 1912, his academic performance as undistinguished as it had been at
Boston Latin—Ds, Cs, a handful of Bs, and a lone A to show for four
years—but his record socially and as an athlete (again on the baseball
team) was impressive if not stellar.

From Harvard, he went directly into banking—or at least as directly as his Irish Catholic heritage allowed in Brahmin Boston. In
1912, only one Boston-area bank had an Irish president, and the barriers to entry into finance were so formidable for men of his ethnic and
religious pedigree that Rose Fitzgerald—the daughter of Mayor John
Francis "Honey Fitz" Fitzgerald, who became his college sweetheart
and whom he married in 1914—was always puzzled as to why he chose
banking over all other possible professions. The reason, of course, was
place. Banking was just the place for a young Bostonian on the outside

looking to get on the inside. Unable to enter banking as an officer, Joe decided to become a bank examiner, a state civil servant. He served in this position only briefly when, thanks to his father's banking connections, the opportunity to acquire a controlling interest in the Columbia Trust Bank came his way in 1913. And so he became, at twenty-five, not only Boston's second Irish Catholic bank president but the nation's youngest bank president.

After marrying Rose, Joe left it to her to choose a house—not in East Boston, however, but in Brookline, across the Charles from Cambridge. It was unmistakably an upscale suburb, but it was not Brahmin. In contrast, say, to Beacon Hill, where only old money mattered, in Brookline, money, new or old, spoke equally loud and clear. Yet even the new house in the new place was not, Joe judged, quite the right *place* for his first son to come into the world. As Rose's first pregnancy ran its course, Joe rented an oceanside summerhouse on the fine gray sands of Hull on the Nantasket Peninsula in Plymouth County. It was an idyllic location, amid cool ocean breezes and salt air. For the impending birth, Joe arranged for not one but two prominent physicians to be on hand, along with an obstetrical nurse and a housemaid. He was determined to leave nothing to chance when it came to ushering his firstborn into the world. The event occurred on July 25, 1915, precisely nine months and eighteen days after he and Rose were wed. Joseph Patrick Kennedy Jr. was born, if not effortlessly—he did weigh ten pounds—at least without complication. The Kennedys were fortunate indeed.

Having chosen the place, summoned the doctors, and made the preparations, Joe Kennedy Sr. did not linger to hover and dote. He had bought the best care money could buy and planned everything to the last detail; now he went about his business as usual, leaving the baby entirely to Rose, the nurse, and the maid.

*   *   *

IT WAS THE WAY THE FATHER would treat all nine of his children, especially the first two, Joe Jr. and Jack. He would prepare, he would purchase, he would pull strings and smooth the way. He would counsel, yet he would not hover. He was, in fact, often absent, especially when he got into the movie business beginning in the 1920s and started spending large blocks of time in Hollywood (either at his desk or in the arms of some star or starlet). Yet he never let go.

Mindful of a heritage of Irish famine, hard work, and early death, Joe Sr. also appreciated his more immediate heritage: a father who made a fortune as well as political connections that propelled him across the Inner Harbor from East Boston to Boston proper by way of Cambridge. He intended to raise his children as Catholics, Irish Catholics. He had not run from that, and he did not want any of them to run, either. But, clearly, he wanted to position them—especially his firstborn and namesake—to suffer fewer of the social and professional exclusions he had circumvented if not always overcome. Joe Jr. did move effortlessly through the first years of the childhood his father had prepared for him. He had come into the world as a ten-pound package of perfect health, and he only grew stronger. The birth of a second son, John Fitzgerald Kennedy, on May 29, 1917, frail and sickly from the start, introduced into the family a rare discordant note of worry—yet, by sheer contrast, the ill health of the younger son also served to underscore the phenomenal vigor of the elder.

If Joe Sr. left child rearing almost exclusively to his wife, she, in turn, relied heavily on Kikoo Convoy, an Irish nanny from the old country, who lavished on the boys her very genuine love. Rose may have had to struggle to avoid showing Joe Jr. the favoritism that his looks—strappingly handsome even as a toddler, with piercing blue eyes—and his obviously high intelligence commanded. Perhaps as a way of leveling the field, she dressed Joe and Jack in identical sailor suits. But after the results of an IQ test administered by his first teachers revealed Joe Jr. as "gifted," neither Rose nor Joe Sr. could continue to view their sons as existing on the same plane. Rose later admitted, "I didn't think you could have two in one family." To publishing mogul Henry Luce, the senior Kennedy even coldly expressed the judgment that Jack, in contrast to Joe, would not "get very far" because "he wasn't very bright."[2]

To say that Joe outshone Jack sounds like the cliché it would certainly be if it wasn't simply true. Seen together as young children, Joe was the far more brilliant presence, big, handsome, and radiating health, whereas Jack appeared at best his thin, frail echo. He would look up to Joe Jr., who surely loved him, and yet the two were fiercely competitive.

Physically, Jack was rarely a match for Joe. As he later admitted, when they fought, which was frequently, Joe "of course . . . always won."[3]

Their parents seem to have done nothing to discourage the competition or even to referee, let alone stop, the fighting. If anything, consciously or not, they encouraged it. Joe was assigned the favored seat at the dinner table and was most often engaged by his father in conversation. More precisely, he was the go-to target of Joe Sr.'s questions, which were typically about business, politics, and current events. Visitors remarked that Joe Jr. spoke as if he were a copy of his father. Indeed, both the Kennedy parents recruited Joe Jr. as a kind of deputy father to their other children, and he would even stand as godfather to the eighth of the Kennedy children, Jean Ann (born 1928). Yet the actual father himself never let his eldest son become comfortable, let alone complacent, in his position of privilege. If Jack practiced the piano for an hour or studied for a half hour, Joe Sr. presented his namesake with a precise accounting worthy of the banker that he was. The implication was unmistakable. *Jack practiced an hour. You owe me at least that much, if not more.* In fact, Joe Jr. was always expected to make additional deposits to his account, lest his brother catch up to—or even overtake—him.[4]

"Boys will be boys," the old saying goes, and it has usually been the excuse fathers make for the boisterous transgressions they themselves instigate in their sons. In the case of Joe and Jack, however, it was Rose more than her husband who encouraged their aggressive behavior. She dutifully inspected them both before sending them off each morning to Edward Devotion Elementary School—Joe started there in 1920 and Jack followed in 1922—ensuring that their outfits were neat, proper, and altogether befitting their station in life. Yet no sooner did the boys return home from school than Rose insisted they change into clothes that made them look (she later said) "like roughnecks."[5] By no means did Joe Sr. discourage this cultivation of masculine aggression in the pair, but his role was more that of instructor. He was, in fact, less interested in how they comported themselves than in what they knew and what they said.

Whether or not it was the result of their father's incitement to competition combined with their mother's cultivation of a "roughneck" attitude, Joe and Jack were often exuberantly unruly, if not downright obnoxious. They loudly disrupted the silence of the local library, they played on a neighbor's rooftop, and (according to Rose's diary) they formed a "club where they initiate new members by sticking pins into them."[6]

*   *   *

WHEN JOSEPH KENNEDY SR. WAS NOT quizzing the boys or lecturing them, he seemed curiously oblivious of them. One snowy day, when Joe Jr. was just two, his father pulled him on a sled; however, instead of watching the boy—let alone enjoying him—he talked business all the while with an associate while absently dragging his cargo behind him. When young Joe tumbled off the sled, the senior Joe did not even take notice but continued pulling, leaving the toddler behind in a bank of snow.

And yet Joe Sr. was willing to remake the world—or at least that part of it immediately adjacent to him—when he saw his children's lives at stake. In February 1920, shortly after Rose had given birth to a second daughter, Kathleen, Jack came down with scarlet fever during a local epidemic. The frail child quickly became desperately ill, and Joe Sr. found himself in a crisis. Jack needed to be hospitalized—not only to increase his own chances for recovery but to isolate him from Rose, the newborn Kathleen, sister Rosemary, and Joe Jr. The Brookline Hospital lacked a contagion ward and so could not accept Jack. Boston Hospital had a special isolation ward for children, the South Department, and also boasted a staff that included a renowned scarlet fever authority, Dr. Edward Place. The problem was that Jack was not a Boston child, and the ward—overflowing to more than five times its capacity with scarlet fever cases—would not accept a patient from outside of the city. Joe could not buy his way into Boston Hospital. But he could lean on his father-in-law, Honey Fitz, the former Boston mayor, who still possessed sufficient influence to prevail on Mayor Andrew Peters to muscle Jack into the isolation ward—never mind that this meant that some Boston child, like Jack a victim of the epidemic, would be excluded.

After Jack was out of danger, he was sent, with a nurse, to a rented house in Maine to convalesce and was periodically visited by members of the family. While Jack was away, in March 1920, the senior Kennedy decided the time had once again come to move. He sold his house on

Beals Street, choosing a larger corner residence at Abbotsford and Naples Roads in a wealthier Brookline neighborhood. When Jack was fully recovered and safely installed in the new house, Joe Sr. was once again content to turn the boys over to Rose—until, in 1924, he decided to alter their young lives by finding a new school for them. He took them out of Edward Devotion, the local public school, and enrolled them both in the Noble Lower School—the feeder school for the exclusive Noble and Greenough School, which had been established in 1866 as an alternative to Boston Latin for boys whose parents had Harvard aspirations.

Why would Joe Kennedy, an alumnus of Boston Latin, want to place his sons in its alternative? We can only assume that it was for the same reason that some other parents chose it. Boston Latin, some agreed, had admitted too many Jews, immigrants—*and* (for that matter) Irish Catholics. Noble Lower and Noble and Greenough were overwhelmingly Protestant and therefore "solidly American." At the time of their enrollment, the Kennedy boys may well have been the only Catholics in attendance at the lower school. They endured slurs and epithets—mostly directed against their Irish ethnicity rather than their Roman Catholicism. As Joe Sr. saw it, for boys like his—just as for the boy he himself had been—exclusive private Protestant schools provided an obligatory hazing of initiation into a WASP-dominated world of money and influence and power. It was the price of admission.

Joe Jr. paid part of that price to one John Clark Jones III, a boy older and bigger than he, who seems to have made it his personal mission to torture the Irish newcomer. Ultimately, Joe learned to use St. Aidan's Church, located nearby at Freeman and Pleasant Streets, as sanctuary. After outrunning Jones and his followers, he would stand in the doorway of the church and announce that it was a shrine. "You can't touch me here!"[7] Like many Protestants, Joe's tormentors were awestruck by the Catholic mystery and did not dare approach him in the shadow of the "shrine."

In 1926, Noble Lower closed, and Joseph Kennedy Sr. joined a seven-man committee to establish in its place the Dexter School—chiefly to function as the new "lower school" for Noble and Greenough. Now the senior Kennedy not only had his two sons in this bastion of Brahmin Boston, he also had a founding stake in it—a stake financed by a considerable contribution to the building fund.

While Kennedy had bought his boys a secure berth in the institution, and although the other parents treated both him and his wife with respect, they never socialized with the couple. It was clear to the senior Kennedy that his boys would have to earn acceptance the way he had at Boston Latin: not by dint of parental money, or even by academic achievement (despite Joe Jr.'s lofty IQ numbers, he was never close to being a standout student at Dexter), but on the playing field.

Frail though he was, Jack earned a spot on the Dexter baseball team and, later, was quarterback on the football team as well. Predictably, while Jack relied on his wits as a quarterback, Joe Jr. approached the game by applying sheer, unrelenting aggression. He relished the tackle, and he always hit hard. Moreover, he carried that same aggression from the gridiron to the diamond. As an outfielder, he laid claim to every fly ball that came even remotely his way, shouting warnings to his teammates to clear off as he maneuvered himself to catch each hit. As a pitcher, he specialized in a fiery fastball that nobody wanted to catch—except for Jack, who willingly endured the pain that made his mitt seem awfully thin. As a base runner, Joe argued with umpires as if he were every bit their equal in age and authority. No other boy could have gotten away with it, but what would have been seen as poor sportsmanship or ungentlemanly conduct in others came across as nothing more or less than the Kennedy spirit when Joe Jr. let loose. For many, that spirit proved an irresistible attraction.

*   *   *

IN 1922, JOE KENNEDY BEGAN renting for his family a vacation home in Cohasset, some thirty miles southeast of Brookline along Massachusetts Bay. It was yet another change of place suited to his ever-rising status. He might have chosen Nantasket on the peninsula, long familiar to the family as a favorite shore resort for Boston's upper-middle-class Irish Catholics. But Cohasset was far and away the favored preserve of stockbrokers, and, since 1919, Kennedy had been an executive with the brokerage of Hayden, Stone & Co. His Wall Street credentials readily bought him and his family entrée into the small summer community at Cohasset, but when he tried to get into the local golf club, he was quietly turned away—even though he was vouched for by several Harvard classmates.

Joe took his family back to Cohasset for the summer of 1923, but in 1924 he rented a house in Hyannis Port. It was at the time a more down-market community than Cohasset in that it had not been colonized by the Brahmin elite. While it was not as closely associated with Boston's Irish Catholic community as Nantasket, it did have a Catholic church, a golf club—which welcomed Joe's membership—and a yacht club, where both Joe Jr. and Jack would learn to sail, and not just in the bay but on the open ocean. While Jack's sailing experience would stand him in good stead as a PT boat skipper in the South Pacific and although the public would become familiar with photos of the JFK family sailing after Jack entered the White House, it was Joe Jr. who became the family's master mariner at Hyannis Port and an avid race competitor. In 1928, thirteen-year-old Joe Jr. and eleven-year-old Jack were given the first boat of their own. They christened it *Rose Elizabeth* to honor their mother, and when, one afternoon, they saw from their front porch a small boat swamped by a swell, the boys instantly set sail in the *Rose Elizabeth,* reached the capsized little craft, and fished a young boy out of the saltwater. The local paper hailed the Kennedy boys as heroes.

Before that 1928 season was out, Joe Sr. purchased the Hyannis Port house he rented at 28 Marchant Avenue. He immediately enlarged it, and it became the nucleus around which the celebrated "Kennedy Compound" grew over the years. JFK purchased a home nearby in 1956, and fourth son Edward Moore "Ted" Kennedy (1932–2009) bought one adjacent to both houses in 1959, selling it to his older brother Robert F. "Bobby" Kennedy (1925–1968) in 1961.

Of all the Kennedy "places," Hyannis Port would be the most durable and enduring. Intimately identified with no particular ethnic, social, or religious group, it was a place Joe and his family could make their own. "We didn't really go out to other places to play," Ted Kennedy recalled in a memoir. "We didn't go off to other kinds of events. It was all here, all here: all the playing, all the enjoyment, all the fun."[8]

By the late 1920s, Joseph Kennedy Sr. was deeply into the movie business, which had very rapidly propelled him from rising prosperity to world-class wealth. As a stockbroker in a market subject to little government regulation, he had become a master at manipulation. This was neither unusual nor considered unethical in his profession. Unlike most other brokers, however, he understood that if *he* could manipulate, he could also *be* manipulated. A man of great energy and enthusiasm, Joe Sr. was also grounded, for better or worse, by a streak of indelible pessimism. While others could see no end to the boom times, he, on the contrary, believed the equity markets were critically overheated. What made the environment all the more volatile, he believed, was the delusional sense of control most brokers had—they could burn others without themselves getting burned. And so, having acquired mountains of wealth, he began to invest in ways aimed at preservation and protection rather than risk-taking. He took a good deal of his assets out of stocks and put it into real estate, and as the stock market continued to heat up, instead of reinvesting there, he strategically acquired a series of short positions, effectively betting on the imminence of a sudden decline. While he was certainly not the only savvy Wall Streeter to prosper when the great crash of October 1929 came, he was one of comparatively few.

And it was a very good thing. Not only had he just sunk money into purchasing and expanding his Hyannis Port property, he also decided to move his family out of Brookline and to New York. In September 1927, he rented a thirteen-room house in Riverdale, the Bronx, overlooking the Hudson River. That his business interests were now centered in New York—and Hollywood (where he would soon commence a long-term affair with the actress Gloria Swanson)—was reason enough to move, but Joe preferred to justify the relocation in terms of his family, protesting that WASPish Brookline was "no place to bring up Irish Catholic children."[9]

Was Riverdale really any better? Perhaps. But he did not stay there long. In May 1929, just six months after buying and expanding his Hyannis Port house, Joe bought a Georgian-style mansion in Bronxville, Westchester County, a community whose exclusivity at the time extended to a nearly total ban on Jews and Catholics, especially Irish Catholics. Kennedy's protestations against anti-Irish prejudice notwithstanding, it was as if he felt compelled to defy exclusion by repeatedly establishing himself in places where "his kind" were not welcome. Rose was never admitted into the Bronxville Women's Club, and Joe Sr. never even tried for the prestigious—and "restricted"—Bronxville Country Club.

When the family moved to Riverdale, Joe Jr., Jack, and their three oldest siblings enrolled at Riverdale Country School. There, Joe and

Jack played sports as usual, having fiercely prepared with summers of touch football at Hyannis Port—though the adjective *touch* was really a misnomer, given the physical intensity with which the two boys played. It was tackle football by another name. As usual, too, both the older Kennedy boys were very popular in school, despite some anti-Irish slurs. Joe swaggered while Jack charmed. Joe was aggressively attracted to girls—and they almost always reciprocated his attentions—whereas Jack, though certainly the object of much adolescent female attention, was painfully shy. He was even known to duck into the bathroom when it was time for dancing class.

Jack distinguished himself academically at Riverdale, at least in a modest way, by winning a prize for composition in the sixth grade. Joe achieved considerably better grades than his father ever had at prep school, yet they were hardly outstanding, and Joe Sr. became concerned about preparing his firstborn for a high school that would position him to enter Harvard. While he would be content to let his girls continue at the high school Riverdale Country offered, he wanted something more for his namesake—and perhaps for Jack as well. His alma mater, Boston Latin, was a possibility, but Joe Sr. was not eager to thrust his sons back into that Brahmin bastion. He sought counsel from several Harvard classmates, including Russell Ayres, who taught history and coached baseball at Choate, the distinguished boarding school located in Wallingford, Connecticut. Joe Sr. judged Choate sufficiently WASP-ish to get his son into Harvard but not so Protestant that it couldn't tolerate an Irish Catholic. (A Jew was another matter. The Choate application actually included a question as to whether the applicant was "in any part Hebraic."[10])

Joe Sr. did know that it would take some doing to get his son's Riverdale grades up to a point compatible with Choate's selective entrance requirements. Since he was frequently away in Hollywood, he had some of his most important "talks" with his oldest son via letters. He congratulated him on "making up" certain subjects in which his showing had been weak. "I am very proud of your effort and results."[11] Joe Jr. lived for such words, which is doubtless why his father's letters in this and similar vein survive.

Admitted to Choate, Joe Jr. initially bridled at the school's regimentation, which contrasted dramatically with the easygoing atmosphere of Riverdale Country, but Headmaster George St. John took him under his beneficent wing. Whether or not Joe saw it, his father had a hand in motivating such concern. Through the likes of Ayres, Joe Sr. had made it clear that he intended to contribute considerably more than basic tuition to the school. To give Joe Jr. his due, however, the young man ultimately did work hard. For his part, St. John wrote detailed reports to Joe Sr., each missive a masterpiece of criticism cloaked in praise calculated to make a parent proud: "we want [Joe's] best and Joe himself really wants to give it to us."[12] Working together—St. John in person, Joe Sr. by mail—the two men wrought a small miracle of motivation. Mediocre grades gradually became exemplary. The young man's initial attitude toward Choate athletics was halfhearted. Shortly after arriving at the school, he asked his father to arrange horseback riding for him. Joe Sr. replied, by letter, that it was better to concentrate on football. "Perhaps," the elder Kennedy allowed, "both [horseback riding and football] can be done but I would not give up the chance of participating in school athletics for the sake of riding horseback."[13] A father's directive couched in the language of strategic advice, it was vintage Joe Sr.—one adult talking business with another.

After completing the seventh grade at Riverdale, Jack was sent to Canterbury, a Catholic boarding school in New Milford, Connecticut. Both Rose and Joe were afraid to test the boy's delicate health by packing him off to the more academically demanding and somewhat more distant Choate. Arguably, they might have taken comfort in the presence of Joe Jr. there to watch out for him, but they may have been more concerned that the boys' intense rivalry would actually push Jack's health beyond its limits. As it turned out, Jack did not much like Canterbury, and his health deteriorated. He lost weight, and he came close to fainting one day during Mass. Writing to his father about this incident, he comforted himself by remarking that brother Joe was known to have fainted *twice* in church, "so I guess I will live."[14] Alarmed by his son's condition, Joe Sr. took him to Palm Beach during Easter vacation in the hope that the sun, sand, and saltwater would revive him. Shortly after he returned to Canterbury, however, Jack suffered an attack of appendicitis, underwent surgery, and then endured a prolonged convalescence. He never returned to the Catholic school. Instead, come September 1931, he joined his brother at Choate.

By that time, Joe Jr. had completed his second year at the school and was not only a model student but also enormously popular. Apparently his earlier aggressive streak was in remission. While he himself had been the target of the traditional hazing of new students and underclassmen, now that it was his turn to dish out the punishment, he would have no part of it.

We can only guess Jack's feelings as he joined his brother at the demanding school Joe had clearly conquered. Did Jack get the sense that his father had passed down to his firstborn the best part of himself? Even worse, perhaps, did he feel that his father believed he had? Jack rarely missed an opportunity to undercut his brother in the eyes of the senior Kennedy. While Jack was still at Canterbury, before he joined his older brother at Choate, Joe came home on a holiday visit during his first year at Choate. On December 9, 1929, Jack wrote to his father (who was in Hollywood) about how Joe arrived, "telling me how strong he was and how tough." Eager to puncture this boastfulness and exhibit the resulting deflation to Joe Sr., Jack continued: "The first thing he did to show me how tough he was was to get sick so that he could not have any thanksgiving dinner. Manly youth."[15]

There was more, much more in that letter. Jack related how Joe was going to show *him* how to Indian wrestle. "I . . . through [*sic*] him over on his neck." And it was with particular relish that he related how the sixth formers at Choate had beaten up on Joe. "Oh Man he was all blisters, they almost paddled the life out of him." Jack related that Joe had been "roughhousing in the hall" when a sixth former caught him and "led him in and all the sixth formers had a swat or two." Jack's narrative reads as if he had been an eyewitness—but, of course, he was still at Canterbury. Nevertheless, from fantasy eyewitness, Jack ratcheted up his point of view to that of a vicarious participant: "What I wouldn't have given to be a sixth former."[16] Far from reprimanding Jack for his uncharitable—not to say mildly sadistic—attitude toward his brother's comeuppance, Joe Sr. did not even remark on it.

Aggressive? Unfeeling? Sadistic? When twenty-two-year-old Joe Jr. took his five-year-old brother Teddy along on a sailboat race in the summer of 1937, Joe, at a critical juncture, called out to the little boy to "pull in the jib." Teddy had no idea what a jib was and so looked about helplessly. Joe leaped up, took hold of the jib, then grabbed Teddy by the seat of his pants and chucked him into the ocean. After fishing him back up, he dumped the child onto the deck—warning him to keep his mouth shut about what had just happened.[17]

What would Joe Sr. and Rose have done to Joe Jr. had Teddy told the tale (which the youngster related only in adulthood)? Seeing that the boy had survived, there would quite probably have been no consequences. *Both* parents, after all, cultivated intense competition among their sons, disparity in age notwithstanding. The father repeatedly delivered to all his children the injunction "Don't come in second or third." Placing didn't count. Only winning mattered.[18] And, when he was home, he insisted on competing with the two eldest himself, taking on the boys in tennis and golf, both sports at which he excelled and in which he played with maximum aggressiveness. When the youngsters became just old enough—and just good enough—to give their father a run for his money, he simply stopped playing. Clearly he took his own mantra to heart. Coming in second was unacceptable, even if the opponent was one of his own sons. When he could no longer be sure of victory on the court or links, he transformed the dinner table into an intellectual arena of question-and-answer, focusing mainly on current events. That Rose assumed his role as grand inquisitor when he was not present suggests that the pair were in cahoots. Indeed, the boys recalled that their mother sometimes read questions from a list—presumably drawn up by the absent father himself.

By the time of his graduation in spring 1933, Joe Jr. was chairman of the student council, editor of the yearbook, president of his class, and—no third place, no second place, but first place—winner of the Choate Prize, the school's highest academic honor. Moreover, it was Joe's name, not Jack's, that was engraved on the Harvard Football Trophy residing in the school's trophy case. Jack, in the meantime, went out for football—twice—but made it only as far as cheerleader. At 117 pounds, he would likely have been judged too small for the varsity team even if his health had been robust. But it was far from robust. He spent almost as much time in the infirmary as in the classroom. Far from viewing Jack as a malingerer, the Choate administration typically prolonged his confinement, keeping the boy in bed as long as possible. The only sport that looked viable for him at Choate was golf, but Jack had little passion for the game and no confidence in his ability. He wrote to his father that he did have a "slight chance" of making the golf team, but only "because it is rather bad this year."[19]

Joe Jr.'s achievements at Choate were both real and admirable. But, thanks in no small part to the incitement of his parents, Joe could not help but compulsively measure himself against his kid brother. The question is—how much satisfaction, how much confidence, could Joe have derived from indexing his achievements against a sibling whose odds of mere survival so often seemed slim?

* * *

BY THE EARLY 1930s, Joseph P. Kennedy Sr., one of a small cadre of very wealthy men who became even wealthier after the crash of 1929, was quite accustomed to seeing himself portrayed in the media as a financial genius, an entrepreneurial superman, and generally the smartest man in the room. Whatever else he was, the senior Kennedy was never average, and that meant he seldom did the expected. He had sent Joe and Jack to conservative Choate. There Joe had excelled. His course was clear and seemed set. It was nearly the course Joe Sr. himself had followed. And perhaps for that very reason, the father pushed the son into a zag where a zig was expected. Fresh out of Choate, which was filled with the scions of America's conservative elite, Joe Jr. felt the hand of his father on his shoulder, twisting him firmly into a left turn. Instead of Harvard— or the even more exclusive Cambridge or Oxford—Joe Sr. enrolled his firstborn for a year at the London School of Economics.

Academically, it was a highly defensible choice. In the 1930s, the school was a hotbed of leading-edge political and economic thought. Socially, however, it was a decidedly contrarian move. The London School was a center of socialist and even Marxist theory. The economic policy formulated and debated there was highly advanced, but also far removed from the conventions of capitalism on which the senior Kennedy had thrived. It was hardly a place Joe Jr. would have chosen for himself. The school was tailor-made for young intellectuals, for iconoclasts, for mavericks, and Joe Jr., imbued with the values of privilege and validated by academic and popular success against others similarly imbued, was none of these things. Joe Sr. explained to his wife that he wanted his sons to "know the whatnots of keeping" the wealth they would undoubtedly one day have.[20] His strategy in sending Joe Jr. to the radical London School of Economics was to give him a perspective from which he could be returned, later, to Harvard or some other high-end academy of conventional capitalism. Joe Sr. always played the angles, and the London School was a most oblique angle, he believed, that would give his boy a unique insight into mainstream politics and economics. His very faith in his son's essential conservatism, his right thinking, led Joe Sr. to have no qualms that the lad might become a leftist or (what amounted to the same thing) a genuine intellectual.

Did he explain his strategic rationale to his son? We don't know. But what is clear is that Joe Jr. did not question, let alone raise objection to, the strategy. He simply followed—even when his Irish Catholic father led him from the Protestant tutelage of Choate to the mentoring of Harold Laski, a practicing Socialist, lapsed Jew, and outspoken atheist.

The child of a Manchester cotton merchant who was also a leader of the Liberal Party, Laski quickly evolved into an aggressive iconoclast. He embraced eugenics and even married a lecturer on the subject. That she was a gentile and not a Jew outraged and alienated his family. Laski responded by renouncing Judaism and proclaiming himself an atheist. He took a degree in history at Oxford, worked briefly as a journalist, left England to teach at McGill University in Montreal, and also lectured at Harvard and Yale before helping to found, in 1919, the New School for Social Research in New York City. At Harvard he was befriended by Felix Frankfurter, a Jewish immigrant from Vienna, who worked and studied his way up from the Lower East Side ghetto, through the City College of New York, and into Harvard Law School, where he edited the *Harvard Law Review*. Frankfurter became a prominent Manhattan attorney, served as assistant to Henry Stimson, when Stimson was U.S. attorney for the Southern District of New York and then, again under Stimson, after President William Howard Taft appointed Stimson secretary of war. Disillusioned with politics during the Wilson administration, Frankfurter joined the Harvard Law faculty, took time out to serve as Judge Advocate General for the War Department after the United States entered World War I, and, after the armistice, returned to Harvard. There, becoming deeply involved in labor politics and labor law, Zionism, and civil liberties, he helped found the American Civil Liberties Union (ACLU). He was appointed chairman of the Harvard Law School in 1921, continued as an activist in progressive and even radical causes, and, with the election of Franklin D. Roosevelt in 1932, became the new president's close advisor on New Deal law and policy. Although Joe Sr. and Frankfurter were miles apart in upbringing, religion, and social policy, both supported FDR, and in 1933 the senior Kennedy felt close enough to Frankfurter to seek his advice on the education of Joe Jr. It was Frankfurter—like Joe Sr., after all, a product of Harvard—who suggested that the young man not rush off to their alma mater but instead study for a year with his remarkable friend Harold Laski.

Sending his son on such a radical detour seems bolder than it may actually have been. Joe Sr. was not afraid to march to the beat of his own drum, but his strategy was always based on the bottom line. Some viewed Frankfurter and Laski as radicals. The senior Kennedy saw them as men who rode certain radical ideas straight into mainstream success. Neither Frankfurter nor Laski exhorted the masses from a threadbare street corner. On the contrary, Frankfurter was precisely what Joe Kennedy aspired to be: an FDR insider. As for Laski, he was one of the world's most highly respected economic and political theorists. Whatever their beliefs, both men had ended up on top—not in third place or second but in first. And to Joe Sr., that is what counted.

Joe Jr. enrolled, therefore, at the London School of Economics, taking the "General Course," which included German and French, along with history and economics—the latter taught by Laski. Joe Sr. kept up a steady stream of letters to his son, two or three each month. His news always included updates on the family and on football at Choate as well as Harvard. The father wanted to inject the familiar into his son's foreign life, yet, at the same time, in response to news that Joe had chosen an American as a roommate, he counseled his son to develop as many contacts with "foreigners" as possible, arguing that he would "have Americans to live with the rest of your life."[21] He discouraged his son from joining the yacht crew of a round-the-world cruise planned for the summer vacation, telling him that he preferred his returning to the States to spend time with the family, line up his first-year Harvard courses, and get ready for freshman football. Nevertheless, he suggested to Joe that, during the *spring* break, he might travel in France and Italy. "I can arrange for you to meet Mussolini," he wrote, "through Breckinridge Long, the American Ambassador to Italy and also arrange an audience with the Pope." He also advised going "into Germany and see[ing] something of Russia."[22] Kennedy furnished his son with a secondhand Chrysler convertible, purchased in Europe, and, come spring, Joe Jr. and his roommate drove it to Rome, where they had their papal audience and did meet with the U.S. ambassador, though not with Il Duce. From Rome, they drove not to Paris but to Munich.

Based on his talks with Laski, Joe Jr. wrote to his father, he expected to see in Munich evidence of "frequent brutalities." Instead, "I was very much impressed by the enthusiasm and confidence" created by the "policies of Hitler." Joe did allow that one German he spoke to, in Pisa en route to Munich, admitted "that it was regrettable that the Jews had to be driven out," but, aside from that, the man generally approved of the Führer's policies and manifest achievements. That observation was the single passage in the letter even approaching a discordant note. As for Munich itself, Joe was "impressed by the quietness of the city." The only evidence of Nazism he found was the presence of numerous Brownshirts, who, however, "are very nice and polite . . . at least to foreigners, and one sees no sign of brutality." The quiet, the politeness, the orderliness of Munich seem to have instilled in Joe a certain coldness of judgment. He wrote to his father that the German people had been left after the world war "scattered, despondent . . . divorced from hope. Hitler came in. He saw the need of a common enemy. . . . Someone, by whose riddance the Germans would feel they had cast out the cause of their predicament." He praised Hitler's perception as "excellent psychology," remarking that "it was too bad that it had to be done to the Jews." Joe did allow that the "dislike of the Jews . . . was well founded." To his mogul father, he observed that the Jews "were at the heads of all big businesses, in law etc." Joe conceded that it was "all to their credit to get so far, but their methods had been quite unscrupulous." Perhaps to avoid any accusation of vulgar anti-Semitism, Joe Jr. bolstered his argument by citing a comment from Sir James Calder, chief executive of the Distillers Company, with whom his liquor importer father regularly did business. The Jews, Calder had said, so tightly controlled the German legal system that "if you had a case against a Jew, you were nearly always sure to lose it." It was, Joe continued, "a sad state of affairs when things like that can take place." As if in stream of consciousness, however, he also thought it "extremely sad, that noted professors, scientists, artists etc. so should have to suffer," only to insist to his father that, "as you can see, it would be practically impossible to throw out only a part of them, from both a practical and psychological point of view." With blithe indifference—logically argued yet utterly unthinking, unfeeling, and morally vacuous—Joe pressed on: "As far as the brutality is concerned, it must have been necessary to use some, to secure the whole hearted support of the people, which was necessary to put through this present program."[23]

Jack, who visited Germany in 1937 and 1939 (and, after the war, in 1945), developed a distinctly different point of view. During his 1937 trip, he found the Nazis arrogant and the apparent progress in Germany hollow. In contrast to his brother, who "reported" to his father his "observations" of German infrastructure and society, Jack was less interested in what he saw than in what people told him. He freely engaged in conversation with German men and women on the street, including a hotel keeper, who, he noted in his diary, was "quite a Hitler fan." Whereas Joe would have ascribed the hotel keeper's enthusiasm to the material improvements Hitler had brought to German life, Jack noted "that these dictators are more popular in the country than outside due to their effective propaganda." And propaganda, he added, seemed to be Hitler's "strongest point."[24]

Joe observed, recorded, and drew conclusions. Jack asked questions. Whereas Joe tended to lecture his father on the meaning of Nazism in Germany, Jack expressed himself with far more modest skepticism, writing to Joe Sr. that he was certain of few things except for "the almost complete ignorance [of] 95% of the people in the U.S." about what was happening in Europe.[25] The implications of this remark were ambiguous. His correspondent, Joe Sr., could choose to interpret it as support for his own isolationist point of view. Or it could be taken to imply that, were the American people better informed, they would never tolerate the appeasement Ambassador Kennedy enthusiastically supported. Jack loved his father, but he did not want to become a chip off the old block, let alone a surrogate for Joe Sr. and his views.

Just how thoroughly the vocabulary of compulsion blunted any skepticism, intellectual curiosity, and empathy Joe Jr. may have had is evident in the young man's praise of Hitler's "sterilization law," which, he wrote to his father, was "a great thing." Joe Jr. conceded that eugenics might not sit well with the Catholic Church, but he pointed out that "it will do away with many of the disgusting specimens of men which inhabit this earth."[26] Surely the young man had not forgotten that his sister Rosemary, just three years his junior, was developmentally disabled. Just as surely, he also loved her very much. When he was an undergraduate at Harvard, he frequently fetched her from Mrs. Newton, the lady who looked after her, and took her to college dances as his "date." He would do the same in New York, at the Stork Club, and in Hyannis Port, at the yacht club.

For the most part, Joe Sr. welcomed his son's assessment of Hitler's Germany. He replied to his letter on May 4, 1934, telling him that his observations "show a very keen sense of perception" and assuring him that his "conclusions are very sound." He admitted, however, what his son did not concede, that it is "still possible that Hitler went far beyond his necessary requirements in his attitude towards the Jews, the evidence of which may be very well covered up from the observer who goes in there at this time."[27]

It is tempting to speculate that his year at the London School of Economics, among whose students were the Jewish Marxists and Socialists that formed Laski's inner circle, heightened Joe Jr.'s resentment of "the Jews." Laski and his followers were brilliant—and biting. The aggressive competitor in the arena of sport could not compete with them as equals on the field of intellectual argument. Not that Joe ever backed down. When he was at Dexter School, although he was capable of evading bullies by taking refuge in a church doorway, he just as frequently picked fights with bigger, older boys as if to prove to himself—and to anyone looking on—that he could take it. Now, instead of slinking away from Laski's classes, tail tucked between his legs, he followed the professor into his office—Laski was famous for his never-ending office hours and enormous generosity in sharing his time with genuinely inquisitive students—and unashamedly asked him to explain whatever it was that had gone over his head. Laski could be an intimidating presence. In public lectures, he was not above humiliating those who asked foolish questions. But he must have seen in Joe Jr. if not an intellectual spark, a powerful will to make himself understand what at the moment was incomprehensible to him. Whatever Joe felt toward "the Jews," he respected what Laski's Jews knew and understood, and he wanted to understand as well. Laski appreciated his hunger, and he also appreciated the ambition Joe confessed to him—for a political career. Laski noted that others in his class subjected him to "relentless teasing" for his "determination to be nothing less than President of the United States," but, for his part, Laski was drawn to "that smile that was pure magic," and so he shared his time and his mind with the young man and corresponded with the senior Kennedy affectionately and approvingly on the subject of his son.[28]

Indeed, at the urging of his father, Joe accepted Laski's invitation to travel with him to the Soviet Union, where he was scheduled to deliver a lecture in Moscow. Joe Sr. heartily approved, assuring his son that the trip would "give you a very favorable view point in consideration of things here."[29] In other words, seeing conditions in the USSR firsthand would cause him to appreciate Western capitalism all the more. However, to the consternation of his father, the young man who had written admiringly about Hitler and Germany now lectured his father, mother, and siblings on the evident superiority of communism over capitalism. Brother Jack was downright gleeful, writing to a friend that "Joe came back about 3 days ago and is a communist. Some shit, eh."[30] But, as young Ted later recalled, his father responded to this radical table talk by setting "his knife and fork down" and fixing his eyes on his first-born. "'When you sell your car, and sell your boat, and sell your horse, you can talk to me about that, but otherwise *I don't want to hear any more about it in this house!*'"[31]

* * *

DESPITE HIS EXPOSURE to the lapsed Jew and practicing atheist Laski and his expressed enthusiasm for Soviet atheist communism, Joe Jr., at the end of the summer of 1934, dutifully toddled off, with Jack, to the retreat Rose had arranged for them at a Passionist monastery in Brighton, Massachusetts. This act of pious obedience should have been encouraging to Joe Sr. and his wife; however, Father Nilus McAllister wrote to Rose that he was concerned because he found that both boys were "very critical and rather of an inquisitive frame of mind," intellectual traits that he feared might threaten their adherence to the faith.[32]

If Father McAllister meant to imply that the boys needed a stronger dose of piety, the message was apparently lost on Joe Sr. From the austerity of the monastic retreat, Joe Jr. went off to Harvard, armed with an allowance sufficiently generous to indulge himself pretty much however he might want. While we don't know how much he was given, the allotment was accompanied by the senior Kennedy's advice that his son attempt to spend no more than $125 a month, not out of frugal necessity but "merely for the moral effect of trying to live as reasonably as possible." Clearly, therefore, his father had provided more than this sum. In any case, he asked his boy to try the $125 budget "for a couple of months." The subject would be revisited, Joe Sr. wrote, if "it doesn't work."[33] By way of assessing what $125 a month would buy a single young man whose room and board were paid for separately, consider that a blue-collar worker of this period took in about $100 a month and a white-collar worker (in the high-end finance, insurance, and real estate industries) could expect $135.[34] In any case, in addition to his allowance, Joe seems to have gotten whatever he asked for, whether it was train tickets to Palm Beach or the services of no less than headlining crooner Rudy Vallée and his Connecticut Yankees to perform at the Freshman Smoker when Joe Jr. chaired the Smoker committee.[35]

Not surprisingly, Joe quickly won friends at Harvard. He was not only generous with his father's money, but his energy, extroversion, and extraordinary good looks drew male and female admirers alike. At six feet, weighing 175 pounds, he exuded spectacularly good health. Into his youthful Irish face were deeply set piercing blue eyes, and his broad cheeks were perfectly balanced by a broad jaw and subtly dimpled chin. His smile displayed a perfect set of teeth (in contrast to many parents of the era, Rose was scrupulous in matters of dental hygiene and professional dental care), was genuinely warm, and virtually impossible to resist. He possessed, it seemed, all the bounty of the gods, and, in turn, he lavished that bounty on college dances—at which he especially cultivated the company of "nice" Catholic girls—and expensive Manhattan weekends, where he sought the company of café society women and showgirls. About the latter adventures, he was far from discreet, let alone secretive. He relished relating to Harvard chums the intimate details of his amorous excursions. One of these compatriots, Robert Purdy, had the "impression . . . that Joe . . . would never date the same girl twice" and was, in fact, "rough on girls . . . not apparently the kind of guy that nice girls liked to date."[36] Purdy's own fiancée—a college sweetheart—was the target of a Joe Kennedy pass, which (Purdy insisted) she rebuffed. Yet Joe was also able to land dates with the likes of a young Ethel Merman—twenty-six years old in 1934—and Katherine Hepburn, twenty-seven and at the early height of her film career.

Joe went out for football and rugby—the one game more physically brutal than the other. He broke his arm playing football and bashed his head in rugby. As if he were not content to be a football/rugby hero, he endeavored to become a hero beyond the campus and the field, on the streets of Cambridge. When he happened upon a man assaulting a woman not far from Harvard Square, he dove in and fought him. By the time the police showed up, the woman was gone, and the officers encountered nothing more or less than two men rolling around on the sidewalk. They arrested both, and Joe spent the night behind bars. No matter—it made a hell of a story. He told another tale about jumping into the Charles River to save a man from drowning. Frustratingly for him, few of his friends believed the story, ascribing it to an Irish penchant for blarney.

Although there is no evidence that Joe was unduly provoked by those who doubted his tales, he did develop a reputation for a quick, hot temper. Apparently in contrast to his father, who learned never to openly display umbrage in the presence of anti-Irish prejudice or slurs, Joe Jr. was ready to fight anyone who cast aspersions, especially when the target was the "Irish politicians" with which Boston abounded. Among this group, of course, his own maternal grandfather, "Honey Fitz" Fitzgerald, was particularly prominent. During a bull session in Joe's room, his classmate and close friend Ted Reardon started to make a reference to "these city officials," specifically including Honey Fitz. Joe cut him short and sternly ordered him out of the room. Seeing the blue fire in his friend's eyes, Reardon did not protest but instantly made for the door—just in time to avoid a swift kick in the rear. Joe's geniality stopped where any anti-Irish sentiment began, even though Reardon was so close a friend that (according to Robert Purdy) he "waited on Joe like he was a valet." Reardon was a poor boy—his father was wiped out in the crash of 1929—and there was a rumor (perhaps true) that Joe Sr., at Joe Jr.'s request, paid his way through Harvard.[37]

Young Kennedy's temper was accepted as just another aspect of his larger-than-life presence. This also included employing an actual valet—George Taylor, an African American who advertised himself as a "gentleman's gentleman"—paid for out of his allowance.[38] If Joe thought it proper to allocate some portion of his funds on a manservant, he also invested lavishly on more practical needs. He purchased the services of private tutors, a practice that many frowned upon at Harvard. If there was criticism, however, Joe apparently paid it no mind. It was said that he hired tutors to help him through every single subject he took.

* * *

ASSUMING JOE SR. WAS AWARE of his son's heavy investment in tutors, he never expressed the slightest objection to it. In fact, it may well have been the senior Kennedy's idea. What always interested Joe Sr. was the bottom line—not the cost of an investment, but the value it created—and Joe Jr. was clearly doing well at Harvard.

The senior Kennedy could take satisfaction in his firstborn's smooth sailing. He greeted with pleasure Joe Jr.'s announcement that he was majoring in government, suggesting, however, that he add economics to the mix. That would give him a leg up in business and would also be invaluable even if he pursued a life in public service. To Mrs. Felix Frankfurter, Joe Sr. explained that he wanted "to do the best thing for Joe" but by no means wanted "to force on him anything he can't see himself."[39] Yet when Joe had earlier expressed, at Harvard, an interest in studying philosophy, his father acted quickly to steer him away from that course and so was relieved and pleased by his opting instead for government.

Father McAllister had warned Rose that Jack was less compliant—more critical, more questioning—than his older brother. Nevertheless, Joe Sr. was surprised when Jack told him that he would not follow Joe into Harvard but instead would join his Choate friends Lem Billings and Rip Horton, who were Princeton bound.

Joe Sr. did not rise to forbid this, but he did question it. Following his friends? "That's not the real reason, is it, Jack?" he asked.[40]

The young man's response is not recorded, but we can guess that he was not eager to reenter his brother's long shadow. As if intent on retaining some degree of control, Jack's father did insist that, before he began at Princeton, he should follow his brother's example to the extent of spending a year under Harold Laski at the London School of Economics. Jack yielded, somewhat reluctantly sailing in September 1935 for London, where his father had arranged to put him up at Claridge's, the exclusive hotel on the corner of Brook and Davies Streets in the capital's Mayfair section. No sooner did he arrive, however, than he fell ill. He was hospitalized for tests, which produced no definitive results—except for Joe Sr.'s decision that his second son should return immediately to the United States and begin college on this side of the Atlantic, at Princeton.

Six weeks into his freshman year, Jack was back in a Boston hospital. Leukemia was the initial—and terminal—diagnosis, but that was soon changed to "malady unknown." Off and on, he spent two months in the hospital, leaving it in February 1936 without a diagnosis. In an attempt to convalesce, he spent time in Palm Beach and then on a dude ranch in Arizona before finally joining Joe Jr. at Harvard in the fall. Perhaps it was the fatigue produced by sickness that took the fight out of him. This time, he gave his father no argument about following his older brother. There was resignation, too, in what he told Professor Payton S. Wild, the master of Winthrop House, his residence. "Dr. Wild, I want you to know I'm not bright like my brother Joe."[41] Doggedly, Jack even went out for football, managing briefly to find a slot on the freshman A team before being almost instantly dropped to the B team.

Despite his ill health, Jack had filled out to 160 pounds—at six feet tall, still very slim, but not emaciated—and his shyness in the presence of the opposite sex had metamorphosed into a quasi-predatory sexual appetite that trumped even that of his brother. His Choate friend Rip Horton later said that he did not believe Jack "ever made love to a girl, told her how wonderful she was, how sweet she was. I don't think he was sentimental. I don't think he was ever dependent on the companionship of a girl. He always felt they were a useful thing to have when you wanted them, but when you didn't want them, put them back."[42]

Jack may well have viewed sex as one field on which he could compete with Joe as an equal. If Joe had dated Merman and Hepburn, he cozied up to Gertrude Niesen, a voluptuous songstress who was the first performer to record "Smoke Gets in Your Eyes" and was voted "Greatest Torch Singer of 1935" by a fan magazine. Following closely in Joe's footsteps, Jack chaired the Freshman Smoker committee and enticed

Niesen to perform. While securing her services was a coup for Jack, Joe nevertheless managed to horn in. "Get lost, Baby Brother," he told him in front of Niesen. "I'll take over." And take over he did. Niesen found Joe's attentions "very exciting, very flattering, very wonderful. Joe was a *terribly* good-looking guy. He was much better looking than Jack at that particular time." Yet, in hindsight, she wished she had "been a little older and really understood what was going on."[43]

Undaunted, Jack proved a very formidable competitor against his brother. Whereas Joe had developed a reputation as a solid if not brilliant student, a hard worker with a liberal dash of the cad about him, Jack was perceived as a womanizing playboy who occasionally took classes. He avidly sought important social connections, but he was even more avid in making sexual conquests at every level, local waitresses included. While Joe made connections among prominent faculty members, Jack befriended socially well-placed students. It was perhaps inevitable that, after the Harvard-Princeton game one year, as Joe and his teammate Tom Bilodeau entered Manhattan's Stork Club as part of a postgame night on the town, he found Jack already seated ringside in the company of a lovely woman. Avoiding an outright confrontation, Joe tactically retreated to a pay phone, had his brother paged, watched as Jack rose to take the call, and then moved in to swiftly collect the young woman. Late that evening, Joe and Bilodeau entered the family house in Bronxville and narrowly avoided coming to physical blows with Jack, who was fuming—all alone—on the sofa.

But they did not fight. Not that night or any other—not over a woman, anyway. In the end, sexual conquest was an activity in which they shared. If anything, it was the one area in which both paid homage to their father equally. In their attitude toward women and sex, the boys were true and faithful copies of their old man.

*   *   *

EARLY IN JUNE 1938, Ambassador Kennedy secured home leave to attend Joe Jr.'s graduation from Harvard. Through a combination of hard work and, apparently, the services of a cadre of well-paid tutors, the young man was exiting *cum laude*. The ambassador was surely proud of the achievement, yet it occasioned a few embarrassing questions from the press. On May 17, the *Boston Globe* had published a story about the ambassador's imminent homecoming, noting that he was to receive an honorary degree from his alma mater. It is unclear who transmitted this information to the newspaper, but the prospect of such an honor was in the air—not so much because the Harvard faculty was pondering it but more probably because Joe Sr. himself had worked hard (but, he hoped, discreetly) lobbying for it. When, however, no honorary degree was forthcoming, he was forced to deflect questions from the press concerning "rumors" that he had sought the honor. No, no, he explained. It was all the result of the "action of my well-intentioned friends" and it had caused him "considerable personal embarrassment." Alluding to his son's *cum laude* distinction, he protested that one "honors degree" should "be pretty good for one family, I think."[44]

Clearly, however, Joe Jr.'s success—gratifying as it was to his father—had created an intolerable son-father imbalance of honors, especially at a time when many Americans were questioning the wisdom and legitimacy of the ambassador's attitude toward the crisis facing Britain and the rest of Europe. Subsequently, Joe Sr. issued from Hyannis Port a press release saying that he had *turned down* an honorary degree because he could not leave the sickbed of his second son, Jack, to attend the ceremony.[45] Jack was indeed unwell at the time, but the degree offer was an outright fabrication, and Joe Sr. was taking an enormous risk putting it into a press release—a risk all the greater because it was, ultimately, quite gratuitous.

Among the women with whom Joe Jr. was romantically involved was a pretty blond starlet, Athalia Ponsell, to whom he may even have proposed marriage. Within days of his graduation, however, instead of marrying her, he boarded the *Normandie* to follow his father back to London and the embassy. With him was Jack (apparently no longer ailing). On the advice of his father, Jack was going to Europe for a long summer vacation before returning to Harvard to start his junior year. As for Joe Jr., he was to stay longer, filling the year between his graduation from Harvard and his entrance into its law school by functioning as his father's secretary—a position suggested by Felix Frankfurter.

After the summer was in full swing, the Kennedy family left London for Cannes, where Secretary of the Treasury Henry Morgenthau was also on holiday. His son spent time with Joe Jr., including part of an afternoon (according to Henry Morgenthau III) "chasing a shapely brunette in and out of the swimming pool." Jack was present as well, but, as young Morgenthau recalled, he held back, as if consciously suppressing himself in the presence of his older brother.[46]

From Cannes, Ambassador Kennedy cabled the assistant secretary of state for administration, George Messersmith, with a request to officially add Joe Jr. to his staff as his private secretary at the rate of one dollar a year. After some prodding, the apparently reluctant Messersmith replied that State Department rules barred ambassadors from hiring family members. Undaunted, the ambassador decided to use his firstborn unofficially as his eyes and ears. He sent Joe on a continental tour from U.S. Embassy to U.S. Embassy, beginning with Paris and continuing on to Prague, Warsaw, Moscow, the Scandinavian capitals, followed by Berlin, The Hague, and back to Paris. He also wanted to arrange a trip to Madrid, where Joe Jr. could observe and report on the ongoing Spanish Civil War. At Harvard, Joe Jr. had founded a student branch of the Hands Off Spain Committee, an American isolationist organization of which the elder Kennedy enthusiastically approved. Isolationism in the case of Spain meant, in effect, siding with Francisco Franco and the Fascists—which both Joe Sr. and Joe Jr. found easy to do, since the Catholic Church supported Franco in what was seen as a struggle against the godless Soviet-supported anti-Franco Loyalists. At Harvard, Joe Jr.'s isolationism did not merely reflect his father's but actually magnified it. He devoted his senior thesis, "Intervention in Spain," to the subject as it applied to the Spanish Civil War. Joe Sr. would try, without success, to get the thesis published.

Initially, Joe Jr.'s European excursions went no farther than the 400 Club in London's tony West End. He spent many evenings during the waning summer of 1938 in company with London's upper crust as well as the likes of an Argentine polo idol, a Turkish pasha, a baron from the Netherlands, and the daughter of the late great American humorist Will Rogers.[47] He never appeared unpaired, escorting a different beautiful young thing every evening. As summer dissolved into fall, however, he finally left for Paris, where his father had arranged for him to serve U.S. ambassador William C. Bullitt as attaché. (He might be barred from hiring his own son, but a fellow ambassador was not.) In part, the senior Kennedy wanted Joe to learn how diplomacy was done outside of

London, but he also charged the young man with reporting to him on how a well-run embassy functioned under a stellar leader. Bullitt was a Yale graduate (voted the "most brilliant" of the Class of 1913) who quickly acquired leftist credentials even more radical than those of Harold Laski. Divorcing his first wife, the socialite Aimee Ernesta Drinker, in 1923, the following year he married Louise Bryant, the radical journalist and widow of John Reed (*Ten Days That Shook the World*), the ex-pat American chronicler of the Bolshevik Revolution. Bullitt, who had served President Woodrow Wilson during the Paris Peace Conference of 1919, went on to become a European correspondent and a novelist before returning to government service when President Franklin D. Roosevelt appointed him as the first U.S. ambassador to the Soviet Union. He served in that post from 1933 to 1936, during which period his enthusiasm for Soviet communism utterly dissolved. By the time he stepped down, he was a committed anti-Communist and was sent to Paris as the new ambassador to France.

And so emerges Joe Sr.'s secondary motive for sending his son to Bullitt. Here was a brilliant former Marxist whose firsthand experience of a Communist state thoroughly converted him to capitalist democracy. If Joe Jr. had any lingering leftist leanings, two months with Bullitt should set him straight. Armed with a diplomatic passport, Joe called on the U.S. embassies and consulates in Prague, Warsaw, Leningrad, Copenhagen, and Berlin. If anything, his visit to Germany confirmed his earlier enthusiasm over Hitler's achievement. Joe did not harbor anything as grand as admiration for a new level of civilization, but for sheer strength and force of will. He found the Germans "really a marvelous people," and he believed it would be "an awful tough time to keep them from getting what they want."[48] To the degree that this sentiment bolstered his own pro-appeasement and isolationist stance makes its logic spine chilling: The Germans are marvelous, it will be "awful tough" stopping them, so why try? Put another way, it was Joe espousing the doctrine of might making right.

From Berlin, Joe materialized at St. Moritz, the exclusive Swiss ski resort town in which his family was spending Christmas vacation—except for the ambassador, who was once again in the United States. Joe casually appeared with Megan Taylor, a beautiful British figure skater who had just won the 1938 world championship in the sport (a victory she would repeat in 1939). After skating with her, Joe took his own maiden voyage on a one-man bobsled, achieving a run of more than seventy-five miles per hour, very nearly a record. From this, he took up skiing—also for the first time—and succeeded in breaking his arm. Fortunately, the family nurse, Luella Hennessey-Donovan, formed part of the Kennedy entourage. The wounded warrior approached her, requesting nothing more than a "Band-Aid." Telling him that his arm was broken, she bundled him into a sled for a ride to the hospital. After his arm was set and put in a cast, he returned to the rink with Megan. (Bobby and Teddy emulated their brother's daring on the slopes. Bobby sustained an ankle sprain and Teddy, a wrenched knee.)

From the slopes of elite St. Moritz, Joe set off for war-torn Spain. While many young Americans of his age volunteered to fight the Fascists in the International Brigade and the Abraham Lincoln Brigade, Joe came only to observe—but his sympathies lay with Franco, whom he regarded as a pro-Catholic anti-Communist rather than a Fascist strongman (not that Joe particularly objected to Fascism). In truth, Joe admired the leftist American and other Loyalist volunteers he encountered, deeming them brave and sincere in their opposition to Franco, but he also believed that they were dupes of the Communists and therefore tragically misguided. Nevertheless, he was determined to tell all sides of the story as he saw it. He visited Barcelona and Valencia, then, abandoning his diplomatic passport for ordinary travel documents, he talked his way onto a military transport bus and entered Madrid, epicenter of the brutal conflict. What he saw was mostly the privation and squalor of war. He camped out in the abandoned U.S. Embassy before settling in a makeshift American "diplomatic compound" on a side street. While riding with his hosts in their car, he and they were stopped by soldiers, ordered out of the vehicle, and lined up against a wall. Joe produced his U.S. passport, which prompted the soldiers to let them all go.

As a result of his experience, Joe was able to provide his father with some bold vignettes of the conflict, and one of his letters from Spain was even published in the *Atlantic Monthly*. Joe felt profound sympathy for all the victims of the war, but his view of the contest remained unchanged. If Franco had the support of the Catholic Church, he must be in the right and whatever his soldiers did was ultimately justified.

Beyond this, Joe had no compelling point of view about the war and certainly expressed no passion for one side or the other. Encouraged by the publication of his letter, he wrote a series of six articles, which one recent biographer, Laurence Leamer, described as containing isolated passages "full of vividly observed detail, followed by pages with no more verve than a legal brief. What was missing was a sense of politics . . . and his account [was] merely a travelogue of adventure."[49] No one saw fit to publish the pieces. In the end, all Joe derived from his journey through the Spanish Civil War was validation of his own very genuine courage. Beyond this personal benefit, however, neither he nor the world profited.

* * *

AFTER SPAIN, JOE RESUMED touring Europe. To him, Nazi Germany now appeared rather more ominous—but still unstoppable. Moreover, he was less disturbed and depressed by what he saw in Germany than he was fascinated by it, feeling privileged to bear witness to a profound passage in world history. As the summer of 1939 came to an end, Joe joined his family on a Riviera holiday at the Domaine de Ranguin on the outskirts of Cannes. When the U.S. chargé d'affaires in Germany cabled on August 21 that Ribbentrop and Molotov had concluded, on behalf of Hitler and Stalin, a nonaggression pact, Ambassador Kennedy and his family flew from Cannes back to London.

Together, in the British capital, they would experience the start of World War II. With Joe Jr., Jack, and Rose, the ambassador waited out the very first air raid alarm, huddled in the basement of the exclusive Molyneux dress shop. Once the immediate danger had passed, Kennedy set about arranging for the evacuation of U.S. nationals from England, including his own family. Jack returned to Harvard and Joe to Harvard Law.

Perhaps inspired by his brother's *cum laude* showing, Jack had by this time become a far more earnest student and even managed to make the Dean's List by the end of his junior year. Next he threw himself into writing his senior thesis, "Appeasement at Munich." Like many other students, earnest or not, young Kennedy left much for the last minute, and brother Joe, who seemed to observe his efforts with some anxiety, wrote to his father on March 17, 1940, about how "Jack rushed madly

around the last week with his thesis and finally with the aid of five ste-
nographers the last day got it [in] under the wire."[50]

Joe was not overly generous in his assessment of his brother's work,
writing to his father that he had "read it before he had finished it up
and it seemed to represent a lot of work but did not prove anything."
Joe did allow, however, that Jack "said he shaped it up the last few days
and he seemed to have some good ideas so it ought to be very good."[51]
At least two of Jack's political science professors rated the work highly,
Henry A. Yeomans according it *magna cum laude* status and Carl J.
Friedrich—who would earn renown as a leading scholar of totalitarianism—rating it only somewhat lower, as *cum laude plus*. Joe Sr. was
proud of Jack's achievement but was not entirely uncritical of his work.
He not only advised his son to try to "improve the writing," but, while
he agreed with his premise that the British people, not their leaders,
bore the brunt of responsibility for the nation's military unpreparedness, he feared that this interpretation might be seen as a "complete
whitewash" and advised careful revision.[52] Jack had taken the initiative
in sending it to Arthur Krock, a Pulitzer Prize–winning journalist who
was the senior Kennedy's close friend and unwavering champion, for
advice on publishing. At Krock's urging, Jack sent it to Krock's own
literary agent, Gertrude Algase. Joe Sr. approved but advised careful
fact checking and revision. Nor did the ambassador leave the fate of
the manuscript to the whim of the publishing gods. He called in favors
and prevailed on Krock to take a strong editorial hand in sprucing up
the manuscript. He also secured an introduction by media mogul and
Time magazine publisher Henry R. Luce. That was impressive, but Luce
had not been his first choice. Earlier, Joe Sr. had asked Harold Laski to
lend his prestige by writing an introduction but was turned down flat.
Laski's wife, Frida, said in an interview years later that her husband
judged the book to be the work "of an immature mind" and "that if
it hadn't been written by the son of a very rich man, [it] wouldn't have
found a publisher."[53]

Published in 1940, both in the United States and Britain, as *Why
England Slept*, Jack's book was a hit, selling an impressive 80,000 copies and earning young Kennedy $40,000. (He donated the proceeds of
British sales to the city of Plymouth, England, to help it recover from
bomb damage inflicted during the Blitz.) When Jack's friend Charles

Spalding asked him about sales, the young man offhandedly replied that they were "going great," adding "Dad's taking care of that."[54] Indeed, it has long been assumed that Joe Sr. boosted sales by personally funding bulk purchases.

What Joe Jr. felt about his kid brother's publishing success—coupled with his *cum laude* Harvard graduation, the same honor Joe had received—is not recorded. Perhaps this means he said very little about these things. In any case, it is known that Joe Sr. had tried to get some combination of Joe Jr.'s own Harvard thesis, "Intervention in Spain," and his letters from the Spanish front published as a book. This was after Joe Sr. had failed to persuade editors at the *Saturday Evening Post* and the Hearst newspapers to commission from Joe Jr. a series of articles on communism. Having also failed to generate interest from the *New York Times* for an account of the fall of Madrid, Joe Sr. reportedly presented his speechwriter, Harvey Klemmer, with a small mountain of his son's Spanish letters. "Turn those into a book," he told Klemmer, pointing to the pile now on his desk, "and you'll make enough money to send both of your girls to college."[55] The hapless Klemmer dutifully produced a draft—but by the time he did, World War II had begun, and no one was much interested in reading the pro-Fascist views of the son of an increasingly unpopular U.S. ambassador to Great Britain. The project went nowhere, and even the draft has been lost.

Despite having graduated *cum laude* in June 1940 with a Harvard degree in international affairs, despite his having written a near best-seller at twenty-three, and despite his influential father, John F. Kennedy found himself oddly adrift. While his brother had duly entered law school, Jack diverted himself with a desultory audit of some graduate classes at Stanford University while he vaguely contemplated a career as a journalist or a professional author. He spent some time with his father in Hollywood—although he may have spent less time as his father's companion than as "The extra's delight," as he dubbed himself in a letter to friend Lem Billings.[56]

His own honors degree notwithstanding, Joe Jr. felt himself struggling at Harvard Law, even though his father had secured the tutoring services of his close friend, John Burns, who had served as counsel to the Securities and Exchange Commission when Kennedy had chaired it and was now an associate justice of the Massachusetts Supreme Court as well as a Harvard Law School professor. At the end of his first year, Joe stood 200th in a class of five hundred—a respectable showing but far from outstanding.[57]

He did not let his struggles cramp his lifestyle, however. He and his roommates shared a large apartment near Harvard Yard and were ministered to by a pair of African American servants. Nevertheless, classmates reported that Joe was clearly jealous of his brother's recent successes in academics and publishing—and also of his talent as a public speaker. He sought to catch up in the latter category by taking night classes at a local Cambridge institution called Staley's School of the Spoken Word, and he announced to his father his intention to enter politics—immediately—by running for a seat as delegate from Brookline to the 1940 Democratic National Convention. Joe Sr. approved, even though that seat was pledged to FDR's opponent, Postmaster General James Farley, and would likely provoke the president at whose pleasure the ambassador served. In the end, Joe Jr. won "half a seat"—and only just barely—and not only made his political debut (something brother Jack had yet even to contemplate) but also stirred controversy by resisting pressure from Roosevelt's operatives to withdraw support from Farley and throw it instead to FDR. It would have been easier for both him and his father—and certainly more politically expedient, at least in the short run—had Joe Jr. capitulated to the Roosevelt men. But he refused, and Joe Sr. wholeheartedly supported his intransigence. "I think the incident will stand you in good stead," he wrote to his son on July 23, 1940. "After all people do appreciate a straightforward opinion, and that includes those you oppose."[58]

Three weeks into his second year at Harvard Law, Joe registered for the "peacetime" draft under the Selective Service and Training Act that FDR had signed into law on September 14, 1940. He wrote to a friend that he had "become one of President Roosevelt's several million numbers, and am not enthusiastic about said designation. If it starts to really look like war, I doubt if I'll wait for the draft and will instead sign up for whatever service I think might suit me best, perhaps the Navy Air Corps." That was, he observed, "an option many fellows around here"—meaning Harvard—"are talking about." Besides, he continued, "I've always fancied the idea of flying; and I've never fancied the idea of crawling with rifle and bayonet through the European mud."[59] His father was not pleased. Pronouncing naval aviation "the most dangerous thing there is," he offered his son a post with his own former naval attaché, Captain Alan Kirk, who now headed the Office of Naval Intelligence in Washington, D.C.[60]

The son of an "appeaser" and faithless "defeatist," Joe Kennedy Jr. was intent on showing the world that the Kennedys were not afraid of anything. He told his father that he did not want a desk job, and despite his fears for Joe Jr., the senior Kennedy clearly began to realize that the only political future left to *him* now belonged to his eldest son. After all, heroes become presidents. If they live. Even as Ambassador Kennedy did all he could to discourage President Roosevelt from drifting into the British camp, even as he prepared to pull strings to keep his sons safe in some respectable military berth out of harm's way, even as he lived day and night through the early weeks of the Blitz, he thought about how he could maneuver Joe Jr. into the most advantageous, if not safest, position in the military—something on which to build a postwar political career. "I have had with me rather intimately," he wrote to Joe Jr. on September 11, 1940, "Major General Emmons, in charge of the Air Force of the U.S.A., General Strong, second in command of the Army, and Admiral Ghormley, second in command of the Navy, and I have been having discussions about you and Jack." The ambassador continued: "Strong . . . feels that the chance for promotion and for position is much better in the [Army] Air Force[s] than in anything else, principally because it is going to be expanded quickly and because it isn't as hidebound as the regular army."[61]

But Joe had other ideas. In November, he wrote to his father that he was leaning toward joining the Navy Air Corps, in which he could serve with a "chance for some individuality."[62] The ambassador did not argue but instead changed the subject to Jack, writing to Joe that he had pretty well given up on any military role for his younger son. "If he isn't well enough to continue his law school course"—Jack had decided to enter the Yale University Law School, but never actually enrolled—"I don't see how he is going to be well enough to go in the army, but I am going to talk to Emmons and Ghormley about him, so that when you fellows talk your own situations over we will have somebody you can talk with to get good advice."[63]

In June 1941, after completing his second year in law school, Joe signed up for the Naval Aviation Cadet Program. Both he and his father knew that, had he chosen simply to serve in the Naval Reserve, he could have finished law school while also doing his patriotic duty. In a letter to his father, Joe explained his rationale for the more affirmative step of becoming a full-time aviation cadet. As he put it, it was, in fact, the senior Kennedy's doing. In view of his "stand on the war," Joe Jr. wrote, "people will wonder what the devil I am doing back at school with everyone else working for national defense." And that would reflect negatively both on himself and on his father—especially since, Joe Jr. assumed, Jack's chronically poor health would prevent him from serving.[64]

Based in objective fact as it was, the latter assumption must also have given Joseph P. Kennedy Jr. substantial comfort. He had finally pulled ahead of his brother in having made his political debut, and now he would serve in the coming war, from which sickly Jack would almost surely be debarred. As for the hopes, ambitions, and plans he knew his father had for him, Joe added to his letter a reassurance he must have thought both selfless and ultimately superfluous: "It seems that Jack is perfectly capable to do everything, if by chance anything happened to me."[65]

As Joe Sr. had predicted, Jack's poor health—in particular, his lower back problems—did result in a medical disqualification from acceptance by the army. But the second son persisted in seeking some form of military service, and, instead of trying to talk him out of it, the ambassador again reached out to Captain Kirk, who, in turn, wrote to Captain C. W. Carr at Chelsea Naval Hospital: "The boy has taken the attitude that he does not wish his father's position used in any way as a lever to secure him preferment." This said, Kirk continued: "This is an excellent point of view but, nevertheless, it has occurred to me he might be helped in one way—vis., his physical condition."[66] Jack was accordingly given the most cursory of medical exams and immediately commissioned as an ensign. What is more, Kirk directly appointed Jack to serve under him, in Washington.

Certain that war would come to him, Joe Jr. now also knew that that, when it came, he would not have the war to himself.

CHAPTER 2

MOST DANGEROUS

"THE GODS," EURIPIDES WROTE, "VISIT THE SINS OF THE FATHERS upon the children."[1] The November 10, 1940, *Boston Sunday Globe* interview, in which Ambassador Kennedy had blandly declared that "[d]emocracy is finished in England," created outrage throughout much of the United States.[2] The senior Kennedy made no secret of his presidential aspirations. This single interview ensured that he never would see them—or any other future political aspiration he had for himself—fulfilled. Yet despite having committed political suicide, he continued unabashedly in his course of defeatism. Even after Hitler's conquest of Poland, Denmark, Norway, Belgium, the Netherlands, Luxembourg, and France, and even as American journalists such as Ernie Pyle and Edward R. Murrow were writing and broadcasting stories of gallant England's lone stand against Nazi tyranny and the courage of Londoners under Hitler's bombs, Ambassador Kennedy told reporters that the "whole reason for aiding England is to give us time . . . to prepare. It isn't that [Britain is] fighting for democracy. That's the bunk." Instead, he assured the reporters, England was fighting for nothing more than "self-preservation, just as we will if it comes to us."[3]

* * *

WHETHER NAVAL FLIGHT TRAINING was a way of standing up to his father, atoning for the old man's sin of appeasement—a position Joe

Jr. himself had echoed, reinforced, and defended—satisfying his father's ambitions for him, or achieving all of these objectives, the young man had to slog his way through pilot training. Naval flight instruction was demanding—significantly more demanding than that given to U.S. Army Air Forces aspirants—but some cadets took to it more naturally than others. Kennedy was not a natural. After months of ground school, he flew with an instructor over Jacksonville, Florida, in a two-seat, single-engine primary trainer for an extended period, from mid-November 1941 until December 9, before his instructor finally decided (two days after Pearl Harbor) that his student was ready to solo. After a mere five minutes of solo flight, one takeoff and one landing, Cadet Kennedy graduated from primary to basic training.

He proved as mediocre in phase 2 training as he had been in phase 1. "This student does not absorb instruction readily," one instructor wrote. "He does not remember things from one day to the next." Another complained: "[S]tudent does not look where he is going . . . flies with head in cockpit too much . . . afraid of inverted spins; consequently recovery [from the spin] uncertain."[4]

A talented pilot—a natural—*sees* and *feels;* Joe Jr. spent his time trying to *remember* what he was supposed to do next. The strain told on him. Unlike his younger brother Jack, who had always been frail and thin, Joe Jr. had a robust physique. After a few weeks of basic, however, he had lost twenty pounds and looked hollow in the chest. Only the conviction that failure was not a Kennedy option drove him to complete primary and initial basic flight training. Sheer will fueled him. Doubtless to the surprise of his instructors, he graduated to the advanced phase of basic training, where he drew the usual critical comments, becoming so unnerved by them that the flight surgeon ordered a week's rest, classifying him as "temporarily incapacitated" on account of "accumulated stresses."[5]

Was he, at bottom, afraid to fly? Probably not. According to his few flying buddies, his concern was not the many hazards of flight but his descending position in the class ranking. Everyone seemed to be pulling ahead of him, and, in the end, Kennedy graduated seventy-seventh out of eighty-eight pilots. His final instructor put the best possible face on his performance, calling him "cheerful," with a "cooperative disposition and a strong, forceful character." He noted that his "handling of regular and additional duties has been satisfactory, but he is expected to improve . . . as he gains experience in naval service."[6]

After graduating from the full basic course, Joe went into operational training at the naval air station on Florida's Banana River, today part of the NASA space center named for his brother. Here he learned to fly the Martin PBM Mariner, a twin-engine patrol bomber flying boat whose most distinctive features were its V-angled stabilizer, with inwardly canted vertical fins, and its gull wings from which two pendulous floats were hung. The "gull" appellation referred not just to the birdlike dihedral bend in each wing, but also to the fact that the wings actually flapped in flight, rising and falling as much as six feet at the tips. The PBM Mariner never achieved the fame of the ubiquitous PBY Catalina, but it was a more advanced aircraft and offered greater military capability. Operationally, the PBM was more complex than the PBY, demanding from the pilot greater attention to procedural detail yet not as much sheer flying skill. Never an instinctive pilot, Joe actually took to the flying boat. He graduated from operational training at the end of July 1942 with better instructor appraisals than he had ever before received.

Designed for long-range reconnaissance and antisubmarine patrol, the PBM lumbered along at an unhurried 211 miles per hour and, in its patrol bomber configuration, carried a .30-caliber machine gun and five .50-cals, along with a dozen 800-pound bombs, which could be swapped out for torpedoes. Crews appreciated its formidable armament, but they enjoyed even more the creature comforts the PBM offered. The capacious boat hull was furnished with amenities familiar to the deluxe Pan Am Clipper civilian airliner, including bunk beds, a full galley—with refrigerator!—and what the naval personnel called a "head" (toilet). Kennedy liked the plane, and he wanted to keep flying it.

The next logical step after operational training was combat flying with an antisubmarine squadron. While Joe did not want to put off getting into the action, he was determined to get into it on his terms. Fresh out of flight school, he knew he would be assigned as a junior flight officer, a job he saw as mostly a lot of scut work, from plotting map fixes to carrying the command pilot's luggage. He knew what his father would advise: *Work the angles. Get what you want.* Well, with just three hundred flying hours under his belt, there was no way he would be assigned a left-hand seat in the cockpit. The command position required at least a thousand flying hours. The quickest way to get them was to volunteer to be an instructor, and so he stayed on at Banana River for the rest of 1942, piling up cockpit time.

When Joe finally left for a combat assignment, in January 1943, it was with PBM Squadron VP-203 at Roosevelt Roads Naval Air Base in San Juan, Puerto Rico. He was in command, as he had wanted to be, but there was another problem. This slice of the Atlantic theater was about as far from the action as it was possible to be in a *world* war. Through March 1943, Kennedy spent dreary hours piloting his comfortable plane in search of German U-boats that were, unsurprisingly, nowhere to be found.

For any pilot eager to prove himself in combat, the situation was undesirable. Joe, however, felt a particular urgency. He had never expected Jack to medically qualify for military service of any kind. But he had failed to appreciate the full extent of his father's influence, which essentially got Jack a bogus medical exam. Moreover, instead of being sent for training, as Joe had been, Jack was directly and immediately commissioned. Even more irritating, whereas Joe was still a flight cadet in October 1941, Jack, an ensign, actually outranked him. Joe would soon catch up and gain the gold stripe of an ensign as well, but on July 27, 1942, Jack left his desk at naval intelligence to attend Naval Reserve Officers Training School at Northwestern University in Evanston, Illinois. Completing the training on September 27, he entered the Motor Torpedo Boat Squadron Training Center at Melville, Rhode Island.

Now Joe fumed. As he flew slow patrols over the placid Caribbean, his brother was training to be a PT boat jockey and would soon be headed for the thick of the war in the South Pacific—the navy's biggest show. Salt was added to the wound when news reached Joe that, on October 10, Jack had been promoted to lieutenant, junior grade. Once again, Joe was outranked by his kid brother. Worse still, after completing his PT boat training on December 2, 1942, Jack was assigned to command his own boat, PT-101. Joe could at least find a crumb of comfort in the fact that Jack's squadron was assigned to Panama, not the South Pacific.

But that crumb didn't last long. Instead of meekly accepting Panama, Jack sought a combat assignment, and on February 23, 1943, he managed a transfer to Motor Torpedo Boat Squadron Two, based at Tulagi Island in the Solomon Islands. On April 23, he took command of PT-109 and was tasked with conducting nighttime operations, mainly against vessels resupplying Japanese garrisons on New Georgia Island. That same month, Joe was transferred to a base even farther from the war, at Norfolk, Virginia. Profoundly bored—and intensely jealous of Jack—he gave the royal treatment to his seventeen-year-old brother Bobby, who visited later in the spring. Not only did he take the kid along on a patrol (a serious breach of regulations), he even gave him a turn at the controls (a far graver violation). Shortly after Bobby left, Joe Jr. was finally promoted from ensign to lieutenant, junior grade, and was greatly relieved that Jack at least no longer outranked him.

Yet Jack was unquestionably outperforming him. Handsome and charismatic but never naturally affable, Joe grew downright combative, restless, bitter. He was a man with a chip on his shoulder, and he sometimes picked fights in particularly ugly ways. When, for example, a fellow pilot in his squadron made a rare contact with a U-boat only to let it get away, Kennedy rode the man mercilessly, claiming first that *he* would never have missed, then broadcasting throughout the outfit his judgment that the man was incompetent. Finally, Joe escalated the trash talk to an outright accusation of cowardice, raging that both pilot and crew were just too damned scared to get within range of the U-boat's deck guns.

And that did it. Joe Kennedy Jr. had his first U.S. Navy fistfight, and he took genuine pleasure in pummeling his opponent.

Salvation seemed to come in mid-July when squadron commander Jim Reedy assembled his pilots in Hangar Sp2 and called for volunteers to fly what he characterized as a "very dangerous" assignment. Reedy explained that he had been tasked with forming a new squadron, VP-110, to fly patrol duty over the Bay of Biscay, south of Brest, France, where the Germans had built extensive U-boat pens. The bay's waters were always heavy with "wolf pack" submarine traffic in and out of the pens. With the local airspace thickly patrolled by Luftwaffe fighters, this was no place for slow-moving flying boats. Reedy told his men that volunteers would be trained to fly the PB4Y-1, the navy version of the four-engine Army Air Corps B-24 Liberator. The plan was to train hard throughout the summer, then ship out to a base in England early in the fall.

In response to Reedy's call, most of the assembled pilots raised their hands, either solemnly or with feigned blasé attitudes. Lieutenant Joe Kennedy Jr., however, frantically waved with both hands and was (according to one of his fellow pilots) the "most excited man in the room," a man who (recalled another squadron mate) "wanted to get with that war and get with it fast."[7]

*   *   *

JUST AS THE PBM MARINER was not nearly as well known as the PBY Catalina, so the PB4Y-1/B-24 Liberator lacked the iconic presence of the B-17 Flying Fortress. Yet, just as the PBM was an advance over the PBY, so the Liberator was a more modern design than the B-17, had a slightly higher top speed (290 versus 287 miles per hour), a considerably better rate of climb (to 20,000 feet in twenty-five minutes versus thirty-seven minutes for the B-17), and greater range and bomb load (2,000 miles carrying 8,800 pounds of ordnance, whereas the B-17 could carry no more than 6,000 pounds the same distance). Nevertheless, though it was produced in greater numbers than the B-17 (18,482 wartime B-24s versus 12,731 B-17s in all variants), the B-24 never found as much favor among aircrews or Army Air Forces brass. For one thing, flying it was very hard work. The big plane was notorious for requiring "heavy control forces," meaning that the pilot was often obliged to manhandle the aircraft, using all his strength to turn, climb, or dive it. This meant that it had relatively poor formation-flying characteristics and was downright exhausting to fly over long distances. The B-17 Flying Fortress lived up to its name, as far as aircrews were concerned. It survived almost everything that could be thrown against it. In contrast, aircrews were not happy about the B-24's lightweight construction and the placement of fuel tanks throughout the upper fuselage, trade-offs that gave the Liberator added range and payload capacity but made it more liable to burst into flame when hit by flak or fighter fire.

Unlike their Army Air Forces counterparts, navy PBM pilots were untroubled by invidious comparisons between the Liberator and the Flying Fortress. All they knew was that the leap from two engines to four was a thrill. Add to this the advanced design, the speed, and the firepower, and they were in ecstasy. Never mind that the learning curve was steep. With the exception of the B-29 Superfortress, the Liberator cockpit was far and away the most crowded and complex of any aircraft of the era, bristling with more than 50 indicator dials and some 150 switches. It is a dramatic measure of just how badly Joe Kennedy Jr. wanted to fly this dangerous beast on dangerous missions that he not only managed to make the transition from the PBM to the PB4Y-1 but to do so in a mere six days. Nevertheless, he drew his share of the customary instructor criticism. Master pilot reports called his handling of the aircraft "sloppy" and even "dangerous."[8] Commander Reedy apparently trusted him, however, because he assigned Kennedy to ferry planes from the Consolidated plant in San Diego, California, to the Norfolk, Virginia, naval air base. Through the month of August, Joe typically flew five transcontinental round trips every eight days. Perhaps the assignment was motivated less by Reedy's confidence in Joe Kennedy Jr. than it was by his own sense that the pilot needed as much experience with the PB4Y-1 as he could get.

The many long, routine flights dampened Joe's enthusiasm to the extent that he complained of having signed up to fly combat, not for Pan Am. What was intensely galling him, as he pounded through his ferry duties, was the epic of PT-109. By August 18, the *Boston Globe* published the full story under the headline KENNEDY'S SON SAVES 10 IN PACIFIC.

In September, just before Squadron VP-110 was about to leave for England, Joe brought his CO, Commander Jim Reedy, to the Kennedy compound at Hyannis to celebrate his father's fifty-fifth birthday. Family friend Judge John Burns toasted "Ambassador Joe Kennedy," proclaiming him "father of our hero, our own hero, Lieutenant John F. Kennedy of the United States Navy."[9]

It was too much for Joe Jr.

Jack, it seemed, was the brother who was showing the world that the Kennedys were not afraid of anything. Another family friend present at the occasion, Boston police commissioner Joseph Timilty, later recalled passing by Joe Jr.'s bedroom. From behind its closed door, he distinctly heard a man's sobs.

*   *   *

BY THE END OF SEPTEMBER 1943, Squadron VP-110 was fully installed at Dunkeswell Airfield in Honiton, Devon, United Kingdom. The rain was incessant, the temperatures cold, the accommodations—corrugated iron Nissen huts—miserable. Pointing out in a letter to his parents that he had "to go several miles" for a bath (it was actually a half mile) and that all the hot water is used up by early in the morning, Joe felt justified in observing that "at long last, I'm really beginning to fight the war," as if "the war" were strictly a function of *his* discomfort.[10]

Not that the flying wasn't both grueling and hazardous. Missions consisted of twelve solid hours of patrol over the Bay of Biscay, looking for U-boats while dodging German Ju 88 heavy fighters, which flew rings around the four-engine Liberators, especially in the dark. Patrol schedules followed the U-boat schedules, which invariably ran from midnight to noon. This meant a great deal of night flying, in which the PB4Y-1 would release a steady stream of parachute-slowed phosphorous flares to light the sea and, it was hoped, reveal the occasional German periscope or conning tower. By early May 1944, Joe had flown twenty-five patrols, enough to qualify him for rotation Stateside. Instead of leaving, however, he volunteered for Operation Cork, antisubmarine patrols in conjunction with the June D-Day landings. By July, he was at fifty missions, twice the prescribed quota for rotation.

"When I tried to make casual conversation [with Joe Kennedy Jr.]," a navigator recalled, "I got the positive impression that I was talking about firecrackers to a man valiantly trying to perfect the atom bomb before an impossible deadline."[11]

Anxiously, jealously, zealously, obsessively, Joe volunteered for one extra mission after another, but it always came down to more of the same: a lot of long, hard flying. Beyond question, antisubmarine patrols were dangerous—35 percent of Joe's 106-man squadron had been lost by March 1944. Describing Joe's military career in a memorial volume dedicated to his brother, John F. Kennedy accurately wrote of how "[h]is squadron, flying in the bitter winter over the Bay of Biscay, suffered heavy casualties, and by the time Joe had completed his designated number of missions in May, he had lost his former co-pilot and a number of close friends." Jack told how his brother "refused his proffered leave and persuaded his crew to remain on for D-day. They flew frequently during June and July, and at the end of July they were given another opportunity to go home. He felt it unfair to ask his crew to stay on longer, and they returned to the United States. He remained." By that time, the offer of "a new and special assignment . . . which would require another month of the most dangerous type of flying" had come his way.[12]

For Joe Jr., the missions were exhausting and failed to offer the opportunity for *individual* heroism, even during D-Day. Joe's war took on a kind of dreariness, which was amplified by the conditions prevailing at RAF Dunkeswell. The late fall of 1943 and early spring of 1944 were extraordinarily wet. "Roads were narrow and a constant sea of mud bathed all hands' pedal extremities, or was splashed on their nether regions by passing jeeps or trucks," Joe wrote in the squadron diary, having taken on the job of squadron secretary. He described "an intermittent drizzle, occasionally whipped into a solid wall of water by capricious winds." He wrote of "miniature coke stoves sparsely scattered around the base," which "made it almost impossible to get either dry or warm." As for plumbing, it "was early stone-age and even more widely dispersed than the living sites or aircraft. There was no toilet paper, although rolls of what seemed to be laminated wood were provided plainly stamped with 'Government Property.'" As for "ablutions"—Joe's comically polite term for latrines—both officers and men were obliged to walk a half mile. "No heat either for the body, the soul, or the water was available in this chamber."[13]

Joe christened the squadron's accommodations "Mudville Heights," in which he shared a Nissen hut room with fellow pilot Mark Soden. Each room was equipped with a "miniature coke stove" and a washbasin. There was running water, but no drainpipe attached to the washbasin. A plug covered a hole, beneath which was a bucket to catch the slop. When the bucket was full, the user was expected to tromp outside, through the eternal rain and mud, to the latrine a half mile away. Soden griped that Joe "was always spitting his toothpaste all over the basin," which he never dumped out—apparently not wanting to be the one who filled (and therefore was expected to empty) the waste bucket. "It got so I couldn't stand him and he couldn't stand me." Shortly "before Christmas I complained to him and told him that he ought to do his share even though he *was* Joe Kennedy or whoever he thought he was." Years after the war, Soden reported that things had become "pretty tense" between them, "but he [Joe] had a bottle of whiskey and he offered me a drink and I took a drink and from then on we were fast friends again." Then he gave Soden the whole bottle.[14]

That—the offer of a drink and the bottle to go with it—was vintage Kennedy. The gesture was generous yet tinged with pragmatism. Soden appreciated the whiskey, whereas Joe had little taste for liquor.

Despite the gloom, the danger, and the fatigue, Joe managed to find ways to live well. He knew the best clubs in London and spent his few precious leaves in them, often with a girl and often in company with his sister Kathleen, called by family and friends "Kick." She had fallen in love with England when she was resident there during her father's ambassadorship, and she begged the senior Kennedy and her mother to be allowed to remain in London after the war broke out. Overruled by the ambassador, she sailed back to the States in the early fall of 1939, attended school, and did volunteer work for the Red Cross. In 1941, she went to work as a research assistant to Frank Waldrop, executive editor of the *Washington Times-Herald*. But she never lost her yearning for England in general and London in particular. In 1943, she volunteered to work in a London-based Red Cross service club for GIs. The job brought opportunities to spend time with Joe—and to fall in love with William Cavendish, Marquess of Hartington.

Cavendish—whom friends called Billy Hartington—was a politician by aspiration but, during the war, an infantry officer by vocation. He was stationed at Alton, and Joe Jr. was stationed at Dunkeswell, in Devon. Kick was in London. The three—often accompanied by Mark Soden—took to spending their free time not in London but at a farm they called "Crash-Bang," which was more or less centrally located with respect to Alton, Dunkeswell, and the capital. It was owned by Patricia Wilson, a wealthy woman with children and an absent husband, but young enough to be considered a girl. She took to living in the farm's tile-roofed "gardener's cottage" because she deemed the location convenient yet reasonably far from the Luftwaffe magnet that was London. She was determined to keep her children with her and to keep them safe.

Weekends spent at Crash-Bang created in Joe an admiration for Billy Hartington, even though he was keenly aware of how the prospect of Kick marrying out of the Catholic Church and into the Church of England would wound their father and, far worse, their mother. Joe volunteered for the hazardous mission of collaborating with Kick on a letter to their parents breaking the news, and he stood by her to help

her weather the emotional storm that the news stirred. Kick would later describe her brother as "a pillar of strength . . . in those difficult days." Full of "wise, helpful advice," Joe "stood by me always," she wrote. "Moral courage he had in abundance, and once he felt that the step was right for me, he never faltered, although he might be held largely responsible [by our parents] for my decision."[15] Indeed, brother and sister prevailed on father and mother, who acquiesced to the marriage, if they did not rejoice in it. The event took place in a civil ceremony at the Caxton Hall Registry Office, in London, on May 6, 1944. Joe was the only Kennedy family member in attendance.

Among Joe Kennedy Jr.'s friends and associates, military and civil, the interest was less in Catholic Kick's marriage to Protestant Billy than it was in what everyone assumed to be a growing romance between Joe and the mistress of Crash-Bang. By the summer of 1944, it became common (though quite incorrect) knowledge among Kennedy's circle that he was engaged to a titled English heiress.

Joe did nothing to counter the universal assumption that he was marrying a wealthy English aristocrat. What was his motive for abetting the deception? Amusement? Ego? He knew that Kick's marriage to a marquess made her a marchioness. Did he want his friends to picture *another* Irish Catholic Kennedy marrying into the English Protestant aristocracy? Unhappily married to her second husband (now a British army officer in Libya), did Patricia Wilson see in Joe a potential third husband, and did he encourage that perception?[16]

Wartime London was full of a reckless fatalism that promoted all-or-nothing romances together with all-or-nothing romantic declarations. Crash-Bang was not London, of course, but on June 15, nine days after D-Day and two days after the first V-1 buzz bomb fell on the capital, a V-1 impacted perilously close to the farm. Joe persuaded Patricia to drive him to the crash site, where he dutifully poked around the smoldering debris, looking for the remains of the rocket bomb's guidance system. He found nothing, but the war had undeniably come to Crash-Bang—and with it, perhaps, the romantic and pseudoromantic attitudes bred of war.

Yet this same period brought Joe's final patrol as an antisubmarine pilot. Ordinarily, completion of one tour—let alone the two full tours (and then some) Joe had flown—would mean rotation back to the

States. Joe, however, could have stayed in England—and could have nurtured a full-blown romance—because he was offered a position as assistant naval attaché in London. He turned this down, however, explaining to his commanding officer that he believed his father's tenure as ambassador had created so heavy a diplomatic cloud that he would not be able to function anywhere near the embassy.

It was a plausible explanation. Even so, had he been intent on developing something more with Patricia Wilson, he would almost surely have taken the position, come clouds or clear skies. The more likely explanation was that he *wanted* to put the Atlantic between himself and the woman. But then something better came along, something more than dogged endurance in the face of unrelenting danger, day after day, night after night, flying unheralded antisubmarine patrols. It came in the form of a call for PB4Y-1 pilots to fly the most dangerous mission conceivable. Nothing more specific. Neither Kennedy nor any of the other volunteers were told their mission was to save London. But the promise of danger was, to him, the promise of a fresh chance at heroism of the kind that could be put into a *Boston Globe* headline. On the verge of returning to America, Joe Kennedy Jr. leaped instead at the offer of what brother Jack later described as "another month of the most dangerous type of flying."

CHAPTER 3

THE BITTER FRUIT
OF PEENEMÜNDE

BRITAIN WENT TO WAR ON SEPTEMBER 3, 1939, AND BEFORE THE
end of that month, Ambassador Kennedy, expecting that German air
raids would soon reduce London to rubble, had shipped his family (except for Rosemary) back home. But for week after week, the London
skies were empty and silent. By October, the second month of World
War II, it was hell for Poland, where the war had begun, and the opening of yet another circle of hell for Europe's Jews. But in England and
France, the press was calling it the "phoney war" because, curiously,
so little seemed to be happening on the Western Front. The action was
east of Germany. Neither France nor England was doing very much to
fight Hitler, and Hitler, for his part, was doing little to hurt England or
France.

On October 13, 1939, Kennedy addressed a letter to Jack and Joe,
both now safely returned to the United States, even farther from the war
than the curiously peaceful London embassy. He wrote that he "was de-
lighted to get [the boys'] observations" on public sentiment in America,
even though their report to him was filled with the disquieting news
that their countrymen were turning against peace-loving Prime Minister Neville Chamberlain and in favor of bellicose Winston Churchill,

now serving as first sea lord in Chamberlain's cabinet. The fact was that the father took delight in hearing from his boys—safe as they now were—and in being able to tell them, yes, Americans may take a liking to Churchill, with his warlike ways and his itch to get the United States into the fighting, but they hadn't yet heard the speech Chamberlain made to Parliament the day before. To Kennedy's way of thinking, the man willing to appease Hitler rather than drag his sons into war had come on strong. Chamberlain sternly told Parliament that the only way Britain could acquiesce to Hitler's latest peace proposal, made while his boot was on Poland's neck, was to recognize "his conquests and his right to do what he pleases with the conquered." And *that,* Chamberlain announced, "would be impossible" without "Great Britain . . . forfeiting her honour and abandoning her claim that international disputes should be settled by discussion and not by force."[1]

In short, Chamberlain managed to simultaneously assert national honor as well as the path of peaceful discussion. Ambassador Kennedy assured his sons that this deft rhetorical motion had "swept the boys right back in their corners again." The British people "wouldn't have stood for any other kind of speech, but"—and this was for Kennedy the reassuring part—"it is still amazing how hopeful people are that something will still be worked out."[2]

Hell for Poland, hell for the Jews, to be sure. Yet Ambassador Kennedy did not envision war as hell for anyone else—just an environment that would be very, very bad for business. "I haven't changed my opinion at all about this situation," the champion of appeasement wrote his sons. "I think that it will be a catastrophe financially, economically and socially for every nation in the world if the war continues and the longer it goes on, the more difficult it will be to make any decent arrangement."[3]

War is hell, William Tecumseh Sherman famously observed. To Joseph P. Kennedy Sr., war was not so much hell as a bad business decision. In fact, of more immediate concern to the ambassador than stopping Hitler was appeasing the cravings of Lady Astor, Kennedy's powerful parliamentary ally in opposing Churchill. The war having cut off the flow of sweets, she had asked him to get her some American gum and candy. "I hope somebody is remembering to send [it to her]," he admonished his boys.[4]

*   *   *

EARLY THE VERY NEXT MONTH, on November 4, Captain Hector Boyes, naval attaché at the British embassy in Oslo, Norway, opened an anonymous letter addressed to him. Astoundingly, it offered the delivery of a report on the latest German weapons technology. Ambassador Kennedy knew nothing of this, of course, and even if he somehow had learned of the offer, he doubtless would have had the same initial reaction as Boyes: This is too good to be true, it's a trick, a feint to intimidate British war planners and generally undermine morale. But Boyes also could imagine nothing to lose by following the instructions in the letter, which were to alter the customary sign-on announcement for the BBC World Service broadcast to Germany from "*Hier ist London*" ("This is London") to "*Hullo, hier ist London*." This would signal the embassy's willingness to receive the report.

A week after the altered broadcast was made, Boyes received a small parcel that contained not only a typewritten document—it would become known to history as "The Oslo Report"—but a unique sort of "valve" (the British term for what Americans called a vacuum tube) that was a high-tech sensor for a proximity fuze—a device designed to detonate a bomb or artillery shell when it *neared* its intended target rather than *impacted* it. The applications for a proximity fuze were many. For one thing, detonating at proximity rather than impact meant that a projectile—an antiaircraft shell, for instance—did not have actually to hit its target to damage or destroy it. For another, the explosive blast of most bombs is much more destructive if detonation takes place a certain distance above a ground-based target rather than when it hits the target, since the ground itself absorbs a high fraction of the energy released by the explosion. The report could have been faked, but the vacuum tube was certainly real—and highly innovative. Boyes therefore passed the German text to an embassy translator and then sent both the report and the device to MI6 headquarters in London.

MI6—Military Intelligence, Section 6, Britain's Secret Intelligence Service (SIS)—was unimpressed, despite the insistence of R. V. Jones, PhD, head of the Scientific Intelligence division of MI6, that, a few inaccuracies notwithstanding, the report seemed perfectly reliable. It was, he believed, a genuine leak.

True, the report was submitted anonymously, over a signature that rather unconvincingly read "A German scientist, who is on your side." But had British intelligence discovered the author's identity, the skeptics would have been won over. As revealed after the war, the author was Hans Ferdinand Meyer, a mathematician and physicist who had studied with Nobel laureate Philipp Lenard and who, as of 1936, was director of the Siemens Research Laboratory in Berlin. Intensely critical of the Nazi regime, he would be arrested by the Gestapo in 1943 and spared summary execution only through the intervention of his mentor Lenard, a Nazi supporter who enjoyed great influence in the party. Nevertheless, Meyer would spend the years from 1943 to the German surrender in 1945 being transferred from one concentration camp to another. After the war, he was scooped up in Operation Paperclip, the U.S. military program responsible for harvesting German weapons scientists, the most famous of whom was V-2 rocket scientist Wernher von Braun.

Fortunately for British World War II intelligence, Winston Churchill became acquainted with Dr. Jones, was impressed by him, and saw to his promotion to assistant director of intelligence (science). In this position, Jones used the report to predict air raids and to design countermeasures against German radar and guidance systems. In addition to material relating to proximity fuzes, Jones found most intriguing what the Oslo Report had to say about developments in the field of autopilots, remote-controlled gliders, and remote-controlled projectiles. These were the report's most consequential hints that Germany was vigorously developing guided missiles, which, it would soon be learned, included a winged type today called a cruise missile.

Yet, in 1939, not even Dr. Jones recognized that Germany was far along in developing an operational version of the cruise missile, which the Reich Propaganda Ministry would dub *Vergeltungswaffe* 1 (Vengeance Weapon 1), known variously in English as the V-1 flying bomb, the buzz bomb, and the doodlebug. As for the next hint, it did not come until 1942, and it pointed to an even more advanced weapon. If the V-1 was the world's first cruise missile, the V-2 was its first ballistic missile.

* * *

ON MAY 15, 1942, RAF Flight Lieutenant Donald Wilfred Steventon was flying his Spitfire on the homeward leg of a photoreconnaissance sortie.

His assigned target along this return journey was Swinemünde, a Baltic seaport in Pomerania. What caught his eye, however, was evidence of construction work in another village, this one near the River Peene and called Peenemünde. Although it wasn't part of his mission brief, Steventon snapped a handful of frames, mainly to satisfy his own curiosity. Subsequent analysis of these images revealed circular embankments quite unlike anything previously seen at German military construction sites. Because no earlier aerial reconnaissance existed with which to compare Steventon's photographs, no high-level alarm was sounded. Nevertheless, thanks to the Oslo Report and rumors of German "flying bombs," Duncan Sandys, chairman of a War Cabinet defense committee that would later be named the Flying Bomb Counter Measures Committee, ordered further reconnaissance of the Peenemünde site, and the photos were shared with U.S. intelligence.

In June, four aerial sorties were launched over the Baltic area, including Peenemünde. The "unusual" circular embankments were increasingly visible. These would turn out to be *Prüfstand* VII—Test Stand 7—Peenemünde's primary V-2 rocket-testing facility. In fact, the town, on the northwestern end of Usedom Island off Germany's Baltic seacoast, was home to the Heeresversuchsanstalt Peenemünde: the Peenemünde Army Research Center. A combination missile and aerodynamics laboratory, flight test facility, and V-2 production plant, the complex drew its slave labor force from the small F-1 concentration camp nearby. At the time of the first photographs, however, Allied intelligence could not have fully comprehended just what the facility was. Still, it was apparent to the experts that *something* sinister was happening in the Baltic town. At the very same time, Allied intelligence took note of equally ominous construction near Calais, just across the English Channel from Britain.

At first, Peenemünde and Calais seemed little more than suspicious dots separated by more than six hundred miles on the map of Europe. Soon, however, intelligence reports connecting these dots began to trickle in. On November 4, 1942, at Tel el Mempsra, Egypt, just west of El Alamein, General der Panzertruppe Wilhelm Josef Ritter von Thoma dismounted his burning tank and gazed dolefully at a desert battlefield strewn with dead soldiers—*his* dead soldiers. Thoma offered no resistance when Captain Allen Grant Singer, 10th Royal Hussars, made him a prisoner of war.

After being treated to dinner by no less a figure than the British commander who had defeated him, General (later Field Marshal) Bernard Law Montgomery, Thoma was sent on a long journey to a series of senior officer prisoner of war camps in England and Wales. In these, he was treated so well that he grew complacently comfortable—and was apparently quite unaware that everything he said was being monitored and recorded by MI6. On March 22, 1943, he told fellow prisoner General Ludwig Crüwell about something he had seen back in 1936 or 1937, at "a special ground near Kunersdorf [*sic*]." Apparently, it gave him hope, even in his own defeat. For "these [were] huge things which they've brought up here. . . . They've always said they would go 15 km into the stratosphere and then. . . . You only aim at an area. . . . If one was to . . . every few days . . . frightful." He had spoken to a major at the test site, he told Crüwell, a man "full of hope," who "said 'Wait until next year and the fun will start!'"[5]

On April 22, 1943, a month after Thoma's indiscreet conversation was recorded, a British Mosquito fighter-bomber fitted out for photoreconnaissance returned from photographing bomb damage created by raids against Stettin (today the Polish city of Szczecin). To use up the remaining film in their cameras, the Mosquito crew kept them running as they flew home, down the northern coast of Germany. When British photo interpreters studied the long roll of developed film, they noted in one exposure what they described as an "enormous cloud of steam," twenty-five feet long. Big as it was, the cloud disappeared after no more than four seconds, based on its absence from the next frame. Only later would it become clear that what had been photographed—by mere chance—was a combination of cooling steam and flame shooting out of a V-2 rocket motor in a static test on Test Stand 7. At the time the photo was taken, however, British analysts concluded that it was no more than a test of *some* new munition.

The very next month, May, Allen Dulles, director of the Swiss-based branch of the U.S. Office of Strategic Services (OSS—predecessor of the Central Intelligence Agency), informed American military leaders that Peenemünde was certainly an experimental weapons base and was testing rockets. On May 14, air reconnaissance reported intense activity at that circular construction area in Peenemünde—Test Stand 7, but at the time referred to by Allied intelligence simply as "the Ellipse."

The activity turned out to be a Nazi VIP preparing to witness a V-2 test launch. Three days later, in Watten, near Saint-Omer in German-occupied northern Pas-de-Calais, a French agent reported the existence of what he called "enormous trenches." These were associated with a massive concrete bunker under construction, as well as a rail line and a canal. The bunker, it was later determined, was part of a facility for servicing V-2 rockets just prior to launch. Capable of servicing more than a hundred missiles simultaneously, the Watten bunker was intended to launch thirty-six a day. The facility included a plant to produce liquid oxygen, the oxidizer used to support combustion in the rocket engine. There was also a massively reinforced train station—virtually bomb-proof—to accommodate delivery of missiles and supplies from various production facilities elsewhere in Germany. As we will see, however, the Watten bunker was never completed, let alone made operational.

On June 4, Dr. Jones of MI6 received sketches (made by a Luxembourg-based spy) of Usedom Island, on which Peenemünde was located and where both V-1s and V-2s were being tested. Jones collated the sketches with a report from French Underground agent Leon Henri Roth that slave laborers at Peenemünde reported seeing the "development of a large rocket which made a noise resembling that of 'squadron at low altitude.'" Other forced laborers spoke of facilities that included a "rocket assembly hall," an "experimental pit," and a "launching tower."[6] Eight days after this information was in British hands, a Mosquito photorecon sortie brought back images of "a white-ish cylinder about 35 feet long and 5 or so feet in diameter with fins."[7] It was a V-2, and ten days later, on June 22, a disaffected German officer in the weapons department of the Wehrmacht High Command reported to British agents that "thirty catapults had been constructed" to launch "winged missiles"—V-1s. The officer noted that fifteen of the catapults "were already serviceable."[8] Finally, on June 23, Mosquito reconnaissance revealed a pair of completed V-2s.

* * *

IT WAS TEN O'CLOCK ON THE NIGHT of June 29, 1943. Not that the hour mattered. The Cabinet War Room, a windowless chamber deep below the government offices of Whitehall, London, was in perpetual twilight regardless of the hour. There, Prime Minister Winston Churchill met with his War Cabinet to review the growing mass of intelligence on Germany's "wonder weapons," especially rockets. Gathered about him were his ministers, military chiefs, and Professor Frederick Lindemann—recently ennobled as Lord Cherwell—the Oxford professor who served as Churchill's closest scientific advisor. Cherwell's protégé R. V. Jones, now head of MI6 Scientific Air Intelligence, was also in attendance, as was Duncan Sandys, who reported on current intelligence, including the recorded conversation of General Thoma. Sandys passed around the conference table aerial photographs of Peenemünde that showed several white objects, unmistakably rocket shaped and looking like fuzzy illustrations from some science fiction story.

"We have heard, from Mr. Sandys," the prime minister summarized, "of the real possibility that a long-range bombardment rocket is under development at Peenemünde, the German research station on the Baltic, and that it may quite soon be put into use against us, aimed certainly at London. The size of the device is uncertain but we have heard estimates that a single rocket might create 4,000 casualties killed and injured." The prime minister rapidly did the math, concluding that "if the enemy had the capacity to fire a rocket every hour for a month, the casualties would amount to over two million. We would be forced to evacuate a major proportion of the population of London, with a grave effect on our war effort and on preparations for the invasion of France."[9]

Lord Cherwell interrupted to disagree. He doubted "that a single rocket would cause anything like 4,000 casualties." What is more, he found it "incredible to think the Germans have reached a stage which our own rocket experts tell me would take us more than five years," and he suggested that the objects in the reconnaissance photos could be "either torpedoes or wooden dummies. The whole rocket story may be a great hoax to distract our attention from some other weapon."

Cherwell was Churchill's go-to authority for what he called the "wizard war," the world of high-tech superweapons. Nevertheless, Churchill next presented "Dr. Jones of MI6, who was responsible for piecing together the evidence which enabled us to detect and defeat the enemy's night bomber radio-navigation beams in 1940." Turning to the young man, the prime minister growled, "Now, Dr. Jones, I want the truth!"

"Prime Minister, I have been studying the possible existence of a rocket weapon since December 1942 when a report was smuggled out through Sweden," Jones began. "Since then, there has been a continuous series of reports, many of them identifying Peenemünde as the location of the work, and now we have these quite definite photographs."

He went on to dismiss his mentor's torpedo theory by pointing out "that there is no type of aircraft in Germany capable of carrying a torpedo thirty-eight feet long and six feet in diameter or that could lift ten or 20 tons."

At this, Churchill quipped: "Stop! Hear that, Lord Cherwell. That's a weighty point against you!"

And then Jones continued, next sweeping aside the "deception theory" on the grounds that "if it was a successful deception, we would attack Peenemünde and there is plenty of evidence to show that it is one of their most important air establishments. It's as though we set out some dummy weapons at Farnborough [home of the Royal Aircraft Establishment] to mislead the Germans. It would be a very silly hoax that resulted in it being bombed flat."

Instead of throwing the matter open to further discussion, Churchill brought debate to an abrupt close: "Peenemünde is a very long way east. I am told that it is beyond the range of our radio navigation beams and that we must bomb by moonlight, although the German night fighters will be close at hand and it is too far to send our own." In other words, a bombing mission against Peenemünde would be extraordinarily hazardous. "Nevertheless, we must attack it on the heaviest possible scale as soon as conditions are suitable."

With this, Operation Hydra, an air raid on Peenemünde, was authorized. Carried out on the night of August 17–18, 1943, it was the first blow in the much more ambitious Operation Crossbow, a large-scale strategic bombing campaign directed against the entire V-weapons program. Hydra would prove costly. Of 324 Lancaster, 218 Halifax, and 54 Stirling heavy bombers launched, 40 heavies never returned, and 215 British airmen were killed, as were untold hundreds of civilian slave laborers housed in a nearby concentration camp. The benefit of the costly raid? The deaths of two German rocket scientists and the delay of V-2 test launches for seven weeks. It is impossible to calculate how many British and other Allied casualties the raid prevented, if any. At the very

least, it prolonged by at least seven weeks the lives of some 4,517 eventual V-2 victims—2,754 in London and 1,736 in Antwerp, Belgium.

August 19, 1943, the day after the Hydra raid, Fritz Kolbe, a diplomatic courier in the German foreign service who was secretly opposed to the Nazi regime, offered the British embassy at Bern, in neutral Switzerland, a cache of secret documents he had copied. Convinced Kolbe was a German plant, the Brits summarily showed him the door. He walked through it and did not stop until he had reached the U.S. Embassy. There he received a much warmer welcome from Allen Dulles, who examined the documents and recruited Kolbe, to whom he assigned the code name George Wood. By May 1945, "Wood" had supplied Dulles with a stream of some sixteen hundred extraordinary documents, including details on both the V-2 and V-1 programs. These helped drive Operation Crossbow, which lasted through May 2, 1945, five days before the end of the war in Europe.

An Anglo-American operation, Crossbow was directed "against all phases of the German long-range weapons programme," including "research and development of the weapons, their manufacture, transportation and their launching sites, and against missiles in flight."[10] Principal aspects of Operation Crossbow included providing V-1 defense, formulating and implementing V-2 countermeasures, and carrying out the strategic bombing of sites associated with the operation of these weapons.

*   *   *

THE MISSION FOR WHICH Joseph P. Kennedy Jr. would volunteer was a part of Project Anvil, developed in the context of the strategic bombing portion of Operation Crossbow. But to understand why the struggle to defeat the V weapons called for three distinct approaches, it is necessary to understand the two weapons themselves.

In 1935, the Third Reich unified its military as the Wehrmacht, which encompassed the navy (Kriegsmarine), the air force (Luftwaffe), and the army (Heer). Such unification, however, was more of an aspiration than a fact. In actual practice, the services competed bitterly with one another for resources, honors, and political clout. Relations between the army and the air force were particularly adversarial, and when it was decided to develop advanced long-range weapons, instead

of working together, the army and air force developed their programs separately and competitively.

In 1936, the army decided to create a ballistic missile as an extension of traditional long-range artillery. The army specification called for a weapon capable of delivering a one-ton explosive payload over a range at least ten times that of the infamous "Paris Gun" of World War I. This meant sending a ton of explosive destruction about 165 miles—far beyond anything any conventional cannon could achieve. For that matter, it was also far beyond the range and payload capacity of any rocket that existed in 1936. Meeting the specifications required designing and building a *ballistic* missile, one that followed a trajectory that would take it to the very upper edge of Earth's atmosphere—the stratosphere—and then, drawn by gravity, return to Earth. The ballistic course could take the missile downrange 165 miles (or even more) from its launch point—provided that a rocket motor could be devised to propel it, carrying a ton of payload in addition to fuel, to an altitude sufficient to create a long parabolic chord. In addition, engineers would need to invent a control system capable of preventing the rocket from entering an uncontrolled flight path. Thrust and control: Both of these requirements were radically formidable, calling for a dedicated scientific and engineering team as well as a secure place to build and test prototypes. Peenemünde fit the bill, and the program moved there in 1938.

The missile that became the V-2 was originally designated A-4. The prototyping program began by producing a series of subscale models, finally working up to a test launch of a full-scale prototype—27,600 pounds, nearly forty-six feet in length, with a diameter of five and a half feet—in March 1942. The test failed, as did the next two. Finally, on October 3, 1942, a fourth test flight succeeded. Yet all of the year 1943 was required to complete development—which was disrupted by intensive Allied air raids against Peenemünde. As a result, the V-2 would not be launched as an operational weapon until September 1944.

By any standard, it was a remarkable vehicle. Unlike a jet engine, which "breathes" atmospheric air to support the combustion necessary for thrust, a rocket like the V-2 contains both its own flammable fuel and oxidizer agent, so that it can climb above Earth's oxygen-rich lower atmosphere. The A-4 was fueled by ethanol cut 25 percent with water. The oxidizer was liquid oxygen. To create the high-energy combustion necessary for flight, high-pressure pumps (driven by steam generated by a chemical reaction of highly concentrated hydrogen peroxide and sodium permanganate) circulated the fuel and oxidizer very rapidly through a combustion chamber, the exhaust from which, vented via a specially designed nozzle at the base of the rocket, produced sufficient thrust to achieve a top speed of more than 3,500 miles per hour and a maximum altitude of 55 miles when launched on a long-range trajectory, or 128 miles if launched straight up. Maximum downrange range was 200 miles. As for guidance, four rudders were mounted on tail fins, and four graphite vanes were fixed to the exhaust nozzle, to direct the thrust. A gyroscope system provided lateral stabilization, and an accelerometer controlled engine cutoff at a specified velocity. Once the engine was cut off, the rocket would begin its arc toward a downward trajectory.

Some early V-2 launches were radio guided, but the missiles later used in actual combat relied on static settings made prior to launch. For this reason, the rocket was not very accurate. For example, it could not be aimed to hit a specific structure within a city, but it could be pointed in the direction of a target city and the engine cutoff calculated such that it would hit *somewhere* within the city. Since the Germans intended the V-2 as a means of terrorizing and demoralizing civilian populations, this very crude degree of accuracy was sufficient.

The V-2's payload was a ton of amatol, a violently explosive mixture of TNT and ammonium nitrate typically used in depth charges and naval mines. Although TNT alone produces a higher explosive velocity and explosive shattering capability (called "brisance"), blending it with ammonium nitrate corrects TNT's oxygen deficiency, thereby producing a net increase in energy release during detonation.

The long period of development required to make the V-2 operational discouraged Adolf Hitler, to whom the missile came to seem nothing more than an artillery shell with a very long range and a very high cost. Until the project's chief scientist, Wernher von Braun, promised the army's Long-Range Bombardment Commission in September 1943 that work on the A-4 was very nearly completed, Hitler remained unimpressed. Yet instead of killing the project in mid-1944, when the A-4 had yet to enter production, Hitler was inspired by the unwavering enthusiasm of the charismatic von Braun and his intensely loyal staff of scientists and engineers. Doubtless, wishful thinking made Hitler vulnerable to that enthusiasm. By 1944, the Third Reich desperately needed a miracle if it was to have any hope of victory or, more to the point, of finding some alternative to total defeat. Gambling that the V-2 was that miracle, Hitler pronounced it a "wonder weapon" *(Wunderwaffe)* and ordered its mass production and deployment. Most of the 5,700-plus V-2s produced were built at the Mittelwerk factory tunneled into Kohnstein, a hill northwest of the town of Nordhausen and adjacent to the Mittelbau-Dora slave labor camp. Tens of thousands of forced laborers toiled underground to build the rockets. At least twenty thousand were quite literally worked to death.

*   *   *

WHILE THE ARMY WAS DEVELOPING the V-2, Fritz Gosslau, an engineer for German engine manufacturer Argus Motoren-Gesellschaft, began research on pilotless aircraft. By early 1937, he had developed proposals for a remote-controlled drone. A prototype of a target drone flew in July 1939, and in November he proposed to develop a cruise missile to be mounted under the wing of a manned bomber and launched air to ground, under remote radio control.

In contrast to the army's ballistic missile, which used a rocket motor with a self-contained oxidizer unit, Gosslau's craft was powered by a pulsejet engine, which "breathed" atmospheric air. While the army struggled with the formidable technical problems involved in creating a ballistic missile that reached the stratosphere before beginning its parabolic descent to an earthly target, the Luftwaffe—the German air force—backed the winged pulsejet cruise missile. In 1942, Gosslau was working with the Fieseler aircraft company and was a key member of the team (headed by designer Robert Lusser) that developed the Fi 103, which the Luftwaffe called the FZG 76. With further development, this would become the V-1, an unmanned cruise missile carrying an explosive payload.

The V-1 had two advantages over the V-2. First, it was much cheaper and simpler. The airframe was small: a little over 27 feet in length, with a wingspan of just 17.6 feet and a weight of 4,760 pounds. It could carry an amatol explosive payload of 1,870 pounds—not that much less than the 2,200-pound payload of the V-2. In contrast to the

V-2, which required highly specialized machinery to build, the V-1, essentially a small airplane, could be turned out by any aircraft plant. Its pulsejet engine was also extremely simple, with remarkably few moving parts. Whereas the unit cost of a V-2 was 100,000 Reichsmarks in January 1944 (down to 50,000 RM by March 1945—the rough equivalent of $200,000 1945 U.S., nearly $2.6 million today), each V-1 could be built for just over 5,000 RM ($21,000 in 1945 or $273,000 today). Even more important, as the V-2 program struggled toward producing a reliable weapon, the V-1 program moved along swiftly. Although development work on the V-1 had started later than that for the V-2, by October 1942, numerous test examples were being successfully launched and flown. Moreover, designers began to realize that they did not have to perfect a complex radio-control system. Instead, the guidance system installed on most operational V-1s was a rudimentary mechanical autopilot that used a gyrocompass-damped weighted pendulum device to correct flight attitude fore and aft and another gyrocompass to stabilize yaw and roll. A mechanical counter could be set to close the fuel valve at a predetermined point in flight, so that the engine would die and the aircraft would crash into its target. Accuracy, of course, was minimal with this system, but if the ramp from which the V-1 was launched was properly aimed, the rocket would reliably reach a chosen city-size target and descend on it.

Recognizing that in the V-1 he had an eminently practical weapon, Hitler backed it as an alternative to the V-2—even as he kept that program going as well. He understood that the V-2 offered greater range and moderately greater destructive effect as well as the ability to launch from specially hardened concrete bunkers or—later—mobile launch vehicles. The V-1, in contrast, required a launching system using compressed steam to catapult the rocket bomb along a lengthy inclined launch ramp. These ramps were difficult to conceal, and Allied reconnaissance pilots learned to recognize them because of their resemblance, from the air, to ski jumps.

Ultimately, the Germans would use the exposed vulnerability of launch sites to their strategic advantage. The V-1s originally were to be stored in highly hardened bunkers and distributed to launch sites as needed. Construction of Hitler's "Atlantic Wall," the elaborate coastal fortifications intended to guard against and repel a cross-Channel invasion, consumed huge quantities of concrete, however, and was given priority over the V-1 structures. Generalfeldmarschall Erhard Milch, head of Luftwaffe production, decided to switch from massive bunkers serving relatively few hardened launch sites to so-called light launch sites, which would be built in three *Stellungsysteme* (setting systems). Stellungsystem-I consisted of sixty-four launch sites in the Pas-de-Calais. These were to be supplemented by thirty-two additional reserve sites in Stellungsystem-II. Stellungsystem-III would consist of additional sites southwest of the Seine from Rouen to the Cotentin Peninsula in Normandy. Milch's idea was not only to provide multiple launch points for massive and continuous attacks but also to lure the Allied air forces into widespread attacks that would not only spread their air assets thin but would force them to undertake hazardous daylight bombing missions. Milch believed he could thereby transform the Pas-de-Calais into what he called the "graveyard of the RAF."[11]

The most important advantage the V-2 had over the V-1 was that, as a ballistic missile with a maximum speed of 3,580 miles per hour and a trajectory that took it to between 55 and 128 miles high before it descended to its target, the V-2 was for all practical purposes impossible to defend against in flight. It flew too high and moved too fast to be shot down. In contrast, the V-1 flew at about 400 miles per hour (fast, but still possible to intercept) at an altitude of two or three thousand feet. It was vulnerable to ground-based antiaircraft fire or to the action of fighter aircraft. In fact, as it lacked a pilot and therefore was incapable of evasive maneuvers, the V-1 was, in some cases, more vulnerable, despite its still-considerable speed.

Under Operation Crossbow, four countermeasures were used to defend against V-1 attacks. The first were ground-based antiaircraft guns, which were strategically deployed near the English Channel during June to September 1944 to intercept the approach tracks of the V-1s. In June 1944, British antiaircraft gunners shot down no more than 17 percent of incoming buzz bombs. By August 23, the kill rate rose to an astounding 60 percent and, by the end of the month, to 74 percent. Initially, only one V-1 was destroyed for every twenty-five-hundred shells fired. By the end of the summer of 1944, the ratio was one for every hundred. Still, one of four buzz bombs that made it to the coastline got through the antiaircraft screen.

In a rather more desperate effort to defend the cities and critical military targets, the British deployed large numbers of barrage balloons. During the Blitz, these tethered blimps had been used to defend against low-flying (below 5,000 feet) aircraft, which would collide with blimps themselves or the heavy cables that tethered them to the ground. Some two thousand additional balloons were added to the deployment during the V-1 onslaught in the hope that the fragile craft would be destroyed on contact with the tether cables. This defense brought down fewer than 300 of the 9,251 V-1s fired against England.

To augment the ground-based antiaircraft defense, the RAF used high-speed fighter aircraft. The problem was that, while some fighters could be pushed to match the 400 miles per hour of the V-1, few could do so at an altitude of only three thousand feet. The Hawker Tempest, which had the necessary combination of speed and low-altitude performance, was in short supply. Factories went into accelerated production of the craft, as well as of Supermarine Spitfires with newer Griffon engines, capable of higher speeds at lower altitudes. The RAF also deployed the remarkably fast U.S.-built P-51 Mustang.

Yet it was soon discovered that conventional pursuit techniques were not very effective at downing the V-1s—at least not in shooting them down so that they didn't simply crash to earth and detonate, inflicting the very casualties the fighters were trying to prevent. Accordingly, fighter pilots learned to maneuver their planes so that their wings broke up the airflow above the incoming V-1. This required sliding the fighter's wingtip to within six inches of the lower surface of the V-1 wing. Doing this would flip the V-1 wing up, disrupting the craft's gyros and sending it into an out-of-control dive. As long as this maneuver was executed close to the Channel and away from big cities, the crash and resulting detonation were relatively harmless to civilians.

By September 1944, RAF pilots had learned that adjusting the 20-mm cannon on their Tempest fighters so that their fire converged at precisely three hundred yards was highly effective against the buzz bombs. Similar modifications on other interceptor aircraft made their cannon fire increasingly effective as well. In June 1944, 264 V-1s (including some V-2s) hit south London, claiming 911 lives. In September and October, there were only 12 impacts, resulting in 109 deaths.[12]

But not all of this reduction in deaths was attributable to effective fighter defense. Under Operation Crossbow, British counterintelligence instituted a system of deception to throw off the aim of the V-1s. Unknown to German intelligence, the British had discovered and turned the vast majority of German agents stationed in England. In exchange for their lives, these agents supplied their spymasters with disinformation furnished by British counterintelligence, including inaccurate data on the effectiveness of V-1 and V-2 impacts. The disinformation had to be delivered subtly, since the press regularly reported on bomb damage in London and elsewhere. Silencing the press would endanger the public, who needed to be alerted to areas of damage, so British counterintelligence instructed the double agents to report to their German contacts impacts but to overreport those that had fallen northwest of London. This would give those responsible for aiming the rockets the impression that they were consistently overshooting their targets. As a result, they would make adjustments that would cause the missiles to fall short of their intended targets. The carefully managed program of deception tended to direct a significant number of launches away from London—or, at least, away from the most densely populated areas of the city.

* * *

BY THE EARLY FALL OF 1944, the V-1 threat to England was abated because the Allied invasion of Europe had overrun most of the coastal launch sites. They would be moved, however, and just as the volume of V-1 launches was reduced, the volume of V-2 launches was dramatically increased. On August 29, 1944, Adolf Hitler ordered V-2 attacks to begin as soon as possible, and, starting in September, at least 3,172 were launched, killing some 9,000 civilian and military personnel before the launches ended in March 1945.

The architects of Operation Crossbow recognized that measures against incoming V-1s, though improving, were inadequate and that using these same measures against V-2s would be totally ineffective. They also believed that, at some point, the V-2 attacks would supplant the V-1s. The only sovereign protection against the rockets—and especially against the V-2s—was to eliminate the source of the weapons by destroying manufacturing and launch facilities. Such was the ultimate objective of Operation Crossbow, and it was the objective of what the

U.S. Army Air Forces called—in homage to the butterfly *Speyeria aphrodite* rather than the Greek goddess of love—Operation Aphrodite and the U.S. Navy Project Anvil.

Of the V-1s fired at targets in England, most were directed against London, where they killed 6,184 civilians and injured 17,981. V-2 attacks claimed 2,754 civilian lives in London, injuring 6,523. But as hard as the V-1s and V-2s were on the civilian population, their toll on military resources was becoming intolerably heavy. The Pas-de-Calais area never became Milch's "graveyard of the RAF," but it nevertheless monopolized more than a quarter of the Anglo-American Combined Bomber Offensive during July and August 1944. This was at the height of the breakout from the Normandy (D-Day) landings, when every conceivable Allied resource should have been devoted to the advance across France and into Germany.

Although the Allied invasion of Europe significantly disrupted the V-1 attacks against England by September, the V-2s took over with barely an intervening interval. The Allies believed that the V-2s would be launched from massive underground bunkers and fixed launch pads. Allied photoreconnaissance revealed bunkers at Watten and Wizernes—both near Saint-Omer in the far northern Pas-de-Calais *département* of France—and a large launch pad near Chateau du Molay, in the Calvados département of Basse-Normandie. By late 1943, Peenemünde had been so severely bombed that a new concentration camp, Mittelbau-Dora, was built on the outskirts of Nordhausen—an industrial town in the southern Harz region of Thuringia—to supply slave labor to the Mittelwerk plant, recently established to take over V-2 manufacture from Peenemünde. Yet the Allies remained largely unaware of this move and would not strategically bomb Nordhausen until April 3–4, *1945,* little more than a month before the end of the European war.

Even as Operation Crossbow reconnaissance flights were identifying the telltale ski-jump ramps that marked V-1 launching sites and bombing missions were dispatched, heavy bombers were also tasked to hit those structures identified as V-2 manufacturing or launch sites. Neither the bombing efforts against the V-1 nor the V-2 sites seemed to have much effect.

What Allied planners did not realize was that while the complex V-2 required massive manufacturing and supply facilities, the weapon itself could be launched from just about anywhere. The Germans came to understand that the V-2 was actually a highly mobile weapon, and they developed a transport trailer called the *Meillerwagen* ("Meiller vehicle") to take each V-2 from a Technical Troop Area, where the rocket was fitted with its warhead, to the launch point. The Meillerwagen transported the rocket horizontally and was equipped with a lift frame and hydraulics to raise it upright on its firing stand. The trailer also contained tanks, pumping equipment, and hoses for fueling the rocket. Although fueling was in itself complicated and hazardous, the entire process from delivery to the launch site, through erection on the stand, all fueling, and finalizing the position of the rocket, took just 110 minutes. Indeed, by the time Allied bombers were targeting the V-2 bunkers, the Germans had abandoned them for Meillerwagen mobile launches. No sooner was a rocket fired than the enemy moved the launch site to a different place. With nothing permanent to bomb, not only were most of the Allied bombing sorties so much wasted effort, the entire Aphrodite and Anvil programs, intended to destroy the hardened structures conventional bombers could not penetrate, were chasing phantoms—targeting abandoned structures.

But there was no way to know all this as the V-1s rained down and as London, among other cities, waited in dread for assault by the even deadlier V-2s. So the Allied bombers flew, and so Joseph P. Kennedy Jr. and the other men of Aphrodite and Anvil prepared to lay down their lives to save the citizens of London and the other English towns.

CHAPTER 4

NEVER SO LUCKY AGAIN

ONE DAY IN THE SPRING OF 1944, MAJOR HENRY JAMES "JIM" RAND picked up the receiver of his buzzing phone.

"Hello," he rasped—or barked. Either way, it was a voice that signaled, in two short syllables, his state of perpetual impatience.

The woman on the other end of the line asked him to "hold on," took a beat, then announced with some importance, "General Doolittle is calling."

With that, the line went silent, and Rand "held on." Seconds turned to minutes, enough of them to unleash a ration of irritation when the general finally came on the line.

"Jim . . ."

"What the hell do you want?" Rand cut him short. He knew he was speaking to the commanding officer of the Eighth United States Air Force, but when the general failed to respond quickly enough, Rand forged ahead: "Speak up, Jimmy. I'm very busy today."[1]

Clearly, neither party in this conversation was playing by the customary rules of military courtesy. But, then, neither Jim Rand nor Jimmy Doolittle had ever acted according to custom.

The two first met years before the war, when Rand was secretary of the National Aeronautic Association and Doolittle was the goddamnedest test pilot and air racer the world had ever seen. Born in Alameda, California, in 1896, Doolittle grew up far away in Nome, Alaska, where his carpenter father, in search of work, had moved the family. There, Jimmy earned his earliest fame: as a tough young boxer. But by 1908, his mother had had enough, both of Nome and her son's father. With Jimmy in tow, she moved south, to 1235 Catalina Street in downtown Los Angeles. Two years later, Doolittle attended the Los Angeles International Air Meet—the first aviation meet held west of the Mississippi River. There he saw his first airplane, and, two years after this, in 1912, the fifteen-year-old tried his own hand at flying.

"I had found an article in an old January–June 1909 issue of *Popular Mechanics* by Carl Bates, entitled 'How to Make a Glider,'" Doolittle recalled many years later in his autobiography, *I Could Never Be So Lucky Again.*[2] Scraping together spare change and the proceeds from odd jobs, he bought "muslin, wood, and piano wire," followed Bates's plans, and hammered together a biplane airframe. His mother sewed the unbleached muslin for the wings. As for actually flying the thing, Bates furnished, in the pages of *Popular Mechanics,* assurance that "[f]lying a glider is simply coasting downhill on air."[3]

When the glider was completed to his satisfaction, Doolittle put it on a wagon and pulled it up to a modest bluff about fifteen feet high. The craft was essentially a biplane hang glider. Young Doolittle strapped it on his back and ran with it at top speed toward the edge of the bluff. Then he jumped.

Maybe it would have flown—if the tail hadn't hit the lip of the bluff and sent him plummeting. Banged up in the fall, he, at least, was in one piece. The same could not be said for the glider. Undiscouraged, however, Doolittle collected the pieces and resolved to rebuild. He also decided that running would never produce sufficient lift, so, after rebuilding his craft, he tied it to the bumper of a friend's father's car, once again strapped it on, and, as the car picked up speed, "ran faster and faster and soon couldn't run any faster." At that point, "I leaped into the air, put the tail down and planned to ease upward into full flight." Instead, "I was dragged quite a few feet while the glider splintered around me," this time leaving behind less than enough reasonably whole debris to build a new biplane.[4]

Both the failure and the pain were forgotten as soon as Doolittle read in another issue of *Popular Mechanics* about motor-driven monoplanes built by Alberto Santos-Dumont of Brazil and by the Frenchman Louis Blériot—who managed to fly his machine across the English Channel!

"I looked at my wreckage and decided that there was enough left to make a monoplane." While he scrounged a pair of bicycle wheels and labored to design "something that looked like it would fly," Doolittle started saving for a motorcycle engine. Doubtless, it was just as well that a storm destroyed his new creation—on the ground—before he earned the cash for an engine and actually attempted powered flight.[5]

Having run "out of money, out of materials, and out of enthusiasm," Doolittle returned to boxing, winning amateur crowns as a flyweight and then as a bantamweight. As a flyweight, the sixteen-year-old weighed 105 pounds and as a bantamweight, 115. "At about five feet four inches, I was as tall as I was going to get."[6] He went on to box professionally, using the name Jimmy Pierce to evade the attention of his mother, who disapproved of the sport. (Indeed, seeking to divert him from the dangers of boxing, she bought him a motorcycle!) Doolittle graduated from high school and enrolled at Los Angeles City College, then moved on to the School of Mines at the University of California, Berkeley.

After his junior year at Berkeley, Doolittle went to work in a California mine during the summer of 1916. Cut off from the outside world, he was stunned to discover, when he returned to Berkeley to sign up for his senior year, that many of his classmates were leaving their studies to enlist in the military, certain that America would soon be entering the so-called European War. "Without thinking very far ahead," Doolittle wrote in his autobiography, he decided to "join the crowd." But while almost everyone else decided to settle for the infantry, "I held out for what I thought would be a much better opportunity—to learn to fly with the Aviation Section of the Army's Signal Corps," also known as the "Air Service."[7]

Doolittle did learn to fly, but he did not see combat in Europe. Instead, he remained stateside as a flight instructor and also flew air patrols along the Mexican border. Despite the rush to demobilize after the war ended in November 1918, the air service recommended that Doolittle be retained, and he was accordingly commissioned as a first lieutenant. He also began compiling a remarkable record of thinking way outside the box and doing the seemingly impossible. In 1921, he led an expedition to salvage a plane that had made a forced landing in a Mexican canyon during an attempt at a transcontinental flight. The plane was downed on February 10. Doolittle found it on May 3—and, far from merely salvaging it, he stunned his superiors by pronouncing it capable of flight. Once he obtained a new motor, he transported it to the aircraft, along with four mechanics. When the new motor revved into life but indicated low oil pressure, he sent out carrier pigeons with a list of additional parts he needed. As they waited for the parts to be air-dropped, Doolittle and his mechanics hacked out a rudimentary airstrip on the canyon floor. After overseeing the repairs, Doolittle personally flew the plane out.

While he was in the Air Service, Doolittle set about doing everything that could be done in or with an airplane and learning everything that could be learned about the art and science of flight. He enrolled in the Air Service Mechanical School and took the army's Aeronautical Engineering Course. He also completed his undergraduate degree at Berkeley. When he wasn't in the classroom, he earned a reputation that made him one of the most famous American pilots between the world wars—perhaps second only to Charles A. Lindbergh. In 1922, he flew the first *successful* cross-country flight, from Florida to San Diego, California, with just one refueling stop. He completed the flight in an astounding twenty-nine hours and nineteen minutes, making extensive use of primitive navigational instruments to fly day and night in overcast or clear skies. For this flight, the army awarded him his first Distinguished Flying Cross.

In 1923, Doolittle became a military test pilot and aeronautical engineer. The following year, he enrolled at the Massachusetts Institute of Technology for graduate work in aeronautics, earning not only a master's for his work on aircraft acceleration but also a second Distinguished Flying Cross. After receiving his master's, he went on to earn a doctorate and then set about to advance the design of high-speed seaplanes.

While he was still a military pilot, Doolittle became a highly successful air racer, winning the Schneider Cup in 1925 and the Mackay Trophy the following year. Sent by the army on a South American tour to give demonstration flights, he broke both ankles in April 1926 when, doing handstands on a high window ledge in Chile, he fell off and hit the ground below. Despite this supremely painful injury, he went through with a scheduled demonstration of aerial maneuvers in his P-1 Hawk, both ankles bound in casts. The following year, while doing experimental work, he became the first pilot to perform an outside loop, a maneuver that draws tremendous G forces and that, at the time, was universally considered fatal to attempt. Doolittle climbed to 10,000 feet in a Curtiss fighter, dived, and, at 280 miles per hour, bottomed out upside-down before climbing to complete the loop.

It was during these record- (and ankle-) breaking interwar years that Doolittle became acquainted with Rand through Rand's work in the National Aeronautic Association. Doolittle recognized in the rather dumpy little man—like him, both a pilot and an aeronautical engineer—a passionate innovator who, gruff as he was, never complained that an assignment was too hard, too dangerous, or too impractical. When, years after meeting Rand, General Doolittle took command of the Eighth Air Force and asked him to serve as his personal head of technical innovation, Rand jumped at the assignment. He saw in Doolittle a man who regarded the impossible as a personal enemy to be engaged and conquered.

* * *

RAND WAS FAR FROM UNIQUE in his assessment of Jimmy Doolittle. By April 1942, practically every American was in awe of the man. He had resigned his regular army commission early in 1930 and, commissioned a major in the Air Reserve Corps, he worked in private industry, won more high-profile racing trophies, and, as a civilian, advised the military on aviation. On July 1, 1940, during the U.S. "peacetime" military buildup as Europe's Second World War raged overseas, Doolittle returned to active duty, assigned to assist automobile manufacturers in converting plants for aircraft production and to travel to England to gather intelligence on European air power in the war. On January 2, 1942, three weeks after the Japanese attack on Pearl Harbor propelled America into the war, Doolittle was promoted from major to lieutenant colonel and given an "impossible" assignment.

One week earlier, against the relentless drumbeat of one devastating Japanese attack and victory after another—in the Philippines, Wake Island, Guam, Malaya, Thailand, Shanghai, Midway, Guam, Burma, British Borneo, and Hong Kong—President Franklin D. Roosevelt summoned to the White House Army Chief of Staff General George C. Marshall, Chief of Staff of the Army Air Forces General Henry Harley "Hap" Arnold, Chief of Naval Operations Admiral Ernest J. King, and others to announce a top-priority assignment. FDR wanted to strike back at the Japanese, hitting their homeland with a bombing raid at the earliest possible moment. Such a raid, he insisted, was essential to building the morale of the American people and that of the nation's allies.

On the face of it, such a raid was also impossible—what with the United States and its allies manifestly losing the war in the Pacific. The Japanese empire was conquering one Pacific and Asian stronghold after another, pushing out from its home islands a great defensive ring, far beyond anyplace that could be used as a base from which to launch an air raid. At this point in World War II, no combatant, including the United States, possessed bombers capable of transcontinental range.

Each of the military leaders present left the meeting pondering the puzzle. In the days that followed, FDR repeated his call to action with the genial do-or-die insistence of which he was a master. During the second week of January 1942, one of Admiral King's staff officers, Captain Francis S. Low, was inspecting the brand-new aircraft carrier *Hornet* in Norfolk, Virginia. Nearby, he saw an airfield pilots used to practice carrier takeoffs and landings. On it was painted the outline of a carrier flight deck. Something clicked in Low's mind. Could *ground*-based Army Air Forces bombers, big planes with far greater range and ordnance payload than single-engine carrier-based fighters, take off from the deck of an aircraft carrier?

Low took the question to his air operations officer, Captain Donald Duncan. By January 16, Duncan delivered, by way of answer, what he believed was a workable proposal to present to Admiral King. It called for twin-engine North American B-25 "Mitchell" medium bombers to take off from a carrier. Loaded with a ton of bombs and (thanks to modification with extra tanks) enough fuel to fly two thousand miles, the bomber could—in theory, mind you—make it off a carrier deck. Or just barely.

Now, *landing* a B-25 or any other twin-engine aircraft on that deck was another matter altogether. There was simply no way it could be done. However, it might be feasible for the B-25s to attack Japanese cities, then fly to friendly airfields in mainland China. Not that this would be safe by any means; China had been under Japanese invasion since 1937.

In greatest secrecy, Duncan worked with Captain Marc Mitscher, skipper of the *Hornet,* to transform theory into practice by testing the ability of the B-25 to take off in a very short space. By early February, the two commanders had developed a technique enabling the plane to become airborne in as little as 500 feet. The *Hornet*'s flight deck was well over 800 feet long.

When Low and Duncan called on Hap Arnold to report their findings and present their proposal, the air force chief of staff received them enthusiastically. He did not tell them that, ever since the meeting with FDR, he had had his own staff working on much the same thing. It was after meeting with the two navy men that Arnold, without telling him why, asked Jimmy Doolittle to make an intensive study of short takeoffs with the B-25. Having conferred with Low and Duncan, Arnold was ready to explain, and Doolittle was eager to hear him.

After laying out the still rather vague notion of launching medium bombers on an air raid from the deck of a carrier, Arnold looked up at Doolittle tentatively, almost sheepishly. "Jim," he began, "I need someone to take this job over. . . ."

"And I know where you can get that someone," Doolittle interrupted.[8]

For Jimmy Doolittle, the snap decision to undertake the impossible was quite simple. He simply believed that taking off from an aircraft carrier in a medium bomber was no more impossible than taking off from the confines of a Mexican canyon, executing a "lethal" outside loop, or flying stunts with two broken ankles. Moreover, this belief had been corroborated, independently, by two responsible naval officers. To be sure, the mission would be as dangerous as they come. Given the hard reality that no round trip was possible (even Doolittle had to bow before the laws of physics), the mission came perilously close to being suicidal. But everything of significance he had ever done had been perilously close to suicide. When he finally retired from big-time air racing in 1932, he had quipped, "I have yet to hear of anyone engaged in this work dying of old age."[9]

Doolittle threw himself into designing and implementing necessary modifications to the B-25 airframe, mostly provisions to carry additional fuel. This work completed, he engaged in a series of rigorous tests of the aircraft in short take-off. While this was ongoing, he called on Brigadier General Carl "Tooey" Spaatz, at the time Arnold's deputy for intelligence, to come up with industrial targets in Tokyo, Yokohama, Kobe, Nagoya, and a half dozen other Japanese cities. Next, Doolittle trained *himself* to pilot the mission. Satisfied with his own training, he recruited volunteer aircrews. He did not tell them what they were going to do, but he assured them in no uncertain terms that their mission would be extremely dangerous. He then ran them through the same intensive and highly specialized course of training he had designed for himself.

Hornet sailed on April 2, 1942, and was joined en route by the carrier *Enterprise,* which would provide air cover during the approach to the launching point, a position about 400 miles off the Japanese mainland. The ships were scheduled to reach it on April 18. Shortly before dawn on that day, however, enemy picket boats were sighted much farther east than expected. U.S. escort ships quickly sank the pickets, but everyone assumed that their crews had already transmitted radio alerts to the Japanese fleet.

With the critical element of surprise presumably compromised, Doolittle made a desperate decision. He would launch the raid immediately, not 400 miles off the coast but 700. This put the B-25s at the extreme limit of their fuel supply and significantly reduced the chances of reaching Chinese airfields. The already-narrow margin separating a hazardous mission from a suicide mission was now razor thin. The mission was top-secret, so the public would not know if it was called off; however, aborting the mission would be a blow to the confidence of both high command and the president. Doolittle feared that, going forward, they might be discouraged from waging war with sufficient boldness and daring. Besides, his forces were in position to make a strike. They had trained for the mission. If it was abandoned, there would almost certainly be no second attempt.

And so, at about eight o'clock on the morning of April 18, Jimmy Doolittle's B-25 was the first to roll down *Hornet*'s flight deck, which pitched in the swell of a moderately stormy sea. The storm winds, combined with the forward speed of the carrier, gave the pilots a stiff 50-mile-per-hour headwind. Though punishing, it was excellent for lift. The *Hornet*'s flight deck was more than 800 feet long, but fewer than 500 feet were clear for the planes first in line, since all sixteen bombers had to be parked on deck due to their size. Doolittle himself had no trouble getting airborne, but some of the other pilots came close to stalling their aircraft on takeoff. Newsreel footage exists, showing a lumbering bomber rolling down the flight deck and then dipping below its edge, seeming to hang precariously over the waves before finally gaining altitude.

There were sixteen five-man crews in all. One bomber and crew were sent to attack Kobe, another Nagoya, and a third, slated to bomb cloudy Osaka, instead dropped its ordnance on alternate cloudless targets, the Yokosuka naval yard and Yokohama. A fourth plane suffered mechanical problems and was forced to land at Vladivostok, in the Soviet Union. The other twelve raiders bombed Tokyo at noon.

As chance would have it, Japanese civil defense authorities were just then conducting a drill, a mock air raid. This may have diluted the immediate psychological impact of the raid, but it also provided a diversion that helped the bombers escape unscathed. Not a single B-25 was lost over Japan.

In strictly tactical terms, the physical damage inflicted by fifteen medium bombers was minimal. Some fifty people were killed and a hundred structures were damaged or destroyed. However, the injury done to the attitude of invulnerability that pervaded the Japanese government and its military was far more serious. As a result of the raid, the Japanese high command was forced to retain a significant number of aircraft and pilots for home defense rather than commit them to frontline combat. Also, the raid removed official objections to a plan proposed by Admiral Isoruku Yamamoto (architect of the Japanese Pearl Harbor attack) to lure the American fleet into a fatal ambush near

Midway Island. This Japanese plan, as it turned out, would play beautifully into American hands, as the Battle of Midway (June 4–7, 1942) proved to be a hard-won U.S. Navy triumph and the turning point in the Pacific war. For these reasons alone, the Doolittle raid, although it was no more than a tactical pinprick, was a profound strategic victory. Add the tremendously inspiring lift it gave to American and Allied morale, an injection of precious hope grounded in actual achievement, and it was a triumph of far-reaching consequence.

Having successfully completed the raid, the bombers were now critically short of fuel. The crews either landed (or crash landed) them in China or abandoned them, bailing out wherever they could. Almost miraculously, Doolittle and seventy other mission members survived, all eventually finding their way back home. One airman was killed in parachuting from his plane, and eight were captured by the Japanese. Of this number, three were executed and one died in prison.

* * *

TWO YEARS AFTER WHAT EVERYONE CALLED the "Doolittle Raid," Lieutenant General Jimmy Doolittle had the Medal of Honor and command of the Eighth Air Force, and his old friend Jim Rand, having answered his phone call, was asking him what the hell he wanted.

Doolittle returned Rand's tone in kind.

"Jim," he told Rand, "you've been shooting off your mouth about being able to guide a bomb right into a hole. The Germans have a lot of big concrete bunkers in the side of cliffs and hills, in the Pas-de-Calais, twenty-five or thirty miles across the Channel, and they're gonna use 'em to destroy London. We've got to knock 'em out, and our bombers aren't getting the job done. . . . I want you to figure out how to fly a plane into these things and blow them up. And I want you to do it fast. If you don't do it fast, London is done for, and maybe New York, too."[10]

Rand had joined the army as an intelligence officer. His response to Doolittle befit this official duty designation. "What are they gonna shoot out of these sites?" he asked.

"None of your damned business!" Doolittle snapped. Then, more gently: "You just worry about blowing them up. What do you need?"

Rand did not hesitate. What he needed were "priorities." No. What he needed were "top priorities."

Doolittle said he would have them typed up within the hour. (Among the documents Doolittle sent Rand was a card direct from Supreme Allied Headquarters announcing that the bearer was not to be "interfered with in any way" by anyone, that his mission was special and had the highest priority, and that he was authorized to "commandeer any service or civilian transport, interrogate anyone, see any document, and demand any assistance he required." The card was signed by General Dwight D. Eisenhower, Supreme Commander, Allied Forces in Europe.)

Okay, Rand continued. He would also need "flexibility and mobility."

Doolittle said he would have a pair of planes and pilots at his disposal 24/7, adding that if Rand wanted a plane to fly himself, "We can arrange that, too."

Now, *this* did seem impossible. Rand explained to Doolittle that the Air Corps had grounded him. "I'm color-blind."

"You just made a miraculous recovery." Without pause, Doolittle pushed the exchange along: "What else do you need?"[11]

In civilian life, Rand was an engineer and scientist. His first and closest instructor had been his father, James H. Rand Jr., president of Remington Rand, at the time a maker of cutting-edge business machines, the technology of which was advancing toward the emergence of the modern digital computer. (Remington's own computer would be called UNIVAC I and would be bought by the U.S. Census Bureau in 1951.) To Doolittle's "What else do you need?" Rand responded with an off-the-cuff but intricately specific list of electronic parts and equipment. When he had paused long enough to indicate that the list was complete, Doolittle closed with "You'll get it."[12]

Jimmy Doolittle appreciated Jim Rand's qualifications as an intelligence officer, his competence as a technologist, and his enthusiasm and skill as an aviator, color-blind or not. Most of all, Doolittle saw himself and Rand as birds of a feather—not just as pilots but as individuals for whom brilliant improvisation was standard operating procedure. Rand, Doolittle believed, knew as much about emerging German technologies as anyone outside of Germany itself. As recently as 1938, as a civilian, Rand visited Berlin to research a topic that had become something of an obsession: cancer, its causes and cure. Like IBM, Remington Rand had a number of contracts with German firms and even the German government, and the son of the company's president had no trouble getting access to a vast array of technological advances that clearly had no connection to cancer. In effect, he was a spy in plain sight, a military attaché with neither uniform nor portfolio.

Having received much of his formal education at the universities of Vienna and Berlin, Rand spoke fluent German. As an aviator—an aviator who spoke German—he struck up a friendship with Ernst Udet, Germany's second-highest scoring air ace in World War I (Manfred "the Red Baron" von Richthofen was number one) and now a top Nazi general playing a key role in the creation of the modern Luftwaffe. The two became so close that they shared a small apartment during his 1938 Berlin sojourn. Rand did not hesitate to exploit their friendship.

"Ernst, I understand you're making television cameras in one of your war plants. Why?"

Rand had crossed a line and struck a nerve. "I'm not going to tell you that!" Udet exploded. "I could have you put in jail right now for asking such a question! Stick to your cancer research!"[13]

Of course, the reply spoke volumes, and Rand duly reported to the U.S. Embassy that the German military was developing television cameras that could be used for aerial reconnaissance and perhaps for remote-controlled aircraft or missile guidance. Unfortunately, neither the embassy nor U.S. intelligence seems to have made much of this early insight.

With America's entry into the war after Pearl Harbor, Rand enlisted, was commissioned as a second lieutenant, and, as a military intelligence officer, worked undercover in Switzerland, occupied France, and Portugal. Later, he served in the White House. Bored with being a Washington desk jockey, he transferred to the U.S. Army Air Forces antisubmarine patrol service, flying in a night fighter as an observer. After only a few months of this tedious duty, he covertly obtained Remington Rand funding to buy a nightclub in Algiers, from which he operated a North African listening post reporting to army intelligence.

Through his family's connections with the global press, he managed to plant news stories portraying himself as a "draft dodger playboy" who amused himself with an exotic nightspot. It was great cover, but, exposed after only a year, he fled Algiers, accepted a promotion to captain, and, by dumb luck, happened to be on a Liberty ship troop transport in the Mediterranean when a German bombing raid was under way.

The scientist in him honed his powers of close and careful observation. Amid the chaotic explosions and flashes of an ongoing raid, he took note of smoke, illuminated by a flare, trailing from one of the "bombs."

"That's a guided missile!" he exclaimed.[14]

If anyone heard him, no one took notice. But he followed up himself and sometime later learned that what he had seen was a weapon the Allies had dubbed "Fritz X." The Germans called it the Ruhrstahl AG SD-1400X, and it had been developed by Dr. Max Kramer of the Deutsche Versuchsanstalt für Luftfahrt (German Aviation Research Institute) beginning in 1939. It was futuristic looking, with four stubby cruciform wings and an "annular" tail that encircled the rear fuselage. It carried some 3,000 pounds of amatol explosive, and its electromagnetically activated spoilers allowed the bombardier to remote-control pitch and yaw as the bomb descended on its target at hypersonic speed. The bombardier tracked the weapon through his bombsight with the aid of a tail flare. In addition to the remote-control provisions, the weapon had self-correcting roll-stabilization features.[15]

Fritz X was not *quite* a guided missile but, rather, a bomb guidable by radio control in terms of azimuth (side-to-side direction) and range. Telling his superiors in Washington that he had actually seen Fritz X in action, Rand urged that *someone* with authority do *something* about starting a crash program to emulate it. He proposed going the German guided bomb one better by adding to it an onboard television camera, so that the controller (a pilot or bombardier), flying nearby in a manned "mother ship," could see the world from the bomb's point of view and guide the ordnance accordingly.

The idea gained considerable traction. American weapons engineers designed and built a "RAZON" (*range and azimuth only*) bomb, which was radio-controlled—but without the television cameras, which were deemed both too expensive and too unreliable. The engineers also soon gave up on trying to remotely control range, and the name of the program was changed to "AZON" (*azimuth only*). Rand, now promoted to major, was sent to England as AZON's on-the-ground technical chief.[16]

* * *

JIM RAND HAD ANSWERED Jimmy Doolittle's phone call as head of the Air Corps AZON unit. The technology was proving moderately successful. But Doolittle could not settle for "moderate." He wanted *spectacular.* By the time Rand hung up the phone, the paperwork transferring him from the AZON program was in motion. Given whatever priorities, people, and equipment he demanded, Rand took three of his AZON mother ship crews with him to Burtonwood, a Royal Air Force base occupied by the Army Air Corps. The installation was replete with the shops and facilities needed to make extensive modifications to aircraft.

Once Rand had arrived at Burtonwood, Doolittle met him there and briefed him on the basics of what was now officially (though secretly) designated Operation Aphrodite, and then he instructed him to share the briefing with his crews. Accordingly, Rand assembled his men, swore them to secrecy, and laid it out this way: "We're going to take old, used-up B-17s and rip their insides out and replace those insides with high explosives. We're going to equip those B-17s with AZON [actually, so-called double AZON, which also provided limited control over range] and fly them into enemy targets by radio control."[17]

When one of his pilots asked what "enemy targets," Rand replied only that he wished he "knew for sure," but what he could say was that they were top priority and that a lot of bombers had already tried to take them out and had failed miserably.[18] He went on to elaborate on the B-17 modification program by explaining that the aircraft would be transformed into robot planes, remotely controllable in terms of azimuth and, to a limited degree, range. The robot B-17s, he concluded, would be huge AZON bombs with some RAZON capability. They would be operated remotely, but within visual distance of their mother ships. The robot B-17s would be packed with enough explosives to create the biggest blasts of the whole war. Of any war, for that matter.

* * *

IF THE TECHNICAL PROBLEMS WERE FORMIDABLE—given the state of electronic technologies at the time, perhaps implausible if not simply and unavoidably impossible—the human factor was even more daunting. That part of the mission was not Rand's responsibility but Doolittle's. He had flown an all-but-suicidal mission before, of course, and had persuaded others to follow him in it. Moreover, as commanding officer of the Eighth Air Force, he ordered men to their deaths virtually every day.

The Eighth Air Force suffered half of the Air Corps' casualties in World War II: more than 47,000 casualties, of which 26,000 were fatal. For much of the war, aircrews were obligated to fly 25 bombing missions before being rotated to other duty, often back in the United States. The odds of surviving all 25 missions were roughly 7 to 10 *against*. Even so, asking men to fly *inside* the biggest bomb ever built and then to jump out before it was sent into a controlled crash was something different. The Japanese had taken to sending pilots on one-way suicide missions, and the Germans talked about doing so. The American armed forces never did, of course. But this, *this* was getting pretty damn close.

Doolittle had no doubt that he would find plenty of men willing to fly the bomb. Every day he discovered incredible heroism and willingness to sacrifice. Consisting of men who weeks or months before had been "ordinary" civilians, the ranks of the Americans boasted many gallant individuals. The heroism that would be exhibited by the Kennedy brothers was more rule than exception.

Demonstrations of Lieutenant (jg) John Fitzgerald Kennedy's heroism—the revelation of which would reduce his elder brother, Joe, to tears—began when, restless behind the desk his father had secured him, Jack sought a combat assignment and put in for midshipman's school. At the time, Jack Kennedy's girlfriend was the Danish-born newspaper reporter and columnist Inga Arvad, whom he lasciviously dubbed Inga-Binga. While she was still living in Europe during the 1930s and working as a freelance reporter, she had been granted at least three interviews with Adolf Hitler. "You immediately like him," she wrote. "He seems lonely. The eyes, showing a kind heart, stare right at you. They sparkle with force."[19] She attended Hermann Göring's wedding to the German actress Emmy Sonnemann, and she was on cordial terms with Joseph Goebbels. Hitler, who called her a perfect example of Nordic beauty, personally invited her to attend the 1936 Summer Olympics. After she came to the United States, the Federal Bureau of Investigation began tracking her. In November 1941, when Ensign Kennedy joined the Office of Naval Intelligence, the FBI shadowed them both—and tapped their phones.

Ultimately, the FBI concluded that she was no spy, but it nevertheless continued to follow and wiretap the couple. Unlike the FBI, the navy was not convinced that Inga was so innocent. Captain Howard

Klingman, assistant director of the Office of Naval Intelligence, wanted Ensign Kennedy cashiered from the navy altogether, but Kennedy's immediate superior, Captain Seymour A. D. Hunter, replied to Klingman that this might cause a problem because Kennedy was the son of the former ambassador to Britain. He advised instead that Kennedy be transferred to a seagoing unit.[20]

Initially, the ensign was simply shifted to another desk job, far outside of Washington, in South Carolina. Nevertheless, it is difficult to resist the speculation that his affair with Inga Arvad might have encouraged his navy superiors to endorse his application to midshipman school and his eventual transfer to combat service. In July 1942, on his way to Great Lakes Naval Training Station near Chicago, Kennedy stopped in Washington to see Inga. He told her he wanted to come to her apartment. This time she demurred. The affair, she calmly told him, was at an end. But after this last encounter, she telephoned a friend and remarked on how Kennedy looked like a "limping monkey from behind. He can't walk at all. That's ridiculous, sending him off to sea duty."[21]

Without any training, Jack Kennedy had been commissioned and sent directly to the Office of Naval Intelligence. The prospect of combat service was another story. Despite his obvious ill health, he endured the rigors of the Naval Reserve Officer Training Corps and then volunteered for the Motor Torpedo Boat Squadron Training Center at Melville, Rhode Island. Long accustomed to managing sailboats, Kennedy would not have been a bad choice as a potential PT boat skipper, except that the small, fast "patrol torpedo" boats were very hard on those who commanded and crewed them. A man suffering from severe spinal problems had no place on one of these vessels that, in combat maneuvers or rough seas, bucked like broncos. No matter. Jack wanted a PT command.

He must have been well aware of two key facts about PT boats.

First, they were nicknamed floating coffins or plywood coffins for very good reason. Their hulls were made of wood—not conventional plywood, but two planks made of diagonally layered mahogany laminated with a glue-impregnated layer of canvas between them. Light and fast, the craft were built for one job and one job only—to close quickly with a much larger enemy vessel and fire a torpedo into it at short range. Offensively, each PT boat was armed with two to four 2,600-pound Mark 8 torpedoes, each carrying a 466-pound TNT warhead. As for defensive armament, two twin 0.50-caliber machine guns were mounted, often supplemented by a single 20-mm Oerlikon "cannon." In truth, however, the boat's main defense was its speed and maneuverability. Just about any weapon on a larger combatant vessel could sink a PT boat. Among the most potent of these weapons was a ship's bow. In a ramming contest of steel hull against wooden hull, a PT was bound to lose every time. No wonder William L. White's best-selling World War II PT boat novel, published in 1942 and made into a John Wayne movie in 1945, was titled *They Were Expendable.* They were, both boat and crew.

The second fact Kennedy certainly knew was that, during America's early days in the Pacific war, the weeks and months after Pearl Harbor, the news coming back home was universally dismal. There were but two bright spots. One was provided by Jimmy Doolittle and his Tokyo raiders. The other came in the form of stories about the exploits of the PT boatmen—gallant knights galloping through enemy waters in the very thick of the enemy fleet.

The actual war record of the PT boats remains controversial. Few sinkings of Japanese warships were absolutely confirmed. This is probably due more to the notoriously unreliable, often defective Mark 8 torpedoes than to limitations of the boats and their crews. PT boat attacks against Japanese supply barges were more successful, and in the Solomon Islands campaign, the PTs were able to disrupt Japanese supply lines serving frontline troops. But Jack, Joe Jr., and Joe Sr. were not much concerned about the tactical effectiveness of the PT boats. What loomed large for them were the images—and the reality—of heroism the boats evoked. Jack Kennedy had found the possibility of achieving his own personal Jimmy Doolittle moment.

His first assignment, however, was not in the thick of the Pacific war but in the tranquil waters off Panama. As quickly as he could, he managed a transfer to the South Pacific, where he took command of PT-109. The story of what happened on the night of August 2, 1943, near New Georgia Island, is very familiar, of course. His boat was rammed by the Japanese destroyer *Amagiri,* which sliced the wooden-hulled vessel in two.

Two of Kennedy's crew were killed in the collision, and two others were grievously injured. A pair of PT-boats accompanying PT-109 launched torpedoes against *Amagiri*. Those of PT-169 missed, and those of PT-162 failed to launch. Assuming that no one could survive aboard a PT rammed by a destroyer, the two boats departed without conducting even a cursory search for survivors.

In the many years that have passed since that night, some have criticized Kennedy's judgment and seamanship for allowing PT-109 to get into harm's way. In the immediate aftermath, however, no such complaints were raised publicly. And certainly no one can doubt the gallantry, courage, fortitude, and leadership Kennedy exhibited in enabling his crew to live through the catastrophe. He gathered the surviving crew while they were all still in the water and announced that there was "nothing in the book about a situation like this." The question now was to fight or to surrender. "A lot of you men have families and some of you have children. What do you want to do? I have nothing to lose."[22]

The men voted to fight. With that, they clung to what was left of the boat's bow until it became clear that it was sinking. At that point, there was nothing to do but swim for it. The nearest land was occupied by Japanese troops. Kennedy knew that the tiny speck, locally known as Kasolo Island but called by the navy men Plum Pudding Island (and, even before the war ended, officially renamed Kennedy Island), was deserted. Those who were uninjured and good swimmers swam for the island. Those who were wounded or could not swim grabbed floating timber and kicked. Kennedy towed one survivor, too badly burned to swim or cling to the timber, by clenching the strap of the man's life jacket between his teeth. The three-and-a-half-mile swim took four perilous hours.

They had survived, but they were hardly safe. The island was roughly circular, perhaps 300 feet in diameter. Nothing edible grew on it, and there was no source of fresh water. Japanese barges, carrying supplies to the garrisons on nearby islands, passed to and fro continually. To remain here was to be captured or to die. Kennedy therefore swam out to Naru and Olasana islands, hoping to secure food and help. Discovering coconut trees and fresh water on Olasana, he led his men to it.

Whereas the officers and sailors manning the PT squadron's base had already conducted a memorial service for the crew of PT-109, an Australian coast watcher on Kolombangara Island decided to send a pair of friendly islanders in a dugout canoe to look for survivors. They found Kennedy and his men six days after the destruction of PT-109. They had been subsisting on coconuts. Because the islanders' canoe was too small to carry any passengers at all, one islander suggested that Kennedy scratch a message on a coconut, which they would deliver. Kennedy carved:

NAURO ISL. COMMANDER . . . / NATIVE KNOWS POS'IT . . . / HE CAN PILOT . . . / 11 ALIVE / NEED SMALL BOAT . . . KENNEDY.

The islanders set off with their message. A short time later, another canoe arrived to pick up Kennedy and take him to the Australian coast watcher. He radioed, and PT-157 was dispatched to pick up the other PT-109 survivors.

During the entire drama, Kennedy and his crew were officially reported as missing in action. The Kennedy family could do nothing but wait and pray. When word finally came of Jack's rescue, there was relief, which turned to joy when a letter, postmarked August 13, 1943, arrived from Jack himself. "Dear Folks," it began. "This is just a short note to tell you that I am alive—and *not* kicking—in spite of any reports that you may happen to hear."[23]

The only discordant note in the general rejoicing came from Joe Jr. As the boys' father wrote to him later: "When I returned home the other day, Mother told me she had finally heard from you. We were considerably upset that during those few days after the news of Jack's rescue we had no word from you. I thought that you would very likely call up to see whether we had had any news as to how Jack was."[24] On August 29, Joe Jr. sought to excuse his silence in a letter that cited his jammed transcontinental PB4Y-1 ferrying schedule. In pointedly sarcastic reference to his own non-combat duty posts, he signed the sheepish missive "the battler of the wars of Banana River, San Juan, Virginia Beach."[25]

CHAPTER 5

WAR-WEARY

MORE THAN A FEW AUTHORS HAVE WRITTEN ON THE "KENNEDY curse" and the "Kennedy death wish," and it is tempting to apply the title of Nigel Hamilton's biography of young Jack, *JFK: Reckless Youth*, to his older brother.[1] Did Joseph P. Kennedy Jr. have a "death wish"?

He certainly craved adventure and risked death, as when he entered into the heat of the Spanish Civil War, not out of any desire to fight on one side or the other but merely to see the action, and, by reporting on it, to ensure that the public knew he was there. But a yen for action and a desire to exploit danger for the purpose of building a reputation are hardly the equivalents of a wish to die. On the contrary, Joe Jr. was always described as "full of life," and his behavior before his military service never smacked of depression or despair.

It is true that the prospect of flying an explosive-laden aircraft without hope of returning in it is an extreme notion. In the context of 1944, however, it was by no means terribly radical. As mentioned, Jimmy Doolittle and other United States Army Air Forces commanders were, on a daily basis, sending men on missions with a high probability of proving fatal. But, as any World War II combat airman knew, parachuting out of a plane was not normally a planned part of a mission. On the contrary, it was in every sense a last resort. A USAAF survival manual spelled it out: "a controlled crash-landing, with fuel to spare, is preferable to bailing out."[2] The idea of *purposely* jumping out of a plane must have been highly unnerving. Joe Jr. himself put the odds of surviving the experience at 50/50.[3] But it could not have been that much more terrible to contemplate than the prospect of flying into huge airspaces of flak and Luftwaffe fighters. For that matter, if the concept of taking off with tons of high explosive on board seemed suicidal, it was really no more so than taking off with a full load of aviation fuel and a full munitions payload. To be sure, 25,000 pounds of high explosive would make a much bigger explosion than the 4,000-pound bomb load that was normal on long-range B-17 missions or the 8,000-pound payload normal for short-range sorties. Any of these, however, was more than sufficient to blow pilot and crew to bits if something went wrong enough on takeoff. And, not infrequently, something *did* go wrong. Engine malfunctions at takeoff were especially common and could prove deadly. Then, once airborne, the act of getting into formation was always hazardous, with midair collision a distinct possibility—especially given the unpredictable weather that prevailed over British airfields.

Even the Aphrodite/Anvil mission, extreme as it was, was not without some precedent—and not just that of the Japanese *kamikaze*. Henry "Jim" Rand had been working on RAZON and AZON remote-control systems for some time before Doolittle tapped him for Aphrodite. Working with a civilian engineer, Thomas J. O'Donnell, he had essentially invented the AZON bomb and had seen it through testing, production, and actual combat use. There were men—especially in the U.S. Navy—who had more and deeper experience with radio control than Rand had, but none had nearly so much practical combat experience with it.

Much as Aphrodite/Anvil relied on already-familiar technology married to some cutting-edge (and only marginally reliable) electronics, AZON was essentially a standard 1,000-pound general purpose bomb modified with the attachment of remote-controlled fins and a midsection "collar" for additional control. The collar featured preset elevators, which functioned like the preset trim tabs on conventional aircraft control surfaces. The elevators tended to stabilize the falling bomb, preventing roll, which made it easier for the remotely controlled fin surfaces to alter the bomb's azimuth. In addition, gyroscopes damped the effect of remote-control course corrections, preventing the bomb from weaving in flight. The gyros were powered by compressed air, and the onboard radio system and servos that controlled the fin surfaces were powered by a dry cell battery. The battery's usable life, about three minutes, was ample for the span of time required for a 1,000-pound bomb to hit its target. To aid the bombardier in controlling the AZON bomb, Rand emulated the German Fritz X guided bomb by adding a flare that produced a colored streamer of light and smoke. These tracer colors could be varied among red, white, green, or (later) yellow, so that the bombardier could distinguish between individual bombs when several were dropped—although, as we will see, the greatest accuracy was achieved when the guided bombs were dropped not in groups but one at a time.

The bomber aircraft from which the AZON munitions were released was fitted with three radio antennas beneath its tail section. One antenna transmitted a signal at 475 cycles for left deflection, one transmitted at 3,000 cycles for right deflection, and one, operating at 30 to 40 cycles, activated the flare/smoke-generating system. The actual transmitter was a standard, off-the-shelf U.S. Army Signal Corps unit, 25 watts, capable of transmitting on fifteen distinct frequencies.[4]

As mentioned, AZON was something of a technological retreat from RAZON in that it remotely controlled azimuth only, not both range and azimuth. Realistically, the sole purpose of the AZON control system was not *steering* the bomb so much as merely *correcting* deflection errors as it rapidly descended toward its target. Testing suggested it was very good at accomplishing this limited function, with the potential to reduce deflection errors to zero. What is more, Rand's AZON bombs were combat tested. In the early spring of 1944, shortly before the Aphrodite program began, Group H, ten B-24 Liberators and their crews from the 458th Bombardment Group, was diverted en route from the China-Burma-India (C-B-I) theater to Horsham, England, for service in the European Theater of Operations (ETO). Flight crews were given specialized AZON training, personally overseen by Major Rand, and on May 31, 1944, they were dispatched on their first mission—targeting five bridges in France. Through August 25—well after Rand had left his AZON assignment to lead the technical effort in Operation Aphrodite—Group H flew eleven more missions over France. During the rest of August and into mid-September, the group flew another four missions over the Netherlands and Germany. Most of the targets were bridges—tactical targets requiring precision bombing. The final mission, on September 13, was more ambitious: an oil refinery and ammunition depot in Germany. After this, the AZON program was ended, and some of the Group H pilots volunteered to join Operation Aphrodite.[5]

Each Group H B-24 was armed with four AZON bombs, which typically were released from an altitude of 15,000 feet, the minimum required to allow sufficient time and space to adequately control the bomb. Of sixteen AZON missions, six were scrubbed (two due to weather) and two were completed without dropping bombs, due to poor visibility over the targets. Of the eight remaining missions, seven were deemed successful—significant proof of concept for radio remote control, however limited.[6]

* * *

THE UNOFFICIAL PATCH the AZON crews wore on their flight jackets proclaimed them the "Buck Rogers Boys" of the Eighth Air Force. Buck Rogers was the interplanetary rocket jockey who first appeared in pulp science-fiction magazines, a long-running syndicated newspaper comic strip, and a popular movie serial starring Olympic swimmer turned actor Buster Crabbe. A World War I veteran, Buck Rogers takes a hazardous job with the "American Radioactive Gas Corporation," is accidentally contaminated, and, as a result, goes into suspended animation, awakening nearly 500 years later, in the twenty-fifth century. To the delight of sci-fi readers and movie serial audiences, Buck quickly adapts to a future of rocket ships, death rays, and guided missiles. The phrase "Buck Rogers" soon became pop culture shorthand for anything wildly futuristic.

If the AZON crews embraced the realm of science fiction, the reality was that serious discussion of unmanned, automatically controlled "aerial torpedoes" or "flying bombs" had begun even before the nations of Europe and their colonial possessions went to war in the summer of 1914. It was, however, in April 1915 that two citizens of the United States—as yet officially neutral in the "Great War"—pooled their expertise to create what they called a "flying bomb." Like other developers of weapons and weapon systems during this period, the pair spoke of creating a technology that could end this war and all wars. Perhaps more immediately, they also saw a profitable market for any weapon that would give one side or the other an edge.

Peter Cooper Hewitt, whose wealth rested on the mercury vapor lamp he had invented, called on Elmer A. Sperry, founder and president of the Sperry Gyroscope Company, with preliminary sketches for the flying bomb. Sperry's innovative gyroscope technology was already widely used in such marine navigation equipment as the gyrostabilizer and gyrocompass. As early as 1911, the year after he founded his company, Sperry became interested in applying radio control to aircraft. Since both Hewitt and Sperry served on the Committee on Aeronautics and Aeronautical Motors of the Naval Consulting Board, they were in an excellent position to persuade the navy to send a representative from its Bureau of Ordnance to inspect and report on the complete autopilot system they developed. On September 12, 1916, Lieutenant T. S. Wilkinson Jr. flew as observer in the Curtiss flying boat piloted by Sperry's son Lawrence. After taking off, Lawrence Sperry engaged this first-ever autopilot, which took the craft to a predetermined altitude, held a preset compass course, flew over a preset distance, and then, as programmed, sent the plane into a dive—at which point Lawrence intervened to pull up.

Thus, in 1916, the first flying bomb flew, achieving everything short of an actual impact and explosion. Impressed, Wilkinson wrote that the flying bomb was superior to naval guns because of its longer range but added the caveat that its "use in long range attacks against forts and cities is of doubtful military value on account of [the] difficulty of striking at any desired point rather than at random within the limits of the city or fortress."[7] Nevertheless, Wilkinson observed, with extraordinary perspicacity, that the "moral effect of such devices may be great. They are practically indestructible, unless a well-aimed shot disables [the] engine or control devices, and they cannot be driven off [by hostile fire]." In other words, the flying bomb had potential as a terror weapon.[8]

Wilkinson's low-key report failed to kindle much excitement in the U.S. Navy. The British, however, were into the second year of a war whose principal theater, the Western Front, was locked in a bloody stalemate. The military establishment was desperate for any innovation that might bring a breakthrough. Archibald M. Low, remembered today as the father of radio guidance systems, joined the British army soon after war began in 1914. Initially tasked by the War Office with developing a radio-based rangefinder system for coastal artillery, he was in short order promoted to captain and seconded to the Royal Flying Corps (later renamed the Royal Air Force, RAF). His new assignment was to create a radio-controlled flying bomb for use against zeppelins as well as ground targets. To accommodate the radio-control system Low built, aeronautical engineer H. P. Folland, who had designed the superb SE-5 pursuit plane, created the "Ruston Proctor AT," a proto-cruise missile, with a 22-foot wingspan and a weight, complete with 35-horsepower engine, of just 500 pounds. Its initial trial, for an audience of Allied generals on March 21, 1917, was at first impressive, but engine failure resulted in a hair-raising crash that sent the assembled brass scattering for their lives. After a second trial, official interest in the project faded, along with War Office funding.[9]

Just as British enthusiasm for a flying bomb waned, American interest was rekindled after the nation entered the war on April 6, 1917. The navy took the lead. Just eight days after Congress declared war, the Naval Consulting Board recommended allocating $50,000 to Sperry-Hewitt's flying bomb. Secretary of the Navy Josephus Daniels ultimately approved $200,000, and the navy installed Sperry controls in five Curtiss N-9 seaplanes, a floatplane version of the land-based Curtiss JN-4 "Jenny," which was the staple of the U.S. Army's small and primitive air arm. The navy conducted more than a hundred test flights with mostly disappointing results, including numerous crashes. Nevertheless, Sperry wrote to Rear Admiral Ralph Earle "that the time has practically arrived when we have on hand *the gun of the future*."[10] He chose the word "gun" carefully. An admiral might balk at continued costly—and so far unsuccessful—efforts to develop an automatically piloted airplane or a flying bomb. But the *gun* of the future was another matter. The navy whose ships had the best guns would always emerge victorious, and Rear Admiral Earle therefore wrote a report to the chief of naval operations that actually magnified Sperry's less-than-warranted optimism. Earle predicted that the flying bomb would be ready before spring 1919, that it would carry a 1,000-pound payload 75 miles, and that it would do so with an accuracy of 1.5 miles and at a per-bomb cost of $2,500.[11]

In fact, the navy's enthusiasm for "the gun of the future" outlived the Great War, which ended on November 11, 1918. In May 1919, while most of the U.S. military establishment was being demobilized and dismantled, the Naval Aircraft Factory in Philadelphia built ten aircraft expressly designed as flying bombs. All proved so tail heavy that they could be flown only with a pilot on board—and, even then, they frequently crashed. Finally, in 1922, amid a public and political climate of resolute isolationism, the navy finally canceled its flying bomb program.

*   *   *

WHILE WORLD WAR I WAS STILL RAGING, however, the army awakened to interest in a flying bomb. On November 21, 1917, Major General George O. Squier, the army's chief signal officer, was the guest of Elmer Sperry, Glenn Curtiss, and Rear Admiral Earle at one of the navy's unpiloted N-9 demonstrations. Impressed by the aircraft's seven-mile flight under automatic control, Squier wrote to the chairman of the army's Aircraft Board on November 26 that the "time has come" for the U.S. military to take "to Europe something new in war."[12]

The chairman presented Squier's recommendation to the entire Aircraft Board, which duly approved experimental work on a new flying bomb. In December 1917, Squier convened a four-person committee to investigate the potential of the concept. Three of the four reported negatively, but one, Charles F. Kettering, whose wealth and fame rested on his having invented a practical automobile self-starter (he would later rise to the presidency of General Motors), reported enthusiastically on the possibilities of the weapon. For this, he earned himself a lucrative cost-plus contract to develop a practical flying bomb.[13]

In Dayton, Ohio, Kettering gathered a remarkable engineering and manufacturing team to build an aircraft on a rush basis. His own firm, Dayton Metal Products, would engineer the control systems. Elmer Sperry would direct gyroscope technology; C. H. Willis, chief engineer for Ford Motor Company, would design the engine; and no less a figure than Orville Wright, of the Dayton Wright Airplane Company, would supply the airframe. Recognizing that a vital link in all of this would be a pneumatic system for mechanically linking controls to control surfaces, Kettering tapped S. F. Votey, of the Aeolian Player Piano Company, figuring that few pneumatic systems are more complex or more accurate than those designed to convert perforated rolls of paper into live piano music.[14]

The team turned out a biplane that was smaller, simpler, and much cheaper than the craft Sperry had earlier designed with Hewitt and Curtiss for the U.S. Navy. With a length of only 12.5 feet and a wingspan just shy of 15 feet, the aircraft weighed in at 530 pounds when loaded with 180 pounds of high explosive. Its power plant was a 40-horsepower four-cylinder De Palma engine modified by Ford's Willis.[15] Although it was officially dubbed the "Liberty Eagle," everyone who beheld its diminutive dimensions and dihedral wings, diaphanous as a dragonfly's, called it the Kettering Bug.[16]

The Bug was built on a wooden frame covered with muslin and brown wrapping paper doped with a mixture of glycerin and creosote. Borrowing from Sperry's technology, range was controlled by an air log impeller that actuated a mechanical counter—bought whole and unmodified from the National Cash Register Company—which measured distance traveled by counting the number of revolutions of the propeller and, at a predetermined count, actuated pneumatic controls that not only cut the ignition to the motor but automatically folded the Bug's wings, instantly transforming the airplane into a bomb.[17]

Impressed, the army ordered twenty-five Bugs on January 25, 1918—*before* seeing a test flight, which did not take place until July 19. That test and two that followed it included a human pilot. On September 13, the first unmanned launch ended in an immediate crash, as did the next two attempts, on September 14 and October 1. On October 2, the Bug finally flew—for all of nine seconds. But just two days later, it flew under automatic control for a full 45 minutes, covering 65 miles, until it crashed at Xenia, Ohio.

Among those who observed the longest flight was Henry Harley Arnold. One of the army's elite inaugural trio of rated military pilots, he had been taught to fly by the Wright Brothers themselves—that is, once he had overcome his intense fear of flying. Universally known by the nickname "Hap," Arnold would rise to command the U.S. Army Air Forces in World War II, in which he became a driving force behind both the Doolittle Raid on Japan and Doolittle's Operation Aphrodite.

Through the eyes of Hap Arnold and others, the repeated failures of the Kettering Bug looked instead like the auguries of future success. The observers persuaded the army to order seventy-five additional Bugs, and Lieutenant Colonel Bion J. Arnold, in charge of the Bug program, claimed to foresee a time when the Air Service fleet would include 10,000 to 100,000 flying bombs at a unit cost of just $400 to $500. An October 1918 flight of 500 yards was deemed a triumph, and General Squier exuberantly reported to the army's Chief of Staff that "this new weapon, which has now demonstrated its practicability" signals the beginning of "an epoch in the evolution of artillery for war purposes . . . comparable . . . with the invention of gunpowder in the Fourteenth Century."[18]

At the height of the enthusiasm, at the eleventh hour of the eleventh day of the very next month, November, World War I ended. On November 27, 1918, just sixteen days after the armistice was signed, the Dayton project was officially shut down. By that time, only twenty Bugs had been built to completion, along with five finished airframes (sans engines and controls) and eleven aircraft in various other stages of assembly. It was far short of 500 machines, let alone 10,000 to 100,000. Nevertheless, instead of scrapping the few craft on hand, the army quietly continued testing them. All failed, and in March 1920 a stop was put to the program.[19]

*   *   *

IN MAJOR HISTORIES OF MILITARY AVIATION, the early U.S. experiments with flying bombs or aerial torpedoes generally figure as footnotes. This is a misleading view. In the end, the enthusiasm so many officers showed for the devices counts for more than the paucity of successful test results. These officers believed they were dealing with a potentially war-winning weapon, and while most historians of flight frequently refer to the Kettering Bug and its ilk as "forgotten" episodes in aviation, they were hardly forgotten by an influential group of World War II–era engineers, aviators, and military leaders.

If the World War I experience *hinted at* the potential of unmanned flight, it definitively *proved* its many difficulties. Chief among these was the challenge of launching, let alone flying, an unmanned craft. Most crashes occurred on launching, and among the mere handful of early test launches that resulted in sustained flight, it was apparent that achieving and maintaining stability without a human pilot was supremely difficult. The principal problem, as the pioneers saw it, was not with the theory of unmanned flight but with the limitations imposed by circumstances and the government on executing that theory. While the demands of war drove development, they also curtailed the time available for proper experimentation. The early designers were forced to build pilotless prototypes quickly and get them into the air without adequate testing on the ground. Imprecision was built into a method marked by urgency. The nature of unmanned flight compounded the problem, as it involved many separate technical systems, all of which were, at the time, in early, incomplete stages of conceptualization.

Add to this that a prime requirement of a flying bomb was dictated by economics. A weapon whose successful deployment necessarily resulted in its destruction had to be cheap. This meant using cheap materials and employing construction methods that were just good enough, and no better. Applying cost-cutting specifications to cutting-edge technology was not a combination that boded success.

Finally, the great teacher in the development of any technology is failure. Careful analysis of what does *not* work provides the insight needed to transform failed components into the elements of success. Inherently fragile, intended for destruction, the Bug and its brethren left little of forensic value to examine and analyze after a crash.

While work was moving forward on the Kettering Bug during World War I, Hap Arnold was dispatched to England and France to share test results with the Allies. The value of developing practical pilotless aircraft resonated with the British, and in May 1919, the first spring after the armistice, the Royal Naval Antiaircraft Gunnery Committee requested development work on a radio-controlled target aircraft—what would later be called a target drone. In response, the British Air Ministry authorized development but also moved to purchase such a target aircraft from the United States. Winston Churchill, at the time secretary of state for air in the cabinet of Prime Minister David Lloyd George, squashed the purchase option. He wanted the newly created Royal Air Force (RAF) to develop uniquely British pilotless aircraft. This may have served to stimulate homegrown development in the field, but it also stifled any collaborative synergy between two natural allies. In any case, by the mid-1920s, the RAF had equipped a variety of existing aircraft with radio control and successfully flew them, albeit always with a human pilot on board to monitor the equipment and intervene as necessary.[20]

The goal of the RAF was to create an unmanned flying bomb. Another British agency, the Royal Aircraft Establishment (RAE), which operated independently of the RAF, focused on what would seem the less ambitious objective of designing a target drone. As it turned out, this work advanced pilotless flight more quickly and significantly. By 1924, the RAE managed to catapult launch a programmed gyro-guided (not radio-controlled) target drone that flew well for twelve minutes before its engine died. The next year, an RAE drone flew for thirty-nine minutes.[21]

Encouraged, beginning in September 1925, the RAE turned from target drones to developing a pilotless attack weapon. Whereas the RAF had attempted to marry pilotless technology to existing aircraft, the RAE decided to develop an aircraft purpose-built for unmanned flight. It was dubbed Larynx (Long Range Gun with Lynx Engine). Precise specifications for the aircraft cannot be found, but an existing photograph from July 1927 reveals it to have been a small, stubby monoplane, with a wingspan of approximately fourteen feet and an abbreviated fuselage of perhaps eight or nine feet in length.[22] We know that it was powered not by the small engines used in the flying bomb experiments of World War I but by a formidable 200-horsepower Armstrong Siddeley Lynx IV engine. This gave it a top speed of 200 miles per hour, which was faster than piloted fighters of the era and so made it difficult to shoot down. In its first configuration, Larynx used an autopilot—programmed, not radio-controlled—developed from Archibald Low's design for the World War I–era Ruston Proctor AT biplane.[23]

Work on Larynx began in 1925, but it was not until July 20, 1927, that the aircraft was launched from a cordite-powered catapult fitted to the stern of the destroyer HMS *Stronghold*. While the launch was a success, the flight was not, as Larynx plunged into the waters of the Bristol Channel. The RAE believed that the second launch, on September 1, 1927, resulted in a flight of at least a hundred miles—but observers lost track of the aircraft, which vanished without a trace. The next month, on October 15, a Larynx aircraft flew 112 miles before impacting just 5 miles off target. In 1928, the catapult was transferred to another destroyer, HMS *Thanet,* and two more launches sent the aircraft on flights of 50 miles each. The first of these launches produced an impact 1.6 miles off target, while the second was off by 4.5 miles.

In May 1929, Larynx planes were twice launched from land. In the first attempt, the aircraft overflew its target and disappeared, but the second launch produced a flight that was quite close to plan. Subsequent testing was moved to desert Iraq, territory under a post–World War I mandate awarded to Britain by the League of Nations, but produced mixed results.[24]

On balance, the Air Ministry was unimpressed by Larynx. The RAF briefly took over the project, only to drop it and return to the less ambitious task of developing a target missile. In 1933, the RAF chief of the Air Staff revisited the pilotless programs. As Nazi Germany was on the rise, the threat of air power from that quarter came to seem increasingly real. Accordingly, number-one priority was now given to developing pilotless missiles for air defense. These were to be remotely radio controlled—not from a ground station but from manned "shepherd aircraft," which would maintain visual contact with the pilotless missiles.[25] Each air defense missile required *two* shepherd aircraft for guidance, which made the system's cost prohibitive. Moreover, because the mother ships had to maintain visual contact with the remote missiles at all times, the system could be operated only in daylight—and in clear weather—whereas conventional *manned* fighters could defend English skies day or night, cloudy or clear, and they could do it far more cheaply. The radio-controlled air defense missile program was abandoned in 1936. Along with it, all of the pilotless programs were summarily cancelled, except for one designed to convert obsolescent Fairley IIIF float biplanes into radio-controlled targets.

Three Fairleys were converted. Two, launched from a catapult on HMS *Valiant* in January and April 1932, crashed. A third, launched on September 14, flew for just nine minutes but was recovered. In January 1933, affectionately christened the "Fairley Queen"—a nod to Edmund Spenser's Elizabethan allegory, *The Faerie Queen*—it flew again under radio control as the Royal Navy practiced its gunnery. The navy's guns took two full hours to bring it down. A miserable showing for the gunners, but an admirable demonstration of the Fairley Queen, the demonstration prompted the Air Ministry to order conversion of the relatively inexpensive Tiger Moth trainer into a radio-controlled target plane. Between 1934 and 1943, the Fairley Corporation delivered 420 of the pilotless Tiger Moths, which the company called Queen Bees. Although these were limited to use as a target drones, they were, in fact, the first truly reliable radio-controlled pilotless aircraft.

*   *   *

IN THE UNITED STATES, although development of the Kettering Bug ended by 1920, the army awarded contracts to the Sperry Gyroscope Company and the Lawrence Sperry Aircraft Company (named for and owned by the son of Elmer A. Sperry) for an autopilot system to be installed in three Standard E-1 aircraft and five Verville-Sperry M-1 Messengers. Using radio control, operated from a mother ship flying within a mile and a half of the Messenger, Lawrence Sperry obtained, during May–June 1922, the best results seen to that time with remote-controlled flight. His flying bombs hit the target twice at 30 miles, three times at 60 miles, and once at 90 miles. Lawrence Sperry did not have long to enjoy his triumph, however. On December 23, 1923, he took off in heavy fog across the English Channel, bound for France. When he failed to land, a search was conducted, and his body was recovered from the Channel on January 11, 1924. The army continued testing radio-controlled flight throughout the 1920s but made no headway beyond what Sperry had achieved. As the Great Depression took hold at the end of the decade, funding shortages prompted the abandonment of further work on pilotless aircraft.[26]

Although the army program withered just as it looked so promising, navy interest in pilotless aircraft reemerged during the mid-1930s with an order for high-speed radio-controlled antiaircraft practice targets. By February 1937, the navy had a handful of prototypes that proved quite successful as targets. Lieutenant Commander Delmar Fahrney, who had been assigned as officer in charge of the Radio-Controlled Aircraft Project, directed the building of the targets at a facility he established at the Naval Aircraft Factory in Philadelphia. By this time, the target aircraft were officially being called "target drones," in homage to the Royal Navy's Queen Bee. As the target drones proved themselves, Fahrney championed the idea of adapting them for combat use as what he dubbed "assault drones."[27]

Fahrney's proposal came at a moment in history when technological and global political developments were on converging courses as the world plunged toward a new war. Television was given a spectacular public demonstration at the 1939 World's Fair in New York. Two years earlier, Radio Corporation of America—RCA—had demonstrated an airborne television camera and transmitting equipment to a delegation of Soviet officials for use in an aerial reconnaissance project, and in August 1941, barely five months before Pearl Harbor, a version of the system was tested aboard a U.S. radio-controlled drone. With a camera mounted in the drone's nose, the operator had a pilot's-eye view of the craft's flight. This technology was quickly married to newly emerging radar altimeter technology, providing a far more accurate reading of altitude above actual terrain than was possible with a conventional barometric altimeter, which measured barometric pressure above sea level. The new radar altimeter was available by January 1941.

In the months leading up to U.S. entry into World War II, the navy's assault drone program progressed, albeit slowly. At last, in November 1941, a month before Pearl Harbor, the chief of the Bureau of Aeronautics ordered a hundred obsolescent torpedo bombers to be converted into assault drones and an additional hundred new aircraft purpose-built for assault. But the same awareness of impending war that drove this decision also impeded its implementation. Because the navy did not want to disrupt production of conventional warplanes, it awarded the contract for the purpose-built drones to a company that was not already committed to warplane work. The unintended consequence was production delays born of inexperience. Worse, when Pearl Harbor was attacked on December 7, 1941, the order to convert the existing torpedo bombers to drones was canceled. Obsolescent or not, the manned bombers were now urgently needed to fight the Japanese.

*   *   *

THE UNITED STATES AND GREAT BRITAIN were not the only military powers experimenting with flying bombs. As Jim Rand and others discovered relatively early in World War II, the Germans had developed radio control for use in guided bombs. Later in the war, it became apparent that some V-1s, the most advanced and numerous of World War II cruise missiles, were equipped with radio-control systems—although most employed nothing more advanced than preprogrammed gyro-stabilization systems.

The two most significant German guided bombs were the Henschel Hs 293 glide bomb and, as discussed in chapter 4, the Ruhrstahl AG SD-1400X, which the Allies called Fritz X.[28]

Developed in 1939, the Henschel Hs 293 was the first radio-guided bomb to be used in combat in World War II. Originally, it was totally unpowered, but when it was discovered that the bomb could not reach the terminal velocity necessary to pierce ship armor—warships were the intended targets of this weapon—a booster rocket motor was added. The warhead for all versions of the Henschel bomb was a standard Luftwaffe high-explosive bomb casing packed with 650 pounds of Trialen 105 (15 percent RDX [Research Department explosive], 70 percent TNT, 15 percent aluminum powder). The guidance system was assembled from advanced off-the-shelf German electronics. It included a gyroscope, a radio-control signal decoder, and a radio command link receiver, which controlled solenoid actuators attached to the craft's ailerons and elevators. The entire package was powered by onboard batteries. Used in combat during 1943 and 1944, the Hs 293 sank some 400,000 tons of Allied shipping.

Development of the Fritz X began in 1939 and used the same radio-guidance system as the Hs 293, but employed a more advanced gyroscope for roll stabilization and had a more distinctively futuristic airframe design. Like the Hs 293, the Fritz X was tracked from the launch plane through a conventional bombsight, the operator aided in guiding the bomb to its target by a tail-mounted smokeless tracer flare. The weapon was loaded with 705 pounds of amatol high explosive. Like the more numerous Hs 293 variant, this so-called glide bomb was, in fact, a guided missile, equipped with a powerful rocket booster. The Germans deployed some 1,400 Fritz X bombs—although it is estimated that about half of this number were expended in experimental trials and training.

* * *

EVEN THOUGH THE U.S. Army and Navy had an early interest in pilotless flight, the nation entered World War II far behind Germany in the development of flying bombs, aerial torpedoes, and guided missiles. There was a rush to catch up. On April 9, 1942, naval experimenters tested a torpedo-carrying drone (TG-2)—an old torpedo bomber

* * *

THE GERMAN GUIDED MISSILE PROGRAMS began before World War II, with glide bombs reaching an advanced state of development early in the war and both the V-1 cruise missile and V-2 ballistic missile emerging later as what propaganda minister Joseph Goebbels called *Wunderwaffen* (wonder weapons). In contrast, the U.S. military began with truly grand expectations for guided weapons and then, during the war, steadily narrowed its vision in the hope of producing a class of quick-and-dirty weapons that could be rushed into combat. Jim Rand was very much an agent of this approach.

Before Rand came into the picture, the United States Army Air Forces had experimented with two classes of so-called glide weapons: the BG (bomb glider) series and the GB (glider bomb) series. Only one BG prototype, converted from an existing target drone (the Fletcher PQ 11A), actually flew. Like the BG concept, the GB series were winged bombs, on which work began in 1940–1941. Fourteen GB variants were produced by the Aeronca Aircraft Company, a major producer of general aviation civil aircraft during the 1930s and 1940s. GB-5 was fitted with the high-contrast, target-seeking electro-optical (EO) system; GB-6 had an early version of an infrared heat-seeking sensor; and GB-7 had a passive radar homing device. Only the GB-8 configuration used radio control, with the remote operator tracking and controlling the glider by observing tracer flares attached to its airframe. Some authorities believe that this variant was also equipped with a solid-fuel rocket. Other variants featured modifications of these sensor and control schemes.

The range of experimentation suggested by the variants is impressive, but only the original glider bomb, the GB-1, actually went into production and was issued to the USAAF, late in 1943. The least ambitious of all the GB variants, it was a bomb to which stubby wooden wings, spanning twelve feet, were attached, along with a twin-boom, twin-fin tail assembly. Its gyroscopic stabilization guidance was pre-programmed by the bombardier prior to release. When the bomber approached its target, the bombardier aimed the weapon and released it, letting it glide away from the bomber in the direction of the target. The GB-1 was designed to be launched from shackles mounted under each wing of a B-17, one bomb per wing. The presumed advantage of the glider bomb was that its shallow angle of descent would enable it to hit tall structures. Although the GB-1 was used in significant numbers in raids on Cologne, Germany, during early 1944, it proved very inaccurate and was abandoned. Perhaps a thousand were used in combat.

Jim Rand was intimately involved with a third class of Air Corps glide weapon, the VB (vertical bomb) series. Whereas the BG and GB concepts resembled crude approximations of the German Henschel Hs 293, the VB series was closer to the Fritz X, which had so impressed Rand when he observed it from the deck of a transport in the Mediterranean. The first eight of the series, VB-1 through VB-8, were modified standard USAAF aerial bombs, either one or two thousand pounds. They were fitted with a new tail assembly that carried a gyro-stabilization system, a pair of rudders, and a tracking flare. The gyro stabilization was used to reduce roll so that the radio-controlled rudders could function more effectively.

Airmen raised three objections to the VB weapons. First, with conventional bombs, bomber crews could drop their load and immediately shear away. The VB munitions, in contrast, required the bomber aircraft to remain on course while the bombardier visually guided the bomb onto its target. This greatly increased the bomber's vulnerability to antiaircraft fire, as gunners were able to draw a bead on a plane flying straight and level. Second, those who did embrace the guided bomb concept objected to the azimuth-only limitation and longed for a fully guided weapon. Third, when dropped in quantity, AZON bomb accuracy was significantly reduced. In theory, the bombardier needed to direct only the first bomb dropped. His radio corrections would be automatically applied to all the others. But aerodynamic imbalances in the individual bombs tended to increase dispersal over a target, making the AZON bombs actually *less* accurate than conventional munitions. The problem proved intractable, and so AZON bombs were dropped one by one, on very specific targets that required great accuracy to hit.[36]

* * *

OPERATION APHRODITE AND PROJECT ANVIL emerged from about a quarter century of haphazard experimentation with pilotless and radio-controlled flight. Valuable technologies had been developed, and a

vision of the possibilities had taken shape. Yet the advances were out-
weighed by an abundance of mixed results and outright failures. The
pedigree of the missions now so urgently being mounted against Hitler's
V weapons was full of dubious ancestors.

It was in a spirit of reduced expectations for guided weapons that
the decision to "recycle" war-weary B-17s for use in Operation Aphrodite was made. This bold experiment in raw courage and cutting-edge
but crude technology relied on hand-me-down aircraft flown by pilots
whose mission was twofold: first, to compensate for the deficiencies of a
semi-robotic technology in which the emphasis was clearly on the *semi;*
second, to try to escape death.

Major Rand moved from Burtonwood to Honington, a large RAF
depot. A collection of beat-up B-17s flew into the facility from all
over the European theater. There they were lined up to be attacked by
swarms of airmen who, under Rand's merciless supervision, stripped
them clean. Some worked on the innards, others removed turrets and
guns. As far as anyone could see, they were acting on orders to take
out anything capable of being taken out—with a single exception. They
always left the pilot's seat in place.

With a small group of test pilots, Rand needed to invent the techniques and tactics for the actual attacks. So he rode herd on another
group of airman-technicians, who began installing electronic, radio-
control, and servo-control gear inside the gutted Flying Fortress hulks.
As tests were run and rerun, Rand had his men working like demons,
adjusting, readjusting, uninstalling, reinstalling the equipment.

The first actual flight test was aimed at answering one simple question: Could the B-17, stripped of some four tons of its innermost guts,
including various structural elements, fly level and fly under complete
control? In fact, could it still fly at all? Rand accompanied the pilot who
took the first gutted Flying Fortress up. As they rotated off the runway,
both men looked and listened for the first signs of structural failure. To
be sure, flying the unnaturally light aircraft took some getting used to,
but both pilot and plane quickly passed that test. The bomber could be
controlled, and it didn't fall apart. The next step was to load the aircraft
with 18,500 pounds of sandbags and make certain *that* weight did not
break it. After both tests were completed, Rand's next set of orders sent
his technicians scurrying to install all the wiring, cables, hydraulics,

and electronics necessary to transform these examples of late 1930s
aeronautical technology into futuristic cruise missiles capable of being
precisely controlled remotely by radio.

Rand had more technical experience with radio control in actual
bombing missions than anybody else in the U.S. military. But this *successful* experience was limited to AZON—azimuth-only remote control
of a falling bomb. What Aphrodite called for was radio control not only
of azimuth but of range, attitude, and the detonation of a planeload of
explosives. Moreover, this control had to be exercised not merely to
correct the side-to-side deviation of a falling bomb but actually to fly
a four-engine bomber with a loaded gross weight of roughly 65,000
pounds. For Rand, therefore, the next set of tests was personal. He
boarded a B-17, modified with radio transceivers and television moni-
tors for controlling the robot craft. Cryptically redesignated a CQ-17, it
was to serve as the mother ship—a flying control platform. Rand took
the remote controls to put the robot B-17—the "baby"—through its
paces. A human pilot remained on board to intervene in the event of
failure.

The CQ-17 took off first, followed by the baby, under pilot control.
The baby would circle at just 2,000 feet while the CQ-17 climbed to
20,000, the altitude from which it would take over control of the baby.
The problem was that, for all its technology, and even with two television cameras installed in the baby—one looking out and ahead, the
other trained on the main instrument cluster—the Aphrodite system,
like most of the radio-control systems tried before it, required clear
line-of-sight visibility between mother and baby. And, unsurprisingly,
the English weather was hardly cooperating. Radioing the B-17 pilot to
keep circling, Rand ordered his CQ-17 pilot to descend—and to keep
descending until the baby became visible through the clouds.

It was not until the mother had descended through 6,000 feet that
the baby finally materialized below it. Now Rand took the remote controls and, for the next two hours, guided the baby in turns and dives
with remarkable precision. His delight in the surprising capability of
a system he had originally designed to control azimuth only was tempered somewhat by his discovery that the mother ship, flying in the
thinner atmosphere above the baby, stubbornly kept outrunning it. In
consultation with the combat pilots who would be assigned to control

the babies from the mother ship, Rand agreed that this problem could be countered by the vigorous use of wing flaps, cowl flaps, propeller pitch—anything to increase drag. If all else failed, it was agreed that the CQ-17 pilots would execute as many 360-degree turns as necessary.

Rand's positive reports to his superiors were corroborated by Cass Hough, a veteran test pilot brought in to keep the people of Aphrodite honest. Of one test he flew, Hough reported that the "manner of control is good. Given decent visibility, it is entirely possible for a trained controller to 'plant' the low ship on a target."[37] It was welcome news, coming at the end of June 1944, when V-1s were wreaking havoc on London and other English cities. Lieutenant General Carl Spaatz, the commanding officer of U.S. Strategic Air Forces in Europe, sent a cable to Hap Arnold:

> OUR FIRST FLIGHT TEST WITH MODIFIED AZON UNITS IN WAR WEARY AIRPLANE DEMONSTRATED THE PRACTICABILITY OF THIS MAKESHIFT AND WE ARE GOING AHEAD IMMEDIATELY WITH FOUR MORE WAR WEARIES. . . .

The encouraging report was also skeptically realistic. In place of a phrase like "splendid achievement," Spaatz called Aphrodite what it in fact was, a "makeshift," and a "war weary" one at that. Nevertheless, upon it, Doolittle, Spaatz, and Arnold were placing their hopes for saving London now—and, quite possibly, New York in the future.

The Kennedys at Hyannis Port, September 4, 1931. From left to right: Robert,
John F., Eunice, Jean (on Joseph P. Kennedy Sr.'s lap), Rose (pregnant with Edward "Ted"
Kennedy), Patricia, Kathleen ("Kick"), and Rosemary. Joe Jr. is behind Rosemary, and the
family dog, Buddy, is in the foreground at left.

Photo by Richard Sears, John F. Kennedy Presidential Library and Museum, Boston

Joe Jr. ready for football at the Choate School,
Wallingford, Connecticut.

John F. Kennedy Presidential Library and Museum,
Boston

Joe Jr. on a ski holiday at Saint Moritz, Switzerland, on the eve of World War II, 1939.

John F. Kennedy Presidential Library and Museum, Boston

Ambassador Joseph P. Kennedy Sr., June 20, 1938.

Wide World Photo from Wikimedia Commons

(Above) *The Blitz hits a suburban neighborhood east of London, September 1940.*

National Archives and Records Administration 306-NT-3163V

The excitement of war: Joe Jr., Kathleen, and John F. Kennedy walk to Parliament to hear Prime Minister Neville Chamberlain's speech to the House of Commons responding to the German invasion of Poland on September 1, 1939.

The John F. Kennedy Presidential Library and Museum, Boston

Lieutenant (jg) John F. Kennedy aboard PT-109, 1942.

United States Navy

Lieutenant Colonel James H. "Jimmy" Doolittle and the crew of the B-25 Mitchell bomber that led the daring Doolittle Raid against Japan, April 18, 1942. Doolittle is second from right. His copilot, Lieutenant R. E. Cole, is next to him. Lieutenant H. A. Potter, navigator, is on the right. Staff Sergeants F. A. Braemer and P. J. Leonard are behind.

Wikimedia Commons

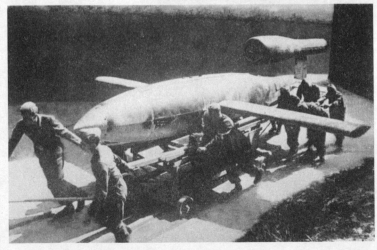

German ground crew haul a V-1 "buzz bomb" from a storage and servicing facility to a launch rail.

Bundesarchiv Bild 148-1973-029A24A

A British military unit fired this captured V-2 from a launch site in Cuxhaven, Germany, during an experimental program called Operation Backfire, October 1945.

Wikimedia Commons

The Union Jack is visible among the ruins of homes in London's Camberwell Road, destroyed in a V-1 raid.

National Archives and Records Administration NWDNS-226-PPL-VBD(13)

A soldier's body and his vehicle burn after a V-2 hits a main intersection in Antwerp, Belgium, November 27, 1944.

U.S. Army Signal Corps photo, National Archives and Records Administration

This B-17G Flying Fortress (Shoo Shoo Shoo Baby) *was restored in the 1980s by members of the 512th Military Airlift Wing, U.S. Air Force. Approximately forty war-weary B-17s were converted for use as flying bombs in Operation Aphrodite and Operation Castor.*

Photo by Master Sergeant Ken Hammon, U.S. Air Force, Department of Defense

This Consolidated PB4Y-1 is the U.S. Navy version of the more familiar B-24 Liberator flown by the U.S. Army Air Forces. Four PB4Y-1s were modified as flying bombs for use in Project Anvil, the navy counterpart to the USAAF's Operation Aphrodite.

San Diego Air and Space Museum Archives via Wikimedia Commons

The V-1 bunker facility code-named Wasserwerk Nr. 1, outside the village of Siracourt in the Pas-de-Calais, was a prime Aphrodite target. Its massively thick reinforced concrete roof, visible here, was built first, and the rest of the facility was excavated beneath it.

Code-named by the Germans Bauvorhaben 21 (Building Project 21) or Schotterwerk Nordwest (Northwest Gravel Works), the V-2 bunker complex near Wizernes and Helfaut in the Pas-de-Calais was better known by its French nickname, La Coupole (the Dome).

An RAF Spitfire MK XI, modified for photoreconnaissance work, took this photograph of Mimoyecques, France, on August 4, 1944—the day of Mission 515, the first four Aphrodite sorties. Note the extensive cratering produced by many prior Allied air raids. None of the Aphrodite missions succeeded in hitting Mimoyecques or any of the other assigned targets.

Naval Air Cadet Joseph P. Kennedy, Jr., 1940.
John F. Kennedy Presidential Library and Museum,
Boston

President John F.
Kennedy and First Lady
Jacqueline Bouvier
Kennedy watch the
America's Cup Race
from the deck of the U.S.
Navy destroyer Joseph P.
Kennedy, Jr., *September*
15, 1962.

Robert Knudsen White
House Photographs,
National Archives and
Records Administration

CHAPTER 6

FOGGED IN

THE "FOG OF WAR" HAS BEEN A FAMILIAR PHRASE AMONG MILItary historians and strategists ever since the Prussian general and theorist Carl von Clausewitz described it in his classic *On War (Vom Kriege),* posthumously published in 1837. "War is an area of uncertainty," Clausewitz wrote. "Three quarters of the things on which all action in War is based are lying in a fog of uncertainty to a greater or lesser extent." What could penetrate this fog? Clausewitz called for "a fine, piercing mind, to feel out the truth with the measure of its judgment."[1] Such minds, hard to come by in war, are nearly impossible to find amid terror.

And the German "vengeance" weapons, V-1 and V-2, were far less weapons of war than weapons of terror. Their inaccuracy and poor reliability meant that they were of marginal tactical value against military targets, but the fact that they could be aimed at a city and hit the city—descending on it out of the day or night sky—made them highly effective agents of terror. Thus Operation Aphrodite and Project Anvil, in all their desperation, were driven less by strategic motives than they were spurred by fear and even panic.

The dense fog created by panic obscures accurate intelligence. The V-1 was followed by the V-2, which was more terrifying than the V-1 because there was no viable defense against it. A ballistic missile, it was the product of technologies all but unknown outside of Germany.

Each V-2 seemed to bear a message from the Third Reich: *We have conquered Europe—and the future too*. Little wonder, then, that rumors
of a new vengeance weapon, the V-3, gave added urgency to Aphrodite.

On July 19, 1944, British intelligence reported on "work of an unexplained nature, including railway sidings, turntables, buildings and
concrete erections . . . proceeding in northwest France." A day later,
the acting chief of staff of U.S. military intelligence sent the British Air
Ministry a summary of a report from the French underground, dated
July 17. It was a remarkably specific list of "characteristics of the V-3"—
a weapon no one had ever actually seen—and included the following
specifications:

Wingspan, 36 meters [118 feet]

Length, 28 meters [92 feet]

Height, 3 meters [10 feet]

Weight, 20 tons

Range, 10,000 kilometers [6,214 miles]

Speed, 700 kilometers per hour [435 mph]

Altitude, "stratospheric"

Charge, 10 tons of high explosive

The summary mentioned that the V-3 "has a crew of one who is sacri-
ficed, but it is understood he will have a parachute supplied. The bomb
explodes on impact."[2]

The Americans wanted to save London, of course, but the range of
the reported V-3—more than 6,000 miles—was clearly intended to be
transatlantic. The target was not London but New York, Washington,
Philadelphia—any number of major American cities. For the leaders of
the Eighth United States Air Force, Hitler's vengeance war was getting
very personal.

In fact, German military planners had been contemplating a long-
range strategic bomber capable of hitting the targets in the United States
as early as 1937 or 1938.[3] A thirty-three page outline plan of the so-
called Amerika-Bomber Project was delivered to Luftwaffe chief Hermann Göring on May 12, 1942. It proposed launching existing heavy
bombers (Heinkel He 277, Junkers Ju 390, and Messershmitt Me 264)
from bases in the Azores, a little over 2,500 miles from New York

City. (Germany planned to lease bases from Portugal, which governed the Azores. Despite Portuguese neutrality, Prime Minister António de Oliveira Salazar was pro-Fascist; however, he ended up leasing Azores naval and air bases to the British empire instead.)

Alternative proposals related to the Amerika-Bomber looked further beyond the conventional. The Huckepack Projekt (Piggyback Project) proposed using an He 177 Greif (Griffin) heavy bomber to carry a smaller Dornier Do 217 "flying pencil" medium bomber as far as its fuel supply would permit. At the point where the larger Greif had just enough fuel to return to its European base, it would launch the smaller Dornier—modified by the addition of a ramjet booster engine—which would make its attack on New York or some other U.S. target, then ditch at a predetermined location off the U.S. Atlantic coast, where a U-boat would recover the crew. Yet another proposal was to build an aircraft carrier to launch attacks by small jet aircraft, a technology in which Germany had taken the lead. Loaded with explosives, the jets would be piloted and the attacks would either be suicide missions or would provide for the pilot to attempt a last-minute bailout. Other ideas called for a radical jet-or rocket-propelled "flying wing" (the Horten H.XVIII or Arado Ar E.555) or a manned or unmanned suborbital winged rocket.[4]

Neither the Amerika-Bomber proposal nor the others resembled the description reported by the French agent and interpreted by British and U.S. intelligence as the V-3. It is believed, however, that winged versions of the V-2 as well as the A9, a more advanced V-2 successor, were tested late in 1944 and/or early in 1945. After the war, plans for an Amerika-Rakete (America Rocket) were discovered. This was a proposed two-stage intercontinental ballistic missile (ICBM), whereas the V-2 and A-9 were both single-stage rockets. No prototype of the America Rocket was ever built.[5]

Yet there really was a V-3. The weapon was not an aircraft or rocket at all but a new type of artillery, a "supergun" the Germans informally called the Fleissiges Lieschen (Busy Lizzie) and officially code-named the *Hochdruckpumpe* (HDP: high-pressure pump).

Although it was unlike any other artillery weapon in existence, the HDP was based on the principle of a multichamber gun, first patented in 1857 by an American arms experimenter. The German invention took the principle much further and made it much bigger. The barrel of the HDP was 430 feet long. Within it, at intervals along its enormous length, multiple propellant charges—solid-fuel rocket boosters rather than conventional explosives—were placed. Each was precisely timed to fire as the projectile passed by en route to the muzzle. The cumulative effect of the multiple charges was calculated to propel a 310-pound, 5.9-inch shell to a muzzle velocity of 4,900 feet per second, sufficient for an effective range of just over 100 miles.[6] Like any other artillery weapon, the HDP, gigantic though it was, would be most effective if used in a multiweapon battery. The German plan was to create a heavily hardened emplacement to accommodate twenty-five V-3 guns. Together, such a battery could fire 600 rounds an hour, every one of them targeted on London.[7] In a speech made on May 13, 1945, days after the end of the war in Europe, Prime Minister Churchill cited Germany's "multiple long range artillery which was being prepared against London" and remarked that such a weapon, had it become operational, would have delivered "the most devastating attack of all."[8]

Naturally, a weapon as massive as the HDP could not be mobile. Nor could it be fixed in some exposed area, where it would quickly become a target of attack. What was needed was a massive fortification, preferably semisubterranean or earth-fast. An engineer from a German army fortification regiment was tasked with leading the search to find a suitable site. By early 1943, he concluded that a hillside, with a rock core, would be best because the long gun tubes could be placed in "drifts"—inclined tunnels. Additional drifts could be excavated into the hill to accommodate equipment and supplies. An ideal site was found in a limestone hill near Mimoyecques on the Pas-de-Calais—the point closest to England across the Channel. The German military code-named the site *Wiese* (meadow) and began construction, starting with the support tunnels, late in May 1943—well before the HDP weapon itself had even entered the prototype stage. While a battery of twenty-five guns had been contemplated, the construction project was planned to create two gun complexes, each of which would consist of five drift tunnels, each of these, in turn, accommodating five HDP barrels for a total battery of fifty guns. All would be permanently targeted on London and would therefore—in theory, at least—deliver against the city a truly devastating firing rate of 1,200 rounds per hour.[9]

A construction project of this size was bound to be noticed. Agents of the French Underground soon reported the existence of a plan to mount a new offensive against England that was somehow connected to what they called "giant underground mortars," which were served by a railroad link. Early in November 1943, British bombers staged three raids against the construction site. This prompted the German army to scale back the project by suspending work on one of the two complexes, thereby reducing the anticipated battery to the original twenty-five guns. The new construction schedule called for five guns to be ready for firing by March 1944 and all twenty-five guns to be in operation by October.[10]

In the meantime, work proceeded on the HDP gun itself, which was ready for testing early in the spring of 1944. The first firings in April, at Midsroy (now Miedzyzdroje, Poland), a proving ground on the Baltic coast, were disappointing. The barrel failed after only twenty-five rounds were test fired, a setback that prompted an additional reduction in construction work at Mimoyecques, from five drifts to just three. Tests in May were more encouraging, achieving a range of some fifty-six miles—far short of what it would take to hit London, but at least indicating the feasibility of the weapon. Construction therefore proceeded on drifts III through V.[11]

An army of more than five thousand labored to build the fortress. German engineers and a cadre of 430 professional Ruhr Valley miners oversaw Soviet prisoners of war (POWs). The drifts in which the gun barrels were placed were angled 50 degrees to the horizontal and extended 340 feet below the surface of the hill. Where the muzzles emerged at the surface of the hillside was an 18-foot-thick, 98-foot-wide concrete slab with openings to allow the passage of the projectiles. Those apertures were protected by movable steel plates. The drifts that accommodated each HDP tube were precisely oriented on a bearing of 299 degrees, making a direct line to Westminster Bridge in London. Although neither the elevation nor the direction of any of the guns could be changed, range could be adjusted by varying the amount of propellant used in each shot. In this way, much of the sprawling British capital could have been brought under fire.[12]

The Mimoyecques fortress was served by a standard-gauge rail spur off of a major railway. Tracks ran into the hill—the entrances protected by heavily armored steel doors—in a straight-line distance of almost half a mile. The standard-gauge tracks terminated at an unloading platform, which had access to ten galleries that intersected the main tunnel at right angles. Within each of these was a narrow-gauge track used to deliver shells and explosive propellant to the guns. Additional underground chambers had been excavated for use as storerooms and military garrison and gun crew quarters.[13]

In September 1943, after French agents reported the planned use of "giant underground mortars" to mount an offensive against England, Allied photoreconnaissance analysts flagged the railway tracks under construction leading to the Mimoyecques tunnels. The next month, additional aerial photography revealed a beehive of activity at the tunnel entrances. Despite the allusion to underground mortars, Allied analysts did not conclude that the site harbored anything like a supergun but instead assumed that it was a launch facility for rockets or flying bombs. One agent did refer to a "rocket launching cannon"; however, it was assumed that such a device was not an artillery weapon but an apparatus for launching the V-2.[14] In any event, two major Allied air raids were launched against the Mimoyecques site. Under Operation Crossbow, the joint Allied effort to defend against the German long-range weapons program, more than 150 Ninth U.S. Air Force B-26 Martin Marauder medium bombers were dispatched on November 5, 1943. The effectiveness of the mission was somewhat compromised by rain and fog that affected the area.[15] The Royal Air Force bombed the site three days later with 72 medium bombers and was able to report distinct hits, but weather conditions prevented assessing the damage.[16]

Far heavier raids were carried out against Mimoyecques from March through early July 1944. In a dozen raids (nine by the Eighth U.S. Air Force and three by the RAF), more than 2,200 aircraft—most of them heavy bombers—were sent against this single site.[17] Again, damage was difficult to assess—except in the case of the July 6, 1944, raid, in which the RAF's No. 617 Squadron used the newly developed 12,000-pound Tallboy "earthquake bomb," packed with a powerful torpedo explosive known as Torpex.

Developed by Barnes Wallis, the British aeronautical engineer who had designed the spectacularly successful bouncing "dam buster" bombs used against Germany's Ruhr River dams in May 1943, the

Tallboy was specifically intended to be used against the spectacularly hardened German coastal fortifications that made up what Hitler called his Atlantic Wall *(Atlantikwall)*. These were structures against which conventional bombs had proven ineffective. No. 617 Squadron—the fabled "Dambusters" themselves—received special training in the use of a modified Stabilizing Automatic Bomb Sight and had their complement of Avro Lancaster heavy bombers adapted to accommodate the enormous weight of the bomb. Designed to be dropped from 18,000 feet to make an impact of 750 miles per hour, Tallboy could penetrate 16 feet of concrete and blast a crater 80 feet deep by 100 feet across.[18] At least four of the Tallboys dropped on July 6 penetrated a shaft at Mimoyecques, exploded within the complex, and created a huge crater.[19] Not only did the facility suffer substantial damage, some 300 workers—mostly POWs—were killed. This was the raid that prompted Adolf Hitler to personally authorize reduction of the installation to accommodate just five HDPs to be installed in a single drift, while the two other intact shafts were to be used to accommodate two Krupp K5 cannon modified to fire a new rocket-propelled long-range artillery shell. Although far less destructive than the HDP, this shell still had sufficient range to reach targets in England.[20]

* * *

DESPITE EVIDENCE OF SUBSTANTIAL DAMAGE to the Mimoyecques fortress, the V-3 rumors continued to drive Allied missions. Neither British nor American intelligence dared speculate, much less assume, that the facility had been severely degraded, let alone totally disabled. They also had no way of knowing that work on the HDP projectiles themselves was going badly. Flawed aerodynamics was causing them to tumble and fall far short of London. Because of the project's highly compressed schedule, the flaw had gone undetected until more than 20,000 HDP projectiles had already been manufactured.[21]

It was not surprising that Allied intelligence knew little of Germany's technical problems. Somewhat more difficult to account for is the failure of intelligence analysts to appreciate the impact of the Allied ground offensive on Mimoyecques. The Normandy landings had taken place on D-Day, June 6, 1944, and by the end of July, Allied ground forces had advanced to the Pas-de-Calais area, prompting all work at

Mimoyecques to stop. Although no official order to abandon the facility was ever issued, the site was, for all practical purposes, abandoned. The Germans, however, continued to stage a show of activity in the area, and this was clearly effective in persuading Allied analysts that Mimoyecques still presented a threat. The site was designated as one of the targets of Mission 515, the first Aphrodite mission, on August 4, 1944.

Four two-man "jump crews"—a pilot and "autopilot engineer"— were mustered. They would fly the robot B-17 to the point of takeover by the mother ship, set the radio-control system, arm the explosive, and then bail out over the English side of the Channel. Among planners, there was talk about targeting Mimoyecques first, with the number 1 jump crew consisting of Lieutenant Fain Pool and Staff Sergeant Philip Enterline.[22] When the order of the sorties was actually posted, however, Pool and Enterline were assigned to hit another Pas-de-Calais bunker, at Watten. As it turned out, Joseph P. Kennedy Jr. would be assigned to Mimoyecques.

Like Kennedy, Fain Pool had volunteered for special duty described only as extremely hazardous. But the backgrounds from which the two volunteers had come were worlds apart. Pool came of age poor, in the Oklahoma boonies, and he looked the part. Powerfully built, he had a head of thick black hair, high cheekbones, a square jaw, and eyes permanently narrowed by the sun into a sharp squint. If Joe Jr. saw military service as a rite of passage required for a career in politics, Fain Pool wanted nothing more than a life's career in the Air Corps. If Joe had willed his way, clawed his way, into competence as a pilot, Pool was a natural. At the same time, Pool approached flying not as a lone wolf—which was more or less the Joe Kennedy way—but as a team player. He took the greatest pride in his mastery of the art of formation flying. At best, flying missions over heavily defended enemy territory was deadly dangerous. The only thing that could make it more dangerous—suicidal, in fact—was to inadvertently straggle or purposely fly out of formation. The effectiveness of the defensive firepower of a single Flying Fortress was multiplied by the number of aircraft in a tight formation. A formation could pour a massive stream of defensive fire on incoming fighters, and a fighter going after one aircraft in the formation stood a good chance of being shot down by others. A fighter challenging a lone B-17, however, had excellent prospects for destroying it. Pool understood and embraced the value of the formation.

Fain Pool had not hesitated to volunteer. In part, this was surely an example of heroism—heroism accelerated by what was apparently a personal hatred of Adolf Hitler. That sentiment had been born in London, when Pool, on a weekend pass, experienced the effects of a V-1 attack firsthand: civilians—men, old men, women, and children, noncombatants all—suffering death, injury, the loss of their homes and businesses. As Pool saw it, this was not warfare. It was unadulterated malice, and it was evil, and it was all at the behest of the Führer. At the time he volunteered, Pool did not know that his mission would be aimed at taking out vengeance weapon launch facilities, but he imagined that he was volunteering for something important that targeted Hitler in some novel way.

Mixed in with Pool's desire to perform perfectly while delivering some form of payback to Adolf Hitler was a healthy dose of personal pragmatism. The commanding officer of Pool's group chose a small handful of pilots as candidates to volunteer for what was described as a one-way mission that required bailing out. One by one, all of those chosen declined the opportunity, most of them on the very reasonable grounds that they were at or near the end of their tour of duty, which, by this time, consisted of flying thirty bombing missions (up from an earlier quota of twenty-five). In contrast to the others, Pool was less than midway through his tour, having flown just fourteen missions. During those flights, he had seen many comrades wounded, killed, or shot down and captured. Whatever the new mission was, he reasoned, it was likely no more dangerous than flying another sixteen sorties over Germany or some other tract of heavily defended enemy territory. Nevertheless, when he showed up at RAF Honington, where the first of the Aphrodite pilots were being marshaled, and entered the Nissen hut to which he had been assigned, one of the several pilots unpacking their gear looked up, glanced his way, looked down again, and announced, "Hey, fellows, another nut's arrived."[23]

* * *

WHILE FAIN POOL AND THE OTHER VOLUNTEER PILOTS were being mustered at RAF Honington in June 1944, the war-weary B-17s were flying in from all over, to be stripped bare by Major Rand's men. Rand retained a handful of planes for testing purposes and sent the rest to Burtonwood. There, the first ten operational Aphrodite B-17s were modified with the addition of stout wooden beams to take the place of whatever structural elements had been removed earlier. As Rand's men continued to experiment with the control electronics and mechanics at Honington, the Burtonwood technicians installed a suite of radio-control equipment, Rand's specially designed radio altimeter (called ACE—automatic control electronics), and a modified autopilot, as well as servo motors and all the electrical cables and mechanical linkages required to connect the electronics to the servos and the servos to the aircraft's controls.

The Burtonwood men received sporadic instructions from Rand to move this or recalibrate that until, at last, the aircraft were dispatched to Honington, where most of the first ten operational war-wearies were loaded with crate after crate of an explosive called nitrostarch. Similar to nitrocellulose—gun cotton—nitrostarch was first formulated in 1833 by combining nitric and sulfuric acids with starch. The resulting high explosive was used in hand grenades during World War I. Although old-fashioned, nitrostarch had the advantage of a reasonably high degree of stability. A few of the B-17s were loaded instead with an incendiary substance developed in a secret laboratory at Harvard University in 1942. Called napalm—derived from naphthenic acid and palmitic acid, the chemicals combined as a gelling agent—the substance was, in effect, jellied gasoline. It joined the destructive flammability of gasoline to the stick-to-any-surface quality of the gelling agent. Originally developed for use against structures, it was subsequently employed directly against personnel. A flamethrower could quickly coat an enemy combatant with flaming gelatin. The B-17s loaded with napalm were intended to follow up on the attacks by the nitrostarch-loaded robots. Experiments conducted at Eglin Army Air Base in Florida, using rats, demonstrated that if a large enclosure, such as a massive bunker, was breached—by a high-explosive blast, for instance—a cover of flame maintained over that breach for at least ten minutes would suffocate all personnel within the enclosure. Napalm was just the substance to maintain such a cover of flame.

Back at Honington, having flown the B-17 empty as well as loaded with sandbags simulating the weight of the nitrostarch, and having demonstrated the serviceability of the radio-control setup modified from AZON, Rand and his test pilots plunged into the final stages of working out the attacks. The initial idea had been that mother ships and babies should cross the English Channel at altitudes sufficiently high—perhaps 30,000 feet—to be safe from German antiaircraft fire. But the early tests showed that Boeing had designed the B-17 to be so stable that it simply refused to hold a steep dive from a high altitude. A human pilot and copilot could combine their strength to push in and hold the control yoke in order to manhandle the airplane into such a dive, but the servomotors that controlled a robot plane were not nearly as powerful as human muscle. Like one wrestler fighting off the attack of another, the Flying Fortress invariably pushed back, seeking to restore level flight. And the big bomber always won.

Rand formulated a workaround tactic. He decided to fly the mother ship high above the baby. While the mother stayed high out of antiaircraft range, the baby would be maintained at an altitude too low for the aerodynamic characteristics of the B-17 to restore level flight. At first, 2,000 feet was thought sufficient, but even at that low altitude, it was very nearly impossible to keep the robot from automatically leveling off. Rand therefore decided to fly the baby over England at 2,000 feet while the human pilot and electronics expert were still onboard. Just before bailing out, the pilot would set the ACE radio altimeter, which controlled the autopilot, to descend to 300 feet and hold that altitude all the way across the English Channel. As soon as the setting was made, the aircraft would begin to descend. It was critical that the pilot jump by the time 1,000 feet had been reached, to allow his parachute sufficient altitude to slow his fall and save him from a hard—and likely fatal—landing. At 300 feet, when the bombardier, who was controlling the baby from the mother ship, flipped the dump switch on his transmitter, the baby's elevators would go into the full-down position, diving the aircraft into its target. At that low an altitude, even the mighty Flying Fortress could not correct itself into level flight.

It was decidedly what Lieutenant General Spaatz had called it: "a makeshift." The so-called double AZON system Rand had cobbled together consisted of just three controls: a switch that transmitted a signal for a left turn, a switch that did the same for a right, and the dump switch, which snapped the elevators into full-down. There was no way to remotely control the elevators back to a level or up position in order to make the aircraft climb. Once the dump switch was thrown, the baby was almost certainly doomed to dive. Even if the dump switch was quickly released and the slipstream pushed the elevators back to a level position, there would be insufficient altitude available to recover from the dive.

In his earlier work with RAZON and then AZON bombs, Rand had wanted to incorporate a television camera and transmitter to give the bombardier the bomb's-eye view. The technology was deemed both too expensive and too unreliable, and so AZON became strictly a line-of-sight weapon. With Aphrodite, Rand dared to think things would be different. He wanted to install *two* television cameras in the robot aircraft, one focused on the instruments and the other out the front windscreen. But, once again, he was overruled. The V-weapon targets had to be hit and hit urgently, he was told. There was simply no time to work out the complexities of television. Aphrodite would therefore require the mother ship to be in continual visual contact with the robot. To increase visibility, the tops of each baby's wings were painted solid white. Aircrews and ground crews alike dubbed them "snowbirds."

* * *

JUNE WAS ON THE WANE when the small group of volunteer pilots was summoned to a ready room to hear, at long last, just what they had volunteered for. As one of the pilots, Frank Houston, recounted many years later, the briefing officer was terse and humorless. "Essentially," he began, "this is what you will do. You will take off a B-17 carrying twenty thousand pounds of high explosives and nothing else, no co-pilot, no radio operator, no engineer, no gunners, nothing except you and twenty thousand pounds of nitrostarch. After you reach about a thousand feet, you will put the aircraft into a gentle glide and bail out. You will be picked up and returned to your original squadron. Are there any questions?"[24]

That solicitation of questions turned out to be entirely rhetorical. The briefing officer was duly peppered with wide-eyed queries—all of which he declined to answer for reasons of security. After several minutes, he announced, "I've told you all you need to know." With that, the final word: "Dismissed!"[25]

While Houston, Pool, and the other Army Air Corps pilots were doubtless troubled by their unanswered questions, they were, for the most part, lowly first lieutenants and understood that theirs was not to reason why but, when ordered, *to do*—and quite possibly die. They might well have been far more troubled, however, if they had known that their CO, *Major General* Earle Partridge, commanding the Third Bomb Division, which had been assigned to Operation Aphrodite, had his own unanswered questions.[26] He had learned from Major Rand that, because of the B-17's stubborn will to remain in the air despite the best efforts to dive and crash it, the Aphrodite robots would have to be "dumped" from 300 feet while traveling at 180 miles per hour. Partridge understood why this was necessary, but he also knew that nobody had ever done this before, at least not intentionally. He had two crucial questions about it: First, in this maneuver, just where would the B-17 hit the ground? Clearly, this was an important question, seeing that the rationale of a remote-controlled flying bomb was to achieve extreme precision. Partridge knew that the Aphrodite robots were supposed to hit hardened targets that, for about a year now, had apparently resisted destruction from even massive conventional raids. Theoretically, radio control could aim and control the baby, but, even at 300 feet, no one knew for certain what would happen when the dump switch was flicked. Would full-down elevators send the big plane into an instant nosedive, so that it would impact at close to a ninety-degree angle? Or would it take a flatter path and overshoot the target? Partridge's second question was whether a B-17—a war-weary one at that, presumably suffering from metal fatigue—would survive the sudden dive intact. He imagined the high probability that, put through such extreme stress, the baby would simply break up, its wings falling off, so that the pieces would come crashing short of the target.

Whereas lieutenants did not have the option of demanding that superior officers answer their questions, a major general could simply *order* answers to his. And so Major General Partridge ordered one of the division's senior pilots, Captain Carroll J. "Joe" Bender, to get him the answers. It was a tall order, but, demanding as Bender's assignment was, it addressed only what would happen when the dump switch was flicked. Partridge was, in fact, troubled by many more unanswered questions. Some were related to unknowns about the stability of a massive load of crated high explosive—let alone napalm—on takeoff. Unanswered questions included how best to load and distribute the explosives in the airplane, how to fuse it, and how to arm it. Then there was the issue of the bailout. Flying was inherently hazardous, and flying over heavily defended targets to destroy them courted death. So the Air Corps had plenty of experience with bailing out—much of it bad, and all of it predicated on exiting an aircraft whose speed had been reduced to about 100 miles per hour or less. Certainly no paratrooper would intentionally *choose* to bail out at faster speeds. The Aphrodite "jump pilots" would have to exit at nearly 200 miles per hour—and they were far from being highly trained parachutists. (Later, the paratrooper officer who advised Aphrodite's planners assured Staff Sergeant Willard Smith, Lieutenant Frank Houston's assigned electronics expert, that he and the others who jumped would earn the Distinguished Flying Cross. "Well, anybody who knows anything about parachuting can tell you you'll earn it. You want to know about the jolt [of a parachute opening at 200 miles per hour]? Well, imagine yourself running down a road at full speed, and here comes a Mack truck straight at you doing forty miles an hour, and *you jump into the radiator.* That's how it's gonna feel."[27])

To one question Partridge knew the answer only too well. *How much time did Third Bomb Division have to resolve all doubts and begin launching operational missions?* Judging from the relentless goading of Washington and his awareness that Hap Arnold, chief of the whole Air Corps, wanted Aphrodite to work and to work *now,* Partridge knew that the answer to *How much time?* was none, none at all.

For his part, Bender set about getting the answers to the questions he'd been assigned.[28] He went to the U.S. Army Air Forces (USAAF) base at Bovington, near London, where he sat down with an old friend, a colonel who had a head for the physics of flight. Bender took his friend to the Bovington flight line, where they personally measured the key surfaces of the B-17 and cranked this data into a complex series of equations. Bender's friend repeatedly asked him why he needed the information, Bender repeatedly told him he could not say, and, to his credit, the colonel never even tried to pull rank to find out.

From Bovington, Bender went to London, where Boeing maintained a field office. He had no friend here. The company representative collected the specs Bender asked for, placed them on his desk, and then refused to hand them over. He told Bender that extensive security clearances had to be obtained, a process that would take days if not longer. He promised to call Bender when he had the clearances in hand. At present, though, he was off to lunch.

When the Boeing man left, Bender asked his secretary if he could have the pleasure of *her* company for lunch. A rather plain woman, she was unaccustomed to such apparently spontaneous invitations. She accepted and excused herself to visit the powder room in preparation. Bender used her brief absence to snatch the folder of specs from the Boeing rep's desk, then ran out before the secretary returned.

All the figures and calculations said the B-17 would not break up. Bender, however, decided he had to prove this in actual flight. Back at Third Bomb Division HQ, he commandeered a brand-new B-17, dubbed *The Silver Queen,* which had been stripped down for use as a headquarters VIP transport. It was not his plane, and he had no right to fly it, certainly not without a crew. But he ordered the crew chief to prepare it for him nevertheless, and the sergeant knew he had no alternative but to obey the orders of a captain. Bender then put the aircraft through three days of high-G torture. It did not fall apart and so one question, at least, had been answered definitively.

To answer the other—What would happen at 300 feet, 180 miles per hour, when the B-17 was slammed into full down-elevator?—Bender defied death with repeated tests that ended just short of impact. In the end, he was able to report that a loaded B-17 would hit the ground "approximately nine hundred and seventy-five feet after application of full down control"[29] and that, no, the wings would not come off.

* * *

BY THE TIME PARTRIDGE HAD HIS ANSWERS, it was early July, and his Aphrodite volunteers were in the throes of accelerated training. Lieutenant General Spaatz, commanding USAAF in Europe, was already fully committed to Aphrodite. On July 8, 1944, he issued a command memo explaining that his headquarters had set "the Aphrodite project . . . into motion . . . to eliminate the threat of the enemy's large rockets and their effect upon England." Spaatz went on to announce that it was "now contemplated to use at least sixty-five (65) robot aircraft." He specified that approximately 21 of these, "(¼ of the total)," would be "loaded with jellied gasoline"—napalm—and the remaining three-quarters, 44 aircraft, would be "loaded with nitro-starch."[30]

As for the first ten pilots of Operation Aphrodite, they began their practical training knowing nothing beyond what the briefing officer had told them shortly after their arrival at Honington late in June. They were going to fly a B-17 heavily loaded with explosives and bail out. Interviewed some thirty years later by author Jack Olsen, Fain Pool made it clear that the connection between the briefing officer's curt outline of their mission and the jump pilots' initial experience with their modified B-17s was highly tenuous. If he anticipated climbing into a Flying Fortress jam-packed with 20,000 pounds of explosive, he was stunned to find . . . absolutely nothing. As Olsen writes it, Pool gasped out "My God!" again and again. "Where's the co-pilot's seat? Where's the radio? Where's the navigator's table? Where's everything?"[31]

To compound the dreamlike disorientation of having been led into a space made almost numbingly familiar by hundreds of hours of training and some fourteen combat missions, only to find it totally foreign, Pool recognized little of the equipment in the cockpit. There were electrical panels of some sort bolted to a space usually occupied by flight instruments. In fact, the only comfortably familiar controls, other than the yoke itself, were *some* of the autopilot switches.

Despite what must have been a look of utter incomprehension, the officer who showed Pool into the airplane gave no instructions or explanations. After tersely instructing Pool to take the plane up, get the feel of the aircraft, and then return to the field for additional instruction, the officer lowered himself out of the hatch and onto the tarmac.

Left all by himself, Pool located what standard controls remained in the cockpit. Alone on the flight deck—itself an eerily unfamiliar experience—he started the engines and prepared to taxi for takeoff, sliding the side window open and putting his hands out, thumbs up, then quickly flicking his wrists to signal the ground crew to pull the chocks out from the wheels.

A fully loaded B-17 was one giant practical demonstration of Newton's First Law of Motion—dead inertia. Pilots learned to accept the fact that the big plane, loaded with bombs, crew, and equipment, was loath to move forward, as if the steel and aluminum machine were even more reluctant than its flesh-and-blood occupants to become airborne and face fighters and flak. Accordingly, pilots pushed the throttles full ahead, giving the Fortress everything she had until she got off the dime, and then pulled back to a walking speed for the trip to the end of the runway. But empty—stripped bare—the giant lurched ahead as soon as the chocks were out and the brakes released. Pool had to get both hands on the yoke to make sure the aircraft did not roll off into the grass. He pulled the throttles back and then eased them, ever so slightly, forward. Even so, he had to keep coaxing them back as the plane threatened to outrun and overrun the ground crew alongside.

And so he positioned for takeoff. Even for an experienced pilot, a combat-seasoned pilot, a really good pilot—all of which described Fain Pool—takeoff in a four-engine heavy bomber was always a very tense and very long moment. No pilot and crew ever really grew accustomed to lumbering down a runway, watching the approach of the tarmac's end and, with it (usually), a row of trees or buildings on the horizon, before finally "rotating"—lifting off—with scant seconds and yards to spare. Pilots and crews learned to live with the very real possibility of failing to gain sufficient altitude to clear the trees and buildings or failing to rotate at all. Crashes on takeoff were common.

Accelerating toward rotation was typically a rough and rumbling ride. This time, Pool was struck by how supernaturally smooth it was—and then he realized that, less than halfway down the runway, all three sets of wheels were already off the ground. So now he anticipated the next sensation pilots learned to live with but never really got used to—the way a four-engine heavy, once it was airborne, would sink back down as you began your pull into a climb. Happened every time. But not this time. Pool told Olsen that his B-17 assumed a sharp nose-up attitude and climbed—nothing but climbed—and kept on climbing.

It was at this moment that Fain Pool, born and bred on the open plains of Oklahoma, felt curiously unburdened—free. Flying a fully loaded Fortress was like driving a bus (except that people were shooting at you). Flying *this* one was—well, it was *flying*. Inspired, Pool put the aircraft through its paces, coming as close to performing aerobatics as anyone ever had riding four engines.

By midday, all ten jump pilots had flown the stripped-down B-17 and were assembled for a briefing. It was friendlier than before but not all that much more informative. This time, the briefing officer actually *apologized* for having to tell the pilots "so little." When Pool said he had just one question—"When the war's over, can I take one of these planes home with me?"—the HQ man gave him a humorless answer: "When you find out what's going to happen to these planes, Lieutenant, you'll understand why *nobody's* going to take one home." He repeated from the earlier briefing that the planes would be filled with explosives, but he now elaborated by explaining that they would be flown by radio-control into "high-priority targets on the Continent." He apologized— for a *second* time—that he could not tell them just what targets they would be.[32]

After letting this summary sink in, the officer drew the broad out-lines of the operational plan. He told Pool and the nine others that each aircraft would take off with a crew of two. The jump pilot—that was each of them—would take the aircraft up and begin flying a rectangu-lar course over eastern England at an altitude of 1,800 feet. (Rand had finally determined that 2,000 was still a bit too high.) While he flew this pattern, the other crew member, an enlisted electronics "expert" (also referred to as an autopilot "expert"), would set up, adjust, and tune the ACE radio altimeter and the autopilot, preparing them for the run on the target. When he had finished this job, he would inform the pilot, who would transmit a code word to the mother ship, which was flying high above—though still in visual contact with the baby. At this point, the mother prepared to take control. *His* job finished, the electronics expert would clamber to the navigator's escape hatch, which was just behind the number 2 engine, and bail out. The pilot would now put the aircraft into a gentle dive, jerk out fourteen cables connected to the nitrostarch loads to arm the explosives manually, and then plug a pair of cables into the arming panel to arm the payload electrically. The ACE was set to level out the dive at 300 feet, at which point the mother ship would assume full control of the baby. But the jump pilot could not wait for his plane to descend to this altitude, which was much too low for a survivable parachute fall. Once he had pulled the lanyard on the arming cables and inserted the electrical-arming plugs, he too had to bail out via the navigator's escape hatch. At under 1,800 feet and traveling at an airspeed of 180 miles per hour, it would be a rough, quite possibly le-thal, jump. Then, with him out of the plane, the mother ship controller would fly the baby across the English Channel and into its coastal target—whatever that was.

Pool said to the briefing officer: "Whew! As simple as that, eh?"

Deliberately overflying the lieutenant's sarcasm, the HQ man replied, "So simple that we don't see how it can fail."[33]

* * *

BEYOND ALLOWING THE JUMP PILOTS to take up unloaded B-17s, there was no further practical training. Procedures were explained and reviewed, right up through arming and handoff to the remote-control pilot in the mother ship and then bailout, but none of these was actually *practiced*. They just had to be *done* when the time came. And so the first mission was scheduled within days of the familiarization flights.

There are worse places to fly out of than England, but you couldn't prove that by the experience of Eighth Air Force pilots and crews. Clear days over England were few and far between. For most flying purposes, some overcast and limited visibility were not reasons to scrub a mission, but Operation Aphrodite depended on maintaining uninterrupted visibility between a mother ship flying at high altitude and the baby flying at just 1,800 feet and descending to 300. This meant holding out for CAVU conditions—ceiling and visibility unlimited: no cloud deck intervening between mother and baby, and no fog. Moreover, CAVU had to prevail on both sides of the Channel, both at the field and over the target. Waiting for this degree of perfection in English Channel weather was like hoping for your number to come up on a roulette wheel.

Days went by, with one mission after another being scrubbed before launch. When CAVU finally seemed assured, it was discovered that the navigator scheduled to fly in the mother ship had failed to return from twenty-four-hour leave by daybreak, per standing orders. This breach of security required automatically scrubbing the mission. As luck and nature would have it, the next CAVU day proved incredibly elusive. Pilots and crews watched and waited. At this point, seven of the ten available B-17s had been fully loaded with nitrostarch and were ready to go. An eighth aircraft had yet to receive its load—napalm—while engineers, armorers, and pilots argued over what kind of container to put the jellied gasoline into. Whereas the solid nitrostarch was judged sufficiently stable to pack into crates, the much more volatile, thick fluid napalm could not just be poured into jerry cans and allowed to slosh around during takeoff and flight. In the meantime, the use of nitro-starch was becoming far from a settled matter. The British had begun to use Torpex—for "TORPedo Explosive"—late in 1942 and were keen on it. Not only was it much more powerful than nitrostarch—an explosives formula with a mid-nineteenth-century vintage—it also was more stable.

The weather, the napalm container conundrum, and the nitro-starch versus Torpex discussion all became temporarily moot on July 7, 1944, when the decision came down from HQ to move all of Operation Aphrodite to another RAF base, Woodbridge, which was closer to the Channel coast—just seven miles inland from the North Sea.

It was, of course, out of the question to fly the explosives-laden B-17s there. In fact, there was never any plan to *land* a loaded baby, something deemed far too dangerous. The only option, therefore, was to unload the seven aircraft, then fly them empty to the new base. The unloaded nitrostarch would be shipped by truck convoy and then re-loaded. The plan was to send each reloaded aircraft to different cor-ners of RAF Woodbridge or even out into the surrounding woods. The idea was that, if one accidentally exploded, the explosion would not ignite a neighboring plane. As it turned out, however, the Aphrodite group's RAF hosts objected to this prudent plan. Nobody wanted even *one* creaky old bomber, loaded with crate upon crate of nitrostarch, parked anywhere near them. British base command therefore ordered all of the Aphrodite aircraft, once loaded, to be parked, together, wing-tip to wingtip, at the far corner of the field. The only personnel to be quartered anywhere near this mass of explosives would be the aircrew and ground crew of Operation Aphrodite. The British, it seemed, had far less concern about the prospect of *Americans* blowing up. If anyone associated with the operation tried to explain to base command that the explosion of seven to ten loaded aircraft parked together would be destructive beyond anything anybody had ever seen, the plea had no ef-fect. The planes, and their personnel, were concentrated for maximum destruction.

Closer to the North Sea, Woodbridge was closer to its targets, but it was also deeper in the soupy fog of Channel weather. Honington, like virtually every other RAF base on which the Eighth Air Force camped out, had been dreary. The gloom of Woodbridge, however, was down-right stygian, and the mixture of restlessness, anxiety, and depression that resulted was compounded by the nagging awareness of the potential for sudden death. Experts had calculated that the nitrostarch packed into a single B-17 could level structures within a radius of perhaps a mile and a half. Now that potential for destruction was multiplied by a factor of seven to ten, with napalm figuring as a wildcard certain only to increase the devastation.

And there was more. Many U.S. pilots stationed in England were morbidly fascinated by the British knack for making the very worst out of the most miserable of situations. Did the beer taste peculiar to the American palate? Yes. Could it be worse? Sure, it could be served warm. How did the Brits serve it on an RAF base? Warm as piss.

Woodbridge was not just a deeply gloomy establishment, in which its American guests were accommodated cheek by jowl with some 200,000 pounds of high explosives and a dash of jellied gasoline, awaiting the rarity of CAVU weather to fly off to probable, if not certain, death, it was also a very special facility. Its runways were abnormally wide and long: a quarter mile by a full two miles, to accommodate badly damaged aircraft, which were often barely under control. Woodbridge was the designated field of last resort for those craft, bombers as well as fighters, wounded in action. There were plenty of dull hours that needed to be passed at Woodbridge, and the Americans passed them by watching desperate emergency landings, many of which ended badly—in explosions, flames, sirens, injury, and death.

Bad to worse—to worse still. Any number of the crippled aircraft that flew in—or tried to fly in—to Woodbridge were the victims not of Luftwaffe fighters or German flak but of overzealous British antiaircraft crews, who were counseled, taught, and ordered to assume that anything coming toward them was the enemy. Every Aphrodite pilot had a story about surviving a particularly hairy mission over Germany only to be fired on in the friendly skies over England. The Aphrodite pilots knew that, because of the extraordinary security surrounding their operation, no flight plans would be filed prior to a mission. The random B-17 that belly landed and then burst into flame at Woodbridge today, they understood, might have been shot to hell not by the enemy but by British ack-ack. Any of them could meet the same fate.

Shortly after arriving at Woodbridge, the mother ship crews—not the jump pilots—were summoned to Bushy Park, in Greater London, location of the headquarters of the U.S. Strategic Air Forces in Europe, where General Spaatz had authorized the most thorough briefing yet. They were told in no uncertain terms that their mission was to destroy vengeance weapon launch facilities—facilities so well hardened that conventional bombing had proved ineffective against them—which were designed to launch the destruction of London. Their mission, therefore, was to save London.

Now that the mother ship crews had been told, they returned to Woodbridge and passed the information to the jump crews. This made the impact of the friendly fire danger even more crippling to morale. The Aphrodite personnel now knew that they were not merely allies of the British; they were tasked as their saviors. And yet they were being forced by their British hosts to bunk down beside tons of high explosives and then to fly into the teeth of a reckless policy of unrestricted antiaircraft defense. It was exasperating, infuriating, and depressing.

This changed, however, when the mother ship crews related some additional aspects of their briefing. According to British intelligence, they said, the Nazis did not plan to stop with London. They were creating transatlantic vengeance weapons, and their primary target was New York City.

Jump pilot Frank Houston spoke for everyone when he responded: "So we're going to save everybody's ass. Then how come we don't have fried chicken and fresh eggs once in a while? Did they tell you that?"[34]

One of the mother ship pilots replied that they had been told Churchill himself "was watching every move we [make], and they [have] all kinds of British decorations for us, starting with the British Distinguished Flying Cross. And one of the American generals said we'd all get the American DFC, too."[35]

"I'd rather have the fried chicken and fresh eggs," said Houston.[36]

*   *   *

ON THE NIGHT OF JULY 11, some jump pilots were immersed in a game of red dog poker when one heard the drone of a distant aircraft engine. Looking up from his cards, the man motioned for silence. As the sound approached and increased in volume, the veteran pilots gathered at the table were certain that what they heard was the distinctive sound of a Junkers Ju 88, whose twin engines, always slightly out of sync, beat the air like giant eggbeaters. The Ju 88 was a dreaded Luftwaffe workhorse—a speedy tactical bomber, dive bomber, and night fighter.

Was it going to attack Woodbridge? The American pilots knew that, as an emergency airfield, Woodbridge was not customarily a target. There was an unspoken understanding between RAF and Luftwaffe airmen that neither would attack the other's emergency fields—at least not on purpose—much as neither side would attack the other's field hospitals (at least not on purpose). But what if German intelligence had learned of the presence and mission of the Aphrodite planes and crews?

This thought must have loomed increasingly large as the discordant volume of the twin engines increased. The poker players took shelter under bunks and cupboards—only to strain their ears as the engine noise diminished, growing distant again. And then, on the verge of relief, there was a new noise—a loud hiss. The crews had learned to recognize this as the sound of the field's high-intensity runway lights, fed by flaming gasoline injected through jets under high pressure and intended to pierce the thick coastal fog. The hiss of the gasoline jets was soon followed by bright lights, and now the pilots were terrified that the English had mistaken a German bomber for a friendly plane in need of help. In showing the incoming aircraft the field, they were showing its pilot-bombardier exactly where to drop his bombs. All anticipated an ungodly nitrostarch-fed blast with a napalm chaser.

Instead, the Ju 88 made at least four passes over the field before throttling back, descending—and landing! Realizing they weren't going to be blown to Kingdom Come, the poker-playing pilots ran out to the field. They were intercepted en route by an RAF military policeman, who told them they had gone far enough and politely but firmly announced that "the field is quarantined."[37]

None of them was ever told what happened to the Ju 88 and its pilot and radio operator. One rumor had it that the German had mistaken the British field for a German one and that, once he was on the ground and realized his error, he gunned his engines in a bid to escape but was stopped by sentries who swarmed the plane, climbed to the cockpit, smashed the canopy with wrenches, and manhandled both pilot and radioman onto the tarmac. Another version held that it was a case of intentional defection. This story was further embellished by the reported sighting of the powder-blue uniform and polished jackboots of a high-ranking Luftwaffe officer, not a rank-and-file Luftwaffe pilot.

There was also a third variant of the story. The Ju 88 pilot was a spy, ordered to fake a defection, touch down, take a peek at Operation Aphrodite, radio coordinates to bombers across the Channel, and then let himself be taken. Although it was the least likely of the three versions, it was certainly the most damaging. In addition to its other roles, the Ju 88 was an aerial recon platform with very sophisticated radio navigational equipment. It bristled with an array of antennas that betokened a technology far in advance of anything on any Allied aircraft. It was certainly possible for such a plane to circle the field and then land, transmitting coordinates and other information all the while. RAF and USAAF commanders had no choice but to assume the worst, and, on July 12, orders were issued to unload the babies and find yet another operational home for Aphrodite. Three days later, on July 15, the entire unit moved to Fersfield, thirteen miles south of Norwich and twenty-five miles from Woodbridge.

Lieutenant Colonel Roy Forrest, USAAF, was put in command of the new base and of the entire Aphrodite operation. At just thirty-one, he was young for his rank, but he was a combat veteran of the European air war, having commanded a B-17 squadron after flying as lead pilot on numerous missions over industrial Germany. Sometimes he led a squadron, sometimes a wing or a group, and, on more than one occasion, an entire air force—a thousand bombers at a time. A cowboy-booted tall-drink-of-water Texan, he counted among his ancestors Confederate general Nathan Bedford Forrest, whom General William Tecumseh Sherman considered so dangerous that he pledged to kill him "if it cost 10,000 lives and breaks the Treasury."[38] The lieutenant colonel cut an unmistakable figure whether in the cockpit—he had led the entire Eighth U.S. Air Force in its third raid on Berlin (March 6, 1944)—or behind a desk, looking like a cross between Errol Flynn and John Carradine. The man was a no-nonsense commander who had fully bought into the man-killing "maximum effort" ethos of the strategic bombing air force in Europe yet who always tried to secure for the officers and men of his command creature comforts and the finer things in life. When he noticed that aircrews adopted every stray dog that came

their way, he built a kennel for them and assigned one of his GI order-
lies the duty of feeding, grooming, and even worming the animals. And
when he grew tired of the kind of war-is-hell hardship Joe Kennedy Jr.
wrote home about—going "several miles" for a bath—he built a toilet
that became an Air Corps legend, complete with hot and cold running
water, shower *and* tub, and even a bidet. Before he debuted it for his aircrews, he commissioned an artistically inclined GI to decorate its walls
with "rustic scenes and nudes"[39] and then announced, "There you are,
gentlemen. Be my guest. This is not a latrine; this is a *men's room*," and,
less elegantly but more to the point: "No more riding the bicycle half a
mile to take a crap."[40]

Forrest prided himself on being a character, but he was deadly serious when it came to the objective of winning the war, and he personally
kicked Operation Aphrodite into high gear. The biggest complaint he
heard from his officers and men was that the demands of absolute secrecy had tangled everything in miles of red tape. Promising this would
end, he instructed everyone to bypass the chain of command and see
him personally to get anything they really needed. From then on, Forrest worked his phone, ordering critical parts from the nearest available sources and then dispatching B-17s to pick them up and fly them
back—immediately.

Yet even the commanding officer was powerless against the weather,
which continued to offer the same miserable conditions that had dogged
the Allied invasion of Normandy on June 6. As RAF Group Captain
James Stagg, meteorological officer for the D-Day operation, had told
Eisenhower and his fellow top commanders, in studying thirty years of
records for the Channel region, he had never encountered such stormy
winter patterns in June. And now they persisted well into July. Meteo-
rologists attached to the Aphrodite mission would predict CAVU for
the morrow only to have the base awaken to angry clouds and thunder-
storms. Powerless to change the weather, Forrest nevertheless thought
he might be able to predict it with greater accuracy. He complained to
the pilot who flew weather recon missions, reading him the riot act for
flying too high to tell anything about the weather at the low altitude
the B-17 babies would inhabit. When the weather pilot explained that
forecasting was *always* done at high altitude, Forrest responded by ordering him to come in at 500 feet and report back. The weather pilot

offered no protest, but, realizing he didn't actually work for Forrest, he went back to his own CO in the weather unit and complained. That officer phoned Forrest, advising him to issue no more orders to *his* pilots. Weather pilots, he added, did not fly at 500 feet, period.

This time it was Forrest who offered no argument. Instead, he slammed down the phone and ordered his personal twin-engine P-38 fighter to the flight line. He went out, climbed into the cockpit, and took off across the Channel for the Pas-de-Calais target area. He was back at Fersfield within an hour.

"Forget it," he complained bitterly. "At low altitude the winds are impossible. You couldn't control a box kite over there, let alone a drone."[41]

It was by no means an admission that weather flights should be left to the weather pilots. On the contrary, the flight persuaded him of the necessity of making weather runs personally. Even if the result was no more than a confirmation of what the weather pilots themselves reported, at least it was a confirmation based on firsthand knowledge. This gave Forrest a modicum of satisfaction, and he must have believed that at least his Aphrodite pilots would feel they were being given the best possible weather intelligence and not being held hostage by the meteorological unit.

Yet as concerned as Forrest was about the morale of his crews, he let himself be guided by what he had been told had happened back at Woodbridge—how a beautiful CAVU day had been lost because a navigator had been given a twenty-four-hour pass and failed to return on time. Forrest therefore refused to let up on the standing order the previous CO had issued back then, an order confining to base everyone associated with Aphrodite. He told his aircrews that they were free to drink as much as they wanted, provided they did so at Fersfield. "Nobody," he said, "is setting foot outside till we get our targets."[42]

Finding himself in the unwelcome and unfamiliar role of jailer, Forrest was thrilled one evening by a sharp *Ten-hut!* announcing the arrival in the officers' club of a short man in a raincoat and flight suit. It was Lieutenant General James H. Doolittle.

That he was CO of the entire Eighth U.S. Air Force was certainly impressive, but all the pilots gathered at the bar saw was the man who had led fifteen B-25s from the deck of the *Hornet* to bomb Japan less than five months after Pearl Harbor—and, scarcely less important, the man who had flown incredibly hot airplanes to legendary victories in the Bendix and Thompson trophy air races before the war.

"Just dropped in to see how you boys were making out," Doolittle announced.

"Yes, sir," Fain Pool managed to respond. "General, sir, it's certainly an honor to have you with us, sir."

Doolittle cut him off: "Honor, my ass. Once in a while I like to have a drink with some real pilots!"[43]

With that, the drinking began in earnest. Never one to overstay his welcome, however, Doolittle shook hands with everyone present and then made his way out the door, into the rain, and into his personal P-47 Thunderbolt. He took off into the teeth of the typically stormy English night, only to loop around, buzz the officers' club, and climb as sharply as only a Thunderbolt—in the hands of a great pilot—could.

*   *   *

DESPITE THE LIFT GENERAL DOOLITTLE'S visit provided, the Aphrodite aircrews, shuttled from one dreary base to another and perpetually idled by weather, were miserable with boredom and frustration. It could have been worse, had they known everything Allied intelligence was telling Eisenhower and his top command about the rapid evolution and proliferation of German vengeance weapons. Captain Harry C. Butcher, Eisenhower's naval aide, wrote to his boss that an eighteen-year-old German, recently captured, "had told our interrogators that the V-2 is the rocket we have been expecting." The specifics of the V-2, Butcher relayed, were a chemically fed explosion that "will destroy by burning an area of (presumably) 25 square kilometers." While the Allies had hitherto considered the vengeance weapons to be exclusively instruments of terror directed at civilian targets for the purpose of eroding the nation's will to continue the fight, the German POW had revealed a new strategic purpose. The "V-2s are to be fired at English ports, so our supplies will be destroyed and traffic to the continent disrupted." Just how committed was Hitler to the V-2? "The prisoner said that V-2 is Germany's last hope of preventing defeat."[44]

Ten days later, Eisenhower received reports of work "of an unexplained nature . . . proceeding in northwest France."[45] Three days after this, on July 22, General Spaatz, commanding the U.S. Strategic Air Forces in Europe, sent USAAF commanding general Hap Arnold a top-secret cable noting that the "test shooting in Poland" of "the large German rocket"—by which he meant the V-2—"is good enough to justify its immediate use against large objectives in England." The cable informed Arnold that Allied intelligence sources had detected "the movement of objects that might be these projectiles to the launching regions in France." Importantly, Spaatz noted that "aside from the grave threat to London, this weapon directly threatens our war effort, since it may be used to destroy communications and port facilities on both sides of the Channel."[46]

On July 27, Britain's home secretary, Herbert Morrison, declared in a meeting of the War Cabinet that a "million people should be evacuated from London as soon as possible," a proposal taken up the very next day by Brigadier General Pleas B. Rogers, at the time commanding the U.S. Army Communications Zone in the European Theater of Operations. Noting that the "best information available to this headquarters" suggested imminent "long range rocket" attacks against England, "particularly the London area," Rogers "recommended that all personnel and activities whose operation in this area is not vitally essential be moved to some other location as expeditiously as possible."[47]

* * *

GROUNDED BY WEATHER IN THE GLOOM of remote Fersfield, Forrest and the Aphrodite pilots knew nothing of the messages marking the inexorable advance of a doomsday clock. They did read the newspapers, however, and they listened to Armed Forces Radio as well as to the BBC. The news of the Allied breakout from Normandy, the advance of the U.S., British, and Canadian armies into Avranches and Brest and thence eastward, was everywhere. Over in the Pacific Theater, the Twentieth Air Force was flying B-29 Superfortresses—aircraft far more advanced than either the B-17 Flying Fortresses or the B-24 Liberators in Europe—against targets throughout Japan. Japanese civilization was being systematically wiped off the map. As for the cities of Germany, every Allied air element in Europe *except* for the group at Fersfield was visiting ceaseless and total destruction on them. Having volunteered for a war-winning mission, the Aphrodite pilots read or heard about it all—even as they themselves sat out the war day after gray day.

Just when it seemed that the tedium, tension, and general level of frustration could not get any worse, the U.S. Navy arrived on the Army Air Corps post.

At first, it was no more than a small detachment of radio-control specialists. The Air Corps personnel took an immediate dislike to them. That was to be expected in a military driven by a tradition of interservice rivalry, but the specialized nature of the newcomers sharpened the competition beyond the customary. The Air Corps radio control specialists all worked directly under Major Jim Rand using equipment they cobbled together modified directly from the AZON program Rand had developed to guide bombs dropped from aircraft. The navy specialists had been trained at the Naval Aircraft Factory, which had been established in Philadelphia way back in 1917—about as long as anybody anywhere had been working with radio control. Undeniably, Rand and his men had done an astounding job of quickly improvising a robot-plane control system from a system originally designed to do nothing more than make a few simple corrections to the course of a falling bomb. But the navy specialists showed up with extensive experience in radio control systems that governed not only azimuth but also altitude, range, and speed. The systems were, moreover, fully integrated with television technology. One look at what the Air Corps was up to convinced the new arrivals that the navy was far in advance of their army counterparts.

The navy men were right, of course, and the navy men let Rand and his men know it. There were no fistfights, but there were plenty of hot words, arguments, and plain old trash talk. Worse, however, must have been the awareness among the Air Corps men that the navy boys, obnoxious though they were, actually did know what they were talking about. Their equipment *was* better. A lot better.

And yet no one at Fersfield seems to have suggested that the two services pool their knowledge, experience, and talents, and create something even better than either of them had alone. Instead, both teams waited as patiently as they could for the weather to break. The Air Corps would fly first, but the navy would also have its turn. The point was not to figure out how to work together but to see, once and for all, who could hit the target and who could not.

* * *

SHORTLY AFTER THE ARRIVAL of the navy specialists, Jim Rand approached Colonel Forrest with a remarkable claim: "We can lick the weather!"

Forrest told him he had his attention, and Rand went on to explain that all he *absolutely* needed was visibility "for the drone on the deck"—that is, at 1,800 feet and below—at least if he could use television.[48]

He went on to elaborate. By mounting a TV camera in the Plexiglas nose of the baby and transmitting the resulting video image to the mother ship above, he could give the controller in the mother a drone's-eye view. Therefore, the controller would have no pressing need to visually observe the drone itself. It didn't matter if clouds stood between the low-flying baby and the high-flying mother, just as long as the weather below 1,800 was without fog and clouds—clear enough for a television picture.

We do not know if it was the arrival of the navy technicians, who had already worked with television as part of their radio control system, that moved Rand to reintroduce the idea of TV. It is quite possible that the endlessly adverse weather forced on him the notion of returning to that technology. In either case, Rand took the base commander into his workshop and demonstrated a television setup. Although it was crude, it was usable enough to prompt Forrest to ask how many babies he could equip, say, in a week. Rand complained about the difficulty of getting parts, even with his personal carte blanche from Ike. With luck, he thought he could get one baby rigged for television within a week.

* * *

ON JULY 30, LIEUTENANT JOSEPH P. KENNEDY JR. climbed into T-11, the PB4Y-1 he had been assigned for his role in the Project Anvil mission, and took off on an engineering test flight from RAF Dunkeswell, in Devon. Like the B-17, the navy version of the B-24 was ungodly powerful when it was unloaded and stripped of its usual equipment and defensive guns. After a half hour in the air, it was clear to Joe that the bomber was more than ready. So was he. As soon as he landed, he and his two crewmen went to their quarters to pick up personal gear for what they figured would be no more than a two-week stay as guests of the USAAF at RAF Fersfield. Among his belongings, Joe brought what he called his "treasure chest"—a box stocked with farm-fresh eggs, which he used his money and ingenuity to continually replenish. The eggs were a wartime delicacy he freely shared with fellow pilots and aircrew wherever he went in the European theater. And he also loaded aboard his prized Raleigh English bicycle.[49]

With his two crewmen and their gear loaded as well, Joe took off for Fersfield, some 250 miles to the northeast, a flight over Salisbury Plain, across the Thames, over Oxford and Cambridge, and then over the hills of East Anglia.[50] Reaching that airfield, he eased T-11 through the dull pewter cloud deck, touched down, and, directed by ground personnel, taxied to a far corner of the base. There the aircraft would be checked out by the navy ground crew and readied for loading with Torpex. In the meantime, the navy boys threw camouflage netting over the plane, and no one was allowed near.

Not that there was much to see. Like the Air Corps B-17s at Fersfield, the PB4Y-1 had been stripped of the guns that should have been bristling from the nose, the tail, and the dorsal turret—but there wasn't even a turret, not on this bomber. Inside, there was even less to see. Every accommodation except the pilot's seat had been removed. Copilot's seat, navigator's table, machine gun ammo bins, engineer's tools, standard radio equipment, bomb racks—all hauled out, the plane gutted like a landed fish. The bomb bay, empty, had been shored up with timbers, as if this Liberator were a ship from the days of sail. There was a load of unfamiliar electrical equipment in the cockpit. A slick-looking control panel was fastened right beside a crude plywood "breadboard," which looked like something cobbled together by a none-too-bright middle schooler prodded into the science fair by overachieving parents. The breadboard was a jerry-built mess of wires, lights, and toggle switches.

Joe was directed to a small Quonset hut, which he was assigned to share with Ensign Jim Simpson, one of the navy radio control techs who had arrived a few days earlier. That night, Simpson was shocked to behold his new roommate drop to his knees at bedside to pray. A Southern Baptist himself, it was the first time Simpson had ever seen a Roman Catholic at prayer. But if he harbored any inclination to "anti-Papist" prejudice, it was quickly vanquished by Joe's disarming manner and magnetism. Kneeling Papist or not, Simpson decided he wanted to fly with that pilot.[51]

Joe joined everyone else in the endless wait for CAVU. On August 2, T-11 was given a thorough check of its radio gear and loaded with 25,000 pounds of sandbags, placed in the same positions that would later be occupied by Torpex. With Jim Simpson and radio control expert Wilford "Bud" Willy, Joe squeezed into the aircraft, rolled down the runway, and took off.

The contrast between a flight burdened by twelve tons of sand and the earlier flight in the empty aircraft was startling. Whereas the stripped-down and empty four-engine bomber had seemed the very embodiment of flight, the loaded plane wallowed rather than flew. It was no fun, no fun at all.

Worse for Joe, after he got the feel of the loaded plane, it was time to test the feel of flight under radio control. None the Army Air Corps pilots had been given this opportunity. Their first experience of "hands-off" flight would be their first operational mission. When he was ready, he radioed the code word "Spade Flush," signaling John Anderson, the primary control pilot stationed in a twin-engine Lockheed PV-1 Ventura (the aircraft the navy used as a mother ship), to take over.[52] With that, Joe took his feet off the rudder pedals and his hands off the yoke.

Joe Kennedy Jr. was the son of a man whose life and career and aspirations were all about gaining and maintaining control. As a student pilot, Joe was criticized for being too concerned with instruments. A feel for flying did not come naturally to him, but the sheer will to control the airplane did. It must, therefore, have been hard for him to relinquish control to a man in another aircraft, linked to his by nothing but invisible radio waves. Nor could it have helped that flying "hands free" was no joy ride. It was like being chauffeured by a rank beginner. Every change in attitude, altitude, or direction was jerky and hesitant. In the low-altitude test, at three hundred feet, the slowness with which Anderson seemed to react to critical changes in terrain—namely the undulations of the East Anglian hills—was unnerving. But Joe maintained sufficient discipline to refrain from seizing the yoke and taking over. Of course, if Joe Kennedy had had any experience of the army's primitive double AZON system, he would have thought much more highly of what the navy had put together. The system in Kennedy's shiny new PB4Y-1 was far more capable than that installed in the war-weary B-17s.

On the next day, August 3, the PB4Y-1 and Joseph P. Kennedy Jr. were both ready to fly—to beat the Army Air Corps in making the first robot attack against the hardened bastions from which Germany was launching its vengeance against London. But rain and fog, as usual, grounded both the Air Corps and the navy. Having failed to beat his brother Jack to a public demonstration of heroism, Joe now feared that he would fail to beat the men of the United States Army Air Forces as well.

When the armorers began loading his plane, Kennedy and Simpson ambled by to watch. The work party consisted exclusively of black GIs—that's the way it was in the segregated American military of the day—stevedores who formed a human chain between the wheeled ammo carriers and the aircraft's aft hatch, the first man lifting a pine box lined with beeswax, then, twisting at the hips, passing it slowly to the next man in the chain, who took it, swiveled, and passed it on. The work was much harder than it looked. Each box, never manhandled, but gracefully passed as if in solemn ritual, contained fifty, maybe sixty pounds of small, wax paper–wrapped blocks of what looked like butter: primrose in color, not quite translucent. At the end of the chain was a man, feet planted firmly on the tarmac, head sticking up through the open aft hatch, hands extended, palms up, as if in supplication, waiting to receive each box as it came to him. Taking it, he would heft it chest high, turn to face forward, then slide it onto the deck of the aircraft. Inside, other laborers, directed by a white naval officer, carried each box forward and lowered it gingerly into place, one atop another, filling every conceivable space, beginning with the place where the copilot's seat should have been, then working back, box upon box, toward the rear of the sixty-some-foot-long bomber.[53]

The loading went ahead like a slow-motion machine, smooth and precise, until the end man, the man with his head in the plane's belly, caught the bottom of one box on the lip of the hatch, scraped the knuckles of one hand, and lost his grip. The box slipped down, hung up briefly in the hatch, and then slid free, falling toward the tarmac. Instinctively, the GI thrust out his foot to take the full weight of the crate's edge on his toe. It had to hurt, badly. At the very least it meant a broken toe, maybe a hairline fracture of the instep. But whatever pain he endured, he kept loading, and not another crate slipped.[54]

Good thing too. The "butter" in each crate was Torpex, the explosive the Royal Gunpowder Factory at Waltham Abbey had developed from a German recipe, mixing an old standby, RDX, also called T4, with TNT and ultrafine aluminum powder to produce a high explosive 50 percent more powerful than TNT alone. The RDX made up 42 percent of the mix, and the TNT 40 percent. Together, these generated the initial release of energy, while the aluminum powder—18 percent—made the explosive pulse last longer and therefore enhanced its destructive force. Beeswax was thrown in to reduce sensitivity to shock and impact, though a six-foot drop onto asphalt would have, at the very least, put the effectiveness of the beeswax buffer to the test. Three hundred forty-seven pine crates of Torpex—21,170 pounds—would be loaded into T-11, equivalent to more than eighteen tons of TNT. Until the detonation of the Little Boy atomic bomb over Hiroshima almost exactly one year later, on August 6, 1945, Kennedy's PB4Y-1 would be the single most destructive explosive weapon in military history.

Kennedy and Simpson did not wait for the final crates to be loaded. Just after the loader caught the falling crate on his toe, Joe nudged Simpson: "Let's get outta here."[55]

Returning to the hut, Joe tried to do some reading, trading to navy radioman Dee Vilan his copy of Henry Bellamann's recent novel, *Floods of Spring,* for *Persons and Places,* by the philosopher George Santayana, whom Joe had met at Harvard—a place that must have seemed a million miles and a thousand years away.[56]

That evening, after a day shrouded in fog, a mission was posted for the following afternoon. T-11 was ready. Joe was ready. But tomorrow's mission would be flown by the Army Air Corps. Fain Pool was listed as the number one jump pilot, with Staff Sergeant Philip Enterline as his electronics expert. The second crew was Lieutenant John Fisher and Tech Sergeant Elmer Most; the third, Lieutenant Joseph Andrecheck and Sergeant Ray Healy; the fourth, Lieutenant Cornelius Engel and Tech Sergeant Clifford Parsons. In addition, a standby crew was posted: Lieutenant Frank Houston and Staff Sergeant Willard Smith.

Joe Kennedy, Dee Vilan later reported, instantly turned "angry and edgy." He must have realized that missions and crews had been posted many times before, whenever the weather looked the least bit promising. Each time, come morning, the mission had to be scrubbed because the predicted CAVU failed to materialize. Of course, if tomorrow's mission was scrubbed, it didn't necessarily mean that Joe would be bumped up ahead of it. And, in any case, the night of August 3 turned perfectly clear and stayed that way. To men accustomed to more than a month of rain, the deep black sky looked like crystal. At sunrise on August 4, 1944, conditions were pure, spectacular CAVU. Word from the other side of the Channel was of the same.

Fain Pool, Phil Enterline, and the other jump and mother crews believed they would be flying that afternoon. All assembled for breakfast, then left for mission briefings. On the way to the briefings hut, they saw no less than Eighth Air Force commander Jimmy Doolittle and Third Bomb Division CO Earle Partridge dismounting jeeps. The generals had each flown in, piloting their personal fighters to Fersfield. When the crews learned that the brass had come early to sit in on the briefings, the reality of the missions became palpable. Aphrodite would attack at last.

CHAPTER 7

THE DRONES
OF AUGUST

FOUR BABIES WERE SLATED TO FLY ON THE AFTERNOON OF AUgust 4, 1944, manned by four two-person crews, with one standby crew available. As they had so many times before, the mother ship and jump crews filed into the briefing hut after breakfast. ("Say, what'd you have for breakfast?" Fain Pool asked his electronics expert, Staff Sergeant Phil Enterline. "Everything except eggs Benedict," he answered. Pool laughed: "The condemned men ate a hearty meal."[1])

Inside the briefing hut, laid out on an array of Ping-Pong tables, were three-dimensional models of the targets assigned to the four sorties collectively designated Mission 515. Having been repeatedly summoned to the hut and briefed, only to have the mission scrubbed on account of weather, the pilots and crews were thoroughly familiar with all of the targets. Indeed, the targets made no difference whatsoever to the jump crews. After taking off and leveling first at 1,800 feet, the jump pilot was to fly a rectangular pattern over the English countryside while his electronics expert set up the autopilot and ACE radio altimeter, then bailed out. The jump pilot would point the aircraft in the direction of the French coast, put it into a gentle dive, set the autopilot to level off at 300 feet, radio the code word "Taxisoldier" to the mother ship to signal that he was leaving his seat, and would then arm the nitrostarch load both manually and electronically before exiting from the navigator's escape hatch. The jump crew would never even see the target.

Major General Earle Partridge, commanding the Third Bomb Division, and Lieutenant General Jimmy Doolittle, Eighth Air Force CO, both attended the briefing and would both fly their own P-38s to observe the mission. Their effort was more than a show of curiosity. Together, they had overseen planning for the extensive support the missions would receive. Much of the time, in the days leading up to August 4, the men of Aphrodite had felt lonely and alone, cut loose by the British and isolated from the rest of the base. Today, however, the Royal Air Force was devoting 250 of its bombers to a diversionary raid against targets of plausible—if not compelling—importance north of Paris. The raid was to commence at three in the afternoon, precisely when the Aphrodite babies would be taking off, in flight, or even beginning their impacts into their targets. The idea was to draw as much of the Luftwaffe as far away from the attacks as possible. In addition, sixteen twin-engine P-38 Lightning fighters—an aircraft whose unconventional twin-boom fuselage prompted Luftwaffe pilots to call it *der Gabelschwanz-Teufel* (fork-tailed devil)—were dispatched to fly cover for the mother ships. More B-17s were sent up for observation and navigation, each of which was also assigned its own fighter cover. Four additional P-38s, equipped for photoreconnaissance, were tasked with capturing the mission in still photos and movies. Two RAF Mosquitoes were specifically detailed to photograph the exit of the two aircrew. Like the P-38, the de Havilland Mosquito was a twin-engine, twin-boom aircraft. Unlike the P-38, it was built mostly of wood. That made it incredibly light for the power it packed—light, maneuverable, and very fast: perfect for getting into position to cover the jumps.

In addition to the U.S. fighters specifically assigned to protect the mission's major operational aircraft, the RAF sent two Spitfire squadrons to cover the entire sortie. Additional Spitfires were dispatched on advance patrol over the Channel to provide early warning of Luftwaffe activity, and the Royal Navy also did its bit, sending out launches offshore on the chance that the jumpers, bailing out so close to the Channel, might overshoot and end up in the drink.

Of greatest concern to all the flight crews, but especially to the men who were actually flying a planeload of nitrostarch, were the trigger-happy English antiaircraft artillery crews. At the last possible minute, word of the mission went out to them to hold their fire. Whatever comfort this provided the men of Aphrodite was tempered, however, by the repetition of instructions that, at the very first sign of friendly fire, the jump crews were to abandon their aircraft. The truth was that no one trusted the AAA crews to remember, much less act on, what they had been told.

Aphrodite personnel were also mindful of the very real danger their mission posed to England, especially to the nearby cities of Norwich and Ipswich. If a baby was shot down over land or, even more likely, if the mother ship failed to establish control over it and it went wild, the devastation 12 tons of high explosives could wreak on the English homeland was horrific to contemplate. The bombardiers in the mother ships had instructions to do everything possible to get control of mis-behaving babies, fly them out over the North Sea as swiftly as possible, and dump them there. If control was impossible to establish, they were to summon the nearest fighters to shoot them out of the sky.

Everyone—and no one more than Major Henry James Rand—knew the radio control system was unreliable. The FM frequencies were subject to interference, especially in a radio environment thick with traffic and plagued by German jamming signals. The equipment, based on inherently delicate vacuum tube technology and hand-soldered connections, was really too fragile to be vibrated by four droning engines and buffeted by low-altitude winds near the turbulent Channel coast. The control surfaces of the B-17—elevators, ailerons, and rudders—were entirely mechanical: a system of linkages designed to be operated not by hydraulics but by muscle, often the combined muscle of pilot and copilot. The necessarily small servo motors available to translate radio-control impulses into physical control actions were no match for human brawn. Even if all the electronics worked, in many situations the mechanical output of the servo systems would simply be insufficient to overcome wind pressure and high-G forces. It was terrifyingly easy for everyone—from engineers to pilots to politicians—to imagine a scenario in which a flying bomb, out of control, suddenly turned 180 degrees from the Channel and headed toward an impact into a nearby village or city or even London itself, which was just a hundred miles from Fersfield. Saving London, it seemed, put a lot people at high risk— including Londoners.

* * *

OF THE FOUR CREWS TAPPED to fly Mission 515 on August 4, Pool and Enterline, designated Crew 1, were assigned to a target the Allies called Watten, near Saint-Omer in France's Pas-de-Calais département. Built by the Germans between March 1943 and July 1944, it was a bunker designed to house, service, and launch V-2 rockets. The Germans code-named it Kraftwerk Nord West (Northwest Power Plant), and the local French authorities called it Blockhaus d'Éperlecques, in reference to its location in the Forest of Éperlecques.

Intended to accommodate 108 V-2s at any one time and to launch as many as 36 daily, the main structure was 302 feet wide and 92 feet high. Its ferroconcrete walls were 23 feet thick in some places, and the build-ing's work areas extended 20 feet below ground. Within the main facil-ity were five massive compressors capable of producing, every day, 10 tons of liquid oxygen—the oxidizer essential to the combustion of the 75 percent ethanol/water mixture that created the V-2's thrust. Extending from the north side of the main bunker was a heavily fortified standard-gauge rail station capable of unloading supplies and every component of the V-2. Once assembled and armed within the main building, missiles were either stored or immediately sent out through the south end of the structure to launch pads. Instead of doors, the south-facing exit portals were protected by massive chicanes, juxtaposed, overlapping barriers designed to deflect the blast of each launch. Another building, located north of the main bunker, housed a heavily reinforced electrical generat-ing station to supply power to the bunker. The original design called for direct connection to the regular power grid, but as German positions in France came under increasingly heavy air attack, the availability of self-contained electricity was deemed essential.[2]

Evidence of construction was first reported by an Allied intelligence source early in April 1943 and was confirmed in May by RAF aerial re-connaissance. On August 27, 1943, the RAF sent 187 B-17s against the site. It was the first of twenty major Allied air raids against Watten prior to Aphrodite Mission 515. At least four of these missions employed the Tallboy "earthquake" bombs specifically designed to destroy highly hardened bunkers and fortifications. Observers reported severe destruction by a Tallboy impact on July 6, but aerial reconnaissance detected continued activity and, from all outward appearances, the facility still seemed viable. Unknown to the Allies—including the commanders of Operation Aphrodite—Adolf Hitler, on July 18, 1944, personally canceled plans to make Watten and the nearby bunker at Wizernes operational. Major-General Dr. Walter Robert Dornberger, the leading military figure in the V-2 program, authorized miscellaneous construction activity to continue at Watten for the express purpose of decoying Allied air attacks. Valuable machinery, including the liquid oxygen generators, were secretly removed and shipped east to the Mittelwerk V-2 factory in central Germany. The mighty Watten bunker was then rechristened Beton Pauschal ("concrete lump") by Dornberger's supremely cynical staff.[3]

* * *

AFTER ATTENDING THE MISSION 515 BRIEFING, Pool and Enterline hopped in a jeep and were driven to a B-17 designated No. 342, after the last three digits of its tail number. There the two men joined the ground crew in making final safety and airworthiness checks. Then Pool did his own walk-around and met up with the crew chief.

"Everything's in order, sir," the crew chief reported. "We'll be leaving you now."[4]

They were unorthodox parting words, especially from an enlisted man to an officer. Not "Anything else, sir?" or "Will that be all, sir?" But *We're outta here!*

Pool could hardly blame him. As he remarked to Enterline, "They don't want to be around when we give her the juice." And as Enterline replied, "Neither do we."[5]

But then Pool looked to the west. A low cloud bank hugged the horizon.

"Hey, look at that!" he said, drawing Enterline's attention to the clouds. The four words were freighted with ambivalence. Were they an expression of disappointment? (Enterline replied as if they were. "Damn!" he cursed. "We'll be scrubbed again, sure as hell.") Or were they words hopeful of reprieve?[6]

Certainly, both men were shaken when they took their places in the cockpit. Additional crates of nitrostarch had been loaded since they last inspected the interior of the plane. The crates were now piled to the very top of every bulkhead. Enterline expressed concern over creating a center of gravity far higher than the B-17 had been designed for. The aircraft was built to haul a lot of weight—but the designers assumed that the great bulk of it would be concentrated in the belly, in the bomb bay, not piled all the way to the overhead.

Pool sought to placate his one and only crew member. "Well, I'll tell you something I've learned, Sergeant. They've got the finest technicians and scientists in the world behind this project, and it's the number one priority in the theater, and I just can't believe they haven't thought of everything. If that nitrostarch is piled high, it's for a reason."[7]

As he surveyed the tiny space left to him and Enterline, a space cramped and stifling, did Pool believe his own words? It no longer resembled an aircraft interior but looked mostly like a solid wall of wooden crates, from deck to overhead, from tail into cockpit, where, in place of the copilot's seat, was just another tightly packed stack of nitrostarch. As if the feeling of being encased in high explosives were not sufficiently unnerving, the men could see wire and cable running everywhere. Some snaked along the floor, some was attached to crates, and all would soon be alive with current—the current necessary to detonate an explosion. In addition to the electric wire and cable was Primacord. The brightly colored rope looked innocent enough—like something you might give a child to play with. In fact, Primacord was a long, continuous core of PETN (pentaerythritol tetranitrate) or RDX (T4), both of which were high explosives considerably more powerful than TNT, around which was wrapped well-waxed textile yarn. Primacord was inserted into every crate of nitrostarch, to detonate along its own length at very high velocity—23,000 feet per second—setting off all of the explosives throughout the huge aircraft in a collective blast that would be, for all practical purposes, absolutely simultaneous.

Pool did his best to look unconcerned by the profusion of wire, cable, and Primacord. He engaged Enterline in the preflight control checklist, focusing their combined attention on that task. When they reached the bottom of the list, Pool flipped the magneto switches that spooled up the inverters, which converted direct current to the alternating current that powered the starter motors of each of the B-17's four engines. Unlike modern inverters, which are all electronic, the World War II–vintage devices were mechanical, rotary apparatuses designed to produce from incoming flat direct current an alternating-current sine wave. When a Flying Fortress pilot flipped the switches, the first thing heard in the cockpit was not the engines coughing into life but the whine of the inverters spinning up. The sound in the cockpit now was familiar—if quite a bit louder than usual. The increase in volume was easy to account for. The inverters were located under the pilot's and copilot's seats. With the copilot's seat gone, there was nothing to muffle the whine of the starboard inverter. What was not at all standard, however, was the sharp summer thunderstorm smell of ozone that filled the cockpit as the exposed inverter on the right side spun up and showered sparks on the nearest crate of nitrostarch and its waxy bright Primacord.

Now it was Fain Pool's turn to express doubt.

"Sergeant!" he shouted. "How stable is that stuff?"

Enterline, who had no place to sit in the cockpit, was kneeling beside Lieutenant Pool. As his posture was distinctly unmilitary, so was his answer. "I haven't the slightest idea. But remember what you said: They've thought of everything."

Pool protested that the "goddamn box" was really close to the inverter. "If one of those sparks takes hold—"

At which Enterline continued in his unmilitary vein: "Don't think about it. We've got enough to do." However, he could not resist commenting on the total absence of personnel anywhere near the taxiway and runway. Not a soul was to be seen. "They certainly show a lot of faith in our scientists."[8]

As the B-17 baby rumbled over the taxiway, it seemed as if the wheels were any shape but round. The crate towers surrounding the men swayed as if buffeted by a strong wind. Enterline expressed concern over the rough ride.

"She's been sitting on that hardstand fully loaded, and the tires have flat spots," he reasoned.[9] It was plausible enough, but the explanation did nothing to stop the crates from swaying. Now that No. 342 was on the move, Pool was sharply focused. Having reached the end of the runway, he applied full power to number four engine, swinging the aircraft into the wind for takeoff. After locking his parking brakes, he throttled up each engine one after the other, all the way, listening to each for a moment before, one at a time, he throttled each back, settling at a 1,000-revolutions-per-minute idle speed.

Pool looked at his watch. One of the keys to being a great formation flier was taking off on time—not a second late and not a second early. While he looked at his watch, waiting for the appointed minute, Pool reminded Staff Sergeant Enterline that he had "only one thing to do on takeoff, but it's important."

"Yeah," Enterline responded. "I know. When we reach sixty, give us a quarter flaps." He took a beat and asked, superfluously, for a confirmation: "Right?"

"Right," affirmed Pool, adding, "We'll never get off without flaps, so it's up to you."[10]

It was 1:40 pm. Takeoff was scheduled for 1:45. Before 1:40, Enterline had insisted that a weather abort would come at any moment. Just after 1:40, Enterline, looking up from beside Pool's seat, held up his sweaty palms.

"Do you get that same feeling?" he asked.

"Yeah," Pool answered. "We're going."[11]

With that, he occupied himself watching the second hand sweep slowly around the dial of his watch. The low drone of the idling engines filled the silence—only to be pierced by a god-awful wail.

Enterline, wide-eyed, asked what it was.

"It's for us. The air-raid siren," Pool said, explaining that he had asked the tower for a time check.[12] With that, he spread his palm and fingers over all four throttles and pushed them forward. Enterline grabbed onto the sides of Pool's seat.

No. 342 lurched ahead and then gathered momentum, slowly. But not *too* slowly—and yet the plane's tail stayed stubbornly down. Pool knew they had passed the point of rotation, the point at which the wheels should be off the ground and the aircraft airborne.

"Goddamn," Enterline heard him mutter as the vegetable garden that supplied the personnel of RAF Fersfield loomed larger and larger in the windscreen. Even though he didn't feel sufficient rotation speed, Pool jerked back on the yoke with all the leverage he could muster. The B-17 shuddered in frank protest, the crates of high explosive vibrating, but the wheels finally left the tarmac. This was followed by the familiar but nevertheless unnerving curtsy dip that was the prelude to the ascent of a heavily loaded heavy bomber. Pool did not even bother to speculate by how many feet—or inches—they would clear the new-growth pines of the forest surrounding RAF Fersfield.

Having cleared them, Pool made no pretense of nonchalance. He punched Enterline gleefully in the arm, thanked the good Lord, and announced, "We're okay! We're airborne!"[13]

To this, Enterline offered an entirely unexpected apology for having put the pilot "through that."

Pool was uncomprehending. "Put me through what?" he asked.

With that, Enterline confessed that he had forgotten to do the one thing he was absolutely supposed to do: set 25 percent flaps. And having confessed, he braced for the explosion—not of 10 tons of nitrostarch but of the officer and pilot he had so blatantly let down.

Pool, however, didn't so much as raise his voice. "We're up now," he said calmly, and then *he* apologized for not having reminded Enterline—a second time. The conversation ended with the two men agreeing that they were both, in fact, "a couple of sad sacks."[14]

Pool felt that Enterline's concern about the high center of gravity inside the overloaded, top-heavy aircraft was amply justified as he found himself very "busy"—the term pilots apply to a flight situation in which either the weather or the state of the aircraft or both present special control challenges. It was not easy to keep his B-17 flying straight and level, and he decided to execute the turns of his prescribed rectangular pattern over England using the rudder only. Basic flight training taught the use of ailerons to make neat, banking turns. In fact, the flat, skidding rudder-only turns Pool began executing would have gotten a student pilot booted out of primary training. It wasn't that Pool was fearful of upsetting the towers of nitrostarch crates. They were packed in too tightly for that. He was afraid, however, very afraid, that the handling characteristics of the B-17 were now so altered that a banking turn would throw the plane into a stall or even a spin from which there would be no recovery.

Once he felt reasonably comfortable with his control of the aircraft, he radioed the mother-ship pilot, Wilfred Ferguson Tooman—known as Pappy—that he was starting his control checks preparatory to turning over the baby for remote control. Tooman was at 21,000 feet, Pool at 2,000. Enterline's job was to check the ACE and set the autopilot. In the reconfigured aircraft, most of these modified controls had been moved from their usual place on the pilot's control panel to the cramped crawlspace under the flight deck. Enterline squeezed through a hole in the deck, landed in the crawlspace, and went to work. Per Major Rand's protocol, the procedure was to set the ACE and autopilot to take the baby to an altitude of 1,800 feet and level off. Instead of leveling at 1,800, however, the B-17 dropped *through* 1,800—and kept dropping.

Pool shouted to Enterline, demanding to know what the problem was. The electronics "expert" could reply only that he didn't *know*. He could *guess,* however. The ACE worked by getting a bounce-back signal from the ground and calculated the altitude accordingly. Enterline speculated that the bounce-back wasn't reaching the ACE, and he suggested descending farther. Pool accordingly eased down to 1,600 feet, but the ACE would not hold there either. He let the B-17 go down another 200 feet. Still no control. At 1,200 feet, however, the radio altimeter finally responded, holding that altitude.

Enterline called out the good news. He could now set the ACE for 300, the altitude at which it would cross the Channel. That the ACE was working was good news. Not so good was the prospect of having to bail out much lower than anticipated. But Pool couldn't worry about that now. The problem with the altimeter had eaten up time. He warned Enterline that they were already halfway around the rectangular checking course. Pool pressed him to get the autopilot set—pronto.

The modified automatic piloting equipment was, like everything else on the babies, mostly an improvisation. Setting up the autopilot was no mere matter of twisting a few knobs in the cockpit. In the crawlspace below the flight deck, Enterline's task was to perfectly balance the three gyroscopes that controlled the aircraft in the dimensions of pitch, roll, and azimuth. Each gyroscope communicated to the outside by means of two lights, three pairs in all. Enterline had to calibrate the instruments while Pool struggled to hold a perfectly straight and level flight. When each gyro was properly set, both indicator lights for that particular gyro would go out. Once all three pairs of lights were extinguished, the gyro was set, and the baby was calibrated to accurately accept radio control.

Enterline had no trouble balancing roll and azimuth. Under his practiced hand, the lights winked off quickly. No matter what he tried, however, one of the warning lights for the pitch gyro—the "up" light—remained illuminated.

That was potentially very bad, but it wasn't conclusive. While the warning lights had been designed to indicate trouble and its resolution, the warning system, like everything else, was far from perfectly reliable. In tests, the glowing lights frequently signified false alarms. Because the "up" light stubbornly refused to go out, regardless of what adjustments Enterline made, there was reason to conclude that the problem was a fault in the warning system, not an actual problem with the pitch gyro. If this assumption was wrong, however, the autopilot, once engaged, would probably put the B-17 into a very sharp climb. Loaded down as it was, the extreme maneuver would almost certainly cause the plane to stall, stand on its tail, and then spiral back to earth, completely and irrecoverably out of control.

Pool became insistent, calling down to the crawlspace: "What's going on?"

"I can't get rid of the up light."[15]

Pool reminded him that time was almost up. He impatiently ticked off the checkpoints already passed—Southwold and Eye—and announced they were nearing Stowmarket. "After that it's Woodbridge," Pool said, "and we jump there!"[16]

Enterline could answer only that he knew but that he just could not get rid of the damned light.

At 3:02, No. 342 flew over Stowmarket, seventy-seven minutes after takeoff. Time to Woodbridge—and mandatory bailout—was just seven minutes. After that lay the English Channel.

Time ran out before the light went out. Pool shouted down at Enterline the order to prepare to jump. Although he had seen false indicator lights in many previous tests, Enterline was not satisfied that this particular light was in error. Even as he centered himself over the open navigator's escape hatch in the belly of the plane, he shouted to Pool, "They'll never be able to dive this thing!"

The only reply Enterline heard was "Get out of here! I can see the coast."[17]

With that, the staff sergeant took off his glasses and put them into the breast pocket of his jumpsuit. He had two parachutes. The main chute was his seat pack, which enclosed a large folded parachute and was held in place by a snap. Enterline connected the snap to a static line, which was anchored to a stout longeron in the aircraft. Instead of counting on the parachutist to deploy his own chute by pulling a ripcord, the planners of Aphrodite relied on the static line to tear open the seat pack when the jumper had fallen a safe distance from the plane. If this somehow failed, the emergency chute, in the chest pack, was equipped with a manual ripcord.

Static line technology was well tested. The paratroops of American and British airborne units, including those who had jumped into Europe on the night before D-Day, had been using it with great success. However, the differences between a paratrooper jumping out of a C-47 and what Enterline was about to do were critical. In the drops that preceded the June 6 Allied landing at Normandy, troopers exited their aircraft at or somewhat above 700 feet. Enterline actually had an advantage of almost twice the altitude. But the C-47 aircraft of D-Day were flying at just 110 miles per hour when the paratroopers jumped, whereas Enterline was leaving an airplane traveling at nearly twice that speed. The sudden deceleration produced by the rapidly opening parachute would be especially violent. Equally important, whereas the paratroops exited through the large side door of their transport, an ample opening easy to clear, Enterline had to squeeze through a belly hatch measuring two by two-and-a-half feet—with seat and chest pack, and traveling very, very fast. The chance of injury was greater than the prospect of emerging unscathed.

After hooking up to the static line, Enterline tottered upright over the narrow hatch, the hurricane-force winds of the slipstream roaring by. He willed himself into the rectangular void and then pushed off into space.

Once lowered into the slipstream's gale, it was impossible to remain perpendicular to the aircraft. As the lower portion of his body was swept up toward the bottom of the fuselage, Enterline felt his head bump against the lip of the hatch, but, remaining conscious, he was dazzled by the flashing alternation of earth and sky in his field of vision. He was not *falling* out of the plane. He was *tumbling*.

That motion stopped abruptly at the end of the static line. When his seat pack tore open, Enterline's parachute poured out and instantly filled with air, pulling him up so violently that he felt himself sliced in two. Looking up, he saw the parachute; looking down, he saw—with almost as much relief—that he still had legs. And now, even as he experienced the negative G's of rapid deceleration, Enterline became aware of a new motion. He was swinging like the bob at the end of an enormous pendulum, his trajectory covering, it seemed to him, hundreds of feet side to side. During his parachute training, somebody had said something about pulling the risers to spill some air out of one side of the chute canopy in order to reduce lateral motion. But, with the ground coming up, Enterline just could not remember the specifics—or even if any specifics had been given. He therefore pulled at the risers randomly, only to realize that his fingers, torn and bleeding, barely worked. It flashed through his mind that he must have instinctively reached out for the lip of the escape hatch when he left the plane. And while he contemplated this, he became aware that the pendulum motion had slowed, though not diminished. Accordingly, he stopped jerking the risers and used his bloody fingers to locate his eyeglasses in his jumpsuit. Surprisingly, he was able to push these onto his face—just in time to see a woman bicycling on the road below. Judging himself to be less than 500 feet above her, he shouted down the only two words he could think of: "Hey, look!"[18]

She must have heard him, because he saw her glance back and start pedaling a lot faster. Just as Enterline caught a glimpse of a group of farmworkers coming up the road, he reached the top of what was now a slow pendulum arc amid the sound of breaking branches. He was in a tree—or, rather, he was falling through the branches of a tree. He instinctively covered his eyes and pressed his feet together, anticipating an impact. In fact, the tree broke his descent and eased him down onto terra firma.

As he related years later, he was on the verge of shouting for sheer joy. Not only was Operation Aphrodite over—for *him*—he was alive. What stopped his expression of jubilation, however, was the realization that he was alive by virtue of sheer dumb luck. If the tree hadn't been there, and if he had hit the ground on the upward arc of his pendulum swing, he would have landed hard—and not on his feet, but on his side, back, or face. It would not have been pretty or pleasant. As it was, retaining his composure turned out to be useful, as he found himself rushed by seven or eight women dressed in the work uniform of the Women's Land Army, a wartime organization of female agricultural laborers. Their pitchforks and hoes were pointed squarely at his chest—though his broad mid-Atlantic American accent (Enterline was from Kittanning, Pennsylvania) instantly dispelled any suspicion that he was a German: "Hey! I just jumped out of an airplane!"[19]

Fain Pool, who was still in that airplane, did his best to suppress his concern over the "up" light on the pitch gyro, which could well mean that the B-17 would climb out of control as soon as he switched to autopilot. Since there was nothing he could do about that now, however, he focused on completing all the tasks he had to get through before he could bail out. The first of these was turning the servo motors on. They would operate the elevators and the *rudder*—since double AZON achieved turns not via ailerons, which caused the aircraft to bank smartly, but by the rudder, which resulted in flat, skidding turns. Next, he switched the autopilot to the "remote" setting. This step was supposed to be performed at 1,800 feet, but because the ACE had failed to respond above 1,200 feet, the baby was flying at that altitude. Pool worried that this discrepancy could throw off the controller in the mother ship, but with the coast rapidly approaching, he had no time to climb back to 1,800. So he called Tooman in the mother ship and pronounced the word "Taxisoldier."

"Watch that first step," Tooman responded in the clear. "It's a son of a bitch!"[20]

Pool now eased the four throttles back from thirty-four to thirty-two inches of manifold pressure, removed his headphones and microphone—a throat model, designed to pick up vocal cord vibrations in the noisy environment of a B-17 cockpit—and eased the baby into a gentle descent. After setting the safety clock, which was wired into the detonation circuit, for a ten-minute electric arming delay, Pool squeezed his way out of the pilot's seat and lowered himself down into the crawlspace toward the navigator's escape hatch. Pool reached for the lanyard that ran alongside the escape hatch. It was connected to fourteen cables attached to fourteen groups of nitrostarch crates. Once pulled out, the explosive load would be set to detonate on impact. Pool tugged, but the cables would not give. He laid both hands on the lanyard and braced his feet against a bulkhead. Then he pulled with all his muscle and body weight. The cables suddenly gave way, sending him sprawling on the catwalk that ran through the crawlspace.

The tug-of-war had consumed valuable seconds—seconds during which the descending B-17 was not only gaining speed but losing altitude. Each fraction of a second that passed made the jump riskier and more difficult to execute.

The manual arming system was backed up by an electric arming system. The two were intended to be redundant, not to ensure safety but to guarantee detonation. Either one was theoretically sufficient to arm the explosives, but one system would compensate for the possible failure of the other. If Pool had been tempted to bypass the electrical arming step, he never told anyone. He turned to the panel adjacent to the escape hatch, noted that the short-circuit indicator lights were out—which was good, since an indication of a short circuit signaled the possibility of premature detonation. He grabbed a pair of telephone switchboard-style jacks hanging loose from the panel and plugged them into the panel, which would energize a pair of fuses as soon as the safety clock timer passed ten minutes. This would arm the load electrically.

All that was left now was to get himself into his emergency chute, which went across his chest and supplemented the seat pack that held the main chute. This done and tightened, he hooked up to the static line and, sitting next to the escape hatch, swung his legs into the slipstream.

The navigator's escape hatch was just aft of the number 2 engine, and the chop-chop-chop of its propeller struck Pool as disconcertingly close. Determined to avoid amputation or worse, he gripped the lip of the hatch on either side, pushed up with his arms to lift his body so that it was centered in the hole, and swung himself back toward the aircraft's tail and as far away from the propeller as possible. What he hadn't thought of was how the resulting angle would put his head in jeopardy. And, sure enough, Pool's forehead scraped the rear lip of the hatch as he fell through it.

Whatever pain he might have felt from the blow to his head failed to register as the parachute, snapping open in the 200-mile-per-hour wind, jerked at the harness that dug into his legs and groin. This impact was followed by an overall numbness; like Enterline, he too thought his legs had been severed. Summoning his courage, Pool looked toward them, discovered they were still with him, and then looked past his feet. The sight of the ground, maybe a mere 500 feet below, was not reassuring. Pool had lost more altitude than he thought before he had been able to leave the aircraft.

Surprisingly, there was even worse to contemplate. Pool could see that he was descending rapidly along a line of high-tension towers and wires, approaching them as if he were approaching a runway. He tugged at his risers in an effort to steer clear, but the descent was so rapid that he had precious little directional control. Pool pictured himself in a shower of sparks and flame—and that picture nearly displaced the reality of his actual descent. Before he knew it, he had slammed into the ground, hard. Instinctively, he staggered to his feet, moved forward two, three, four, or more steps, and pitched headfirst into a ditch. He turned onto his back, gazing at the high-tension wires above him.

Fain Pool began taking inventory in that ditch. There was blood and pain, but nothing actually seemed shattered or broken. And that realization sent him into a kind of drunken ecstasy. The joy of being alive not only propelled him to his feet but set his feet to dancing. Before long, he was back on level ground—laughing and rolling in the grass like a puppy. He later reported hearing the sound of an explosion, which he assumed was his B-17 blowing up prematurely. It didn't really much bother him.

* * *

"TAXISOLDIER!" CRACKLED OVER Pappy Tooman's headset. It was the code word signifying that Pool was leaving the pilot's seat and would, at any moment, bail out of B-17 No. 342.

Piloting the mother ship, a B-24 Liberator rigged out with a double AZON transceiver, Tooman got on the interphone and relayed the code word to his bombardier, Glen Hargis, whose job it was to fly the baby into the target.

Seconds before they received the "Taxisoldier" call, Tooman and Hargis watched Enterline bail out of No. 342. So far, so good. But then seconds more ticked by, and they watched the B-17 descend. The code word had been transmitted when the baby was already well below bailout altitude. Had Pool been hurt? Disabled?

With No. 342 at no more than 600 feet from the earth of coastal England, Tooman and Hargis at last saw Pool shoot out of the navigator's hatch. He was obviously very much alive, though at 200 miles per hour just 600 feet above the earth, it was anyone's guess whether he'd stay that way for long. No matter. Tooman squeezed the interphone switch on his throat mike and spurred Hargis into action: "Let's go! She's all ours!"[21]

"All ours" did not really mean all that much, however. The double AZON system improvised from Rand's AZON bomb course-correction system allowed no more than three points of control. Flip one switch, and you turned the 60,000-pound baby left. Flip another, and you turned it right. The only feedback you had was visual—and, in the case of No. 342, which was *not* equipped with a television camera and transmitter, "visual" meant all that the bombardier, at 21,000 feet, could see of the B-17 at just 300 feet, using a bombsight originally modified for AZON. The bright white paint that had been slapped onto the top surface of the baby's wings did enhance visibility, and on some of the drones, a coat of bright yellow paint was applied to the fuselage, right over the standard olive drab. Still, it was some tall order to pilot a four-engine "heavy," by sight, from more than three-and-a-half miles away.

Whereas the two azimuth controls could be used individually or together to more or less ease the baby one way or another, the third switch was intended as one-time only and strictly binary. Flip it, and it would send the aircraft into a sudden dive based on full down elevators. Turning that switch off *might* allow the elevators to return to neutral, but there was no guarantee. Certainly, there was no way to *raise* the elevators, which meant that the bombardier in the mother ship had no means of making the baby climb.

Hargis was experienced with controlling AZON bombs, but he had never flown any aircraft by remote control, let alone a loaded B-17. There had been no practice runs for him. The operational sortie was his first "solo" mission. He had, however, been briefed on the Watten target, and he carried with him a full target description. He understood from it that the most vulnerable aspect of the target was a fifteen-by-sixteen-foot opening on the east side of the main bunker. The objective, therefore, was to fly the B-17 around its target, to hit it from the east, as close to the opening as possible. Even if a blast door were closed over it, the fortress was still most vulnerable at this point.

Yet the very notion of getting the baby anywhere near that fifteen-by-sixteen-foot bull's-eye—flying it from a vantage point 20,000 feet above—was highly optimistic, to put it mildly. Hargis figured the best he could do was to hit the main building somewhere, anywhere. That, at least, should cause as much damage as a Tallboy, maybe even a lot more.

Of course, that was assuming the baby could be controlled adequately enough to get it across the Channel. And suddenly it began to look as if No. 342 would not make it much beyond the English coastal countryside. Barrage balloons—unmanned tethered blimps—were flying from British ships and moorings in the shallows of the North Sea just east of the coast. Their purpose was to prevent German bombers from coming in low for raids. Each balloon floated at an altitude of 1,500 feet and carried aloft cabling strong enough to ensnare, cripple, or crash any aircraft that blundered into it. Orders had been given to haul in the barrage balloons prior to the launch of Mission 515. Clearly, those orders had been ignored, and Tooman and Hargis watched helplessly as the B-17 baby, flying now at just 300 feet, plowed through the balloon-and-cable thicket—miraculously without snagging anything. Once the aircraft was clear of the balloons, Tooman, on the interphone with Hargis, pronounced this feat of flying precisely what it was: "dumb luck."[22]

He had, however, spoken too soon. Although the baby cleared the barrage balloons and their cables, telltale bursts of flak near the aircraft indicated that British antiaircraft gunners either had not received orders to stand down during the Aphrodite sortie or they just didn't care. Tooman angrily suggested that Hargis steer the baby right into the ack-ack. With the loaded B-17 at just 300 feet, the blast touched off by a direct hit would ensure that English gunners would "never fire on a friendly again."[23] But Hargis continued to fly the prescribed course, easing the baby left, out over the English Channel and on a course for the Pas-de-Calais.

Before long, fresh flak bursts appeared—from the Germans' coastal batteries. As best he could with his two control switches governing the rudder to execute skidding turns, Hargis executed some halfhearted evasive moves. Yet, miracle of miracles, he could see that the baby was headed dead on target. He couldn't promise he'd be able to fly it around and walk it through that fifteen-by-sixteen-foot doorway, but it did look certain he'd at least hit the broadside of the bunker.

Hargis announced excitedly into the interphone that they had "a good one"—"If they [the German flak gunners] don't hit her."[24]

The bombardier was mindful of his briefing instruction to flip the dump switch when No. 342 was 1,000 feet from its target. This distance had been marked on any number of recon photographs, and the bombardier instantly recognized the defining landmark. The location of this dump point was based on the calculations Captain Joe Bender had furnished on orders from Major General Partridge, who had demanded to know just where a baby would hit when it was dumped.

Hargis flipped the switch.

Nothing happened.

Tooman yelled through the interphone to hit it, hit the dump switch! "I did hit it," Hargis protested. "It's not responding."[25]

When the navigator piped in to ask Tooman for their next move, the pilot replied, "We turn the stupid son of a bitch around and try again."[26]

Hearing this, another voice over the interphone pointed out that the baby would draw a lot of flak, now that the element of surprise had been lost. "Screw the flak!" Tooman shot back.[27]

Hargis, in the meantime, voiced his assessment that making a second pass was no use. The baby, he said, just wouldn't respond to the *down* command. Each sortie included two mother ships, a primary and an alternate. Heeding Hargis's assessment, Tooman spoke the code phrase "New umpire," which signaled the alternate mother ship to take over. There *was* a chance that the problem was with the transmitter, not the receiver. The alternate quickly positioned itself, its bombardier flipped his dump switch, and, again, nothing happened.

A frustrated airman on Tooman's B-24 suggested that they just keep the baby flying in a circle until it ran out of gas—then let it go down on its own and blow up something or other.

"Yeah," Tooman responded. "Great idea. Maybe we can wipe out Caen or St. Pol, or maybe we'll just get some nice little French village."[28]

After a few moments, Tooman ordered Hargis to fly the baby directly in front of the German flak battery that had fired on it earlier. He wanted to create a target as tempting as it was impossible to miss.

Tooman did as he was told, the German gunners opened up on the lumbering B-17, but, just as it had passed through a forest of barrage balloon cables, British AAA, and the first round of German flak, it escaped harm even when deliberately exposed. Swearing loudly into the interphone, Tooman ordered another pass. Hargis's next 180 was so wide that it brought No. 342 considerably closer to the German battery.

The gunners opened up. Black flak obscured visibility from the mother ship—but the sudden bright bloom of unholy yellow fire, followed by a blast audible even at 21,000 feet, confirmed that the gunners had scored a hit—wiping out one war-weary, unmanned B-17 as well as themselves. The first sortie of Aphrodite Mission 515 was a total failure, but, thanks to the knowledge that they had at least managed to annihilate one German flak battery, not entirely without satisfaction for the crew of the mother ship.

*   *   *

TEN MINUTES AFTER POOL AND ENTERLINE had taken off in No. 342, Lieutenant John Fisher and Technical Sergeant Elmer Most rolled out to the end of the runway in No. 835. Fisher swung the aircraft into the wind, accelerated down the strip, and lifted off with a full fifty yards to spare. Despite a loaded weight of 60,000 pounds, Fisher's ship took off "like a scalded dog," as Tooman had admiringly observed.[29]

No. 835 was targeted on the Siracourt V-1 bunker,[30] situated a few miles due south, inland, from the Watten bunker. The Germans code-named it Wasserwerk St. Pol (St. Pol Waterworks). While the V-1 buzz bomb had been under development, top Luftwaffe commanders argued over whether the missiles should be launched from massive fixed bunkers or lighter, more mobile bases. General der Luftwaffe Walther von Axthelm favored deploying the V-1s in a great many light installations, which could be camouflaged and moved about. Aware that Hitler wanted to build massive bunkers, Generalfeldmarschall Erhard Milch argued for these instead. Ultimately, however, Milch compromised on a combination of the two approaches. As noted, the light structures were to be widely deployed in three lines, or *Stellungsysteme* (setting systems). As for the heavy *Wasserwerk*-type bunkers, just four were to be built—and, of these four, only Wasserwerk St. Pol, near Siracourt, was ever constructed.

The bunker was built using an ingenious new method intended to provide protection from air raids during construction. Called *Verbunkerung,* the procedure began by building the roof flat on the ground and then excavating beneath it to create the rest of the facility underground and therefore sheltered from attack. The resulting building measured 705 feet long by 118 feet wide and was 33 feet high (or, more precisely, deep). The bunker would function as a massive storage and service facility for V-1 cruise missiles. It was to be connected to two catapult launch rails, the structures Allied reconnaissance pilots called ski jumps. Within the bunker, a chemical gas generator was to create high-pressure steam to actuate a catapult piston that propelled the missile into flight along the 160-foot launch rail.

Despite the Verbunkerung technique, Allied reconnaissance pilots discovered the Siracourt bunker almost immediately after construction began in September 1943. Starting with an attack by 74 U.S. Army Air Forces B-24 Liberators on January 31, 1944, a total of twenty-seven air raids were launched against the site before Fisher and Most took off on August 4. As was the case with the Watten bunker, Siracourt was abandoned by the time Aphrodite became operational. Although both facilities appeared to be intact and even active—misleading Allied planners to conclude that conventional bombing had had little effect on them—neither battered base had ever fired a missile nor ever would.

Beginning with the flawless takeoff, the mission profile of B-17 No. 835 promised perfection. This aircraft was the only one of Mission 515 Rand had been able to equip with television. A camera was mounted in the Plexiglas nose to capture and transmit a bombardier's-eye view. No camera covered the pilot's instruments. Major Rand, who was personally manning the radio controls, nevertheless had a good, if grainy, view.

As Fisher and Most neared the coast, the recon aircraft tasked with marking the parachute landings of the crew flew in close. Suddenly the baby went into a sharp climb. The video image on Rand's tiny monitor shifted from earth to sky. The recon pilots saw one man bail out at what turned out to be the apex of the climb. While this was happening, the voice of pilot John Fisher crackled over the radio: "Taxisoldier! Taxisoldier!"[31] It was the signal that he had left his seat and that the mother ship should immediately prepare to take control.

But none of the three switches at Rand's command was capable of correcting a climb. Nevertheless, the B-17 did begin to level out, and from one of the reconnaissance pilots, who was flying below the baby, came an exclamation that he saw legs dangling out the navigator's hatch. Just then, however, No. 835 entered another steep climb, and the legs withdrew back into the fuselage. With that, the aircraft again leveled out, and, for a second time, legs came out of the aircraft's belly. Before John Fisher could emerge fully, his B-17 jerked up into yet another climb, a climb so steep that the plane soon stalled and fell off on its left wing, tumbling, cartwheel fashion, out of control.

Flickering across Rand's video screen were disjointed images of sky and trees and ground, all whirling together. Rand could manage nothing more illuminating than "She's going down," sputtered into the interphone.[32]

The recon pilot who had earlier reported the emergence of legs from the escape hatch dived in for a closer look at the doomed baby. At 100 feet, he clearly saw a body fall out of the open hatch. Whether or not the man had hooked up his static line did not matter—at 100 feet the parachute would not have the time and altitude to open. Looking down as he climbed out of the dive, the recon pilot saw the aircraft and its pilot hit the ground at virtually the same instant. Aware that a very big explosion was coming, the recon pilot sheared up and away at full throttle.

Fain Pool heard the explosion almost immediately after his own parachute drop had ended in a rough landing. He had mistakenly assumed that it was *his* airplane. Generals Doolittle and Partridge, each flying his own P-38 a bit more than a quarter mile behind No. 835, were buffeted sharply by the blast wave but managed to retain control of their airplanes. The shock impulse tilted one of the navigation B-17s, also within a quarter mile of the impact, sharply to its side. The tail gunner, tucked tightly into his cramped perch, hit his head and suffered a mild concussion.

In USAAF records, the premature loss of B-17 No. 835 and the death of Lieutenant John Fisher were misattributed to the pilot's having "abandoned aircraft too soon."[33] Just before Fisher had taken off, Pappy Tooman had remarked to his copilot that "This is the one that worries me. This guy's been acting jittery all week, and I think he's a little flak happy"[34]—the Air Corps equivalent of what the infantry more formally called battle fatigue. But the cause of the fatal event was clearly a failure of primitive electronics. Technical Sergeant Most, who survived his bailout, later reported that he and Fisher struggled to get the ACE to function—the same device that had caused trouble for Pool and Enterline. In their case, they forced the ACE to work by descending below the 1,800-foot mission minimum, all the way down to 1,200 feet, at which point the ACE received its bounce-back signal from the ground and functioned accurately. Noting that, at 2,000 feet, the ACE inaccurately registered 300 feet, neither Fisher nor Most thought of descending. Instead, Most tried readjusting the device. His efforts triggered the series of sharp climbs.

During his debriefing, Most reported that Fisher ordered him to "get out, and I headed out the hatch with him right after me." Unlike most aircrew members, Elmer Most was a big man—topping six feet and heavyset. He explained: "There wasn't room for me and both my chutes through [the navigator's escape hatch, so] I stuck there, and Lieutenant Fisher put his foot on my shoulder and shoved me through."[35]

* * *

"SEND ANOTHER BABY!" Major Rand bellowed into the radio after John Fisher's crashed airplane exploded into yellow flame in the woods adjacent to the village of Sudbourne. "I'm up here. We might as well get the job done!"[36]

The radio traffic of all the sorties of Mission 515 was broadcast that day over loudspeakers in the two mission-ready rooms at Fersfield—one for enlisted personnel and one for officers, including Roy Forrest, who sat at a desk with radio equipment and could communicate directly with all of the aircraft deployed. When he heard Rand calling for another baby, Forrest asked why. One of the recon pilots radioed back that Fisher's plane had gone out of control, stalled, and then "fell off on a wing and went in." Forrest asked if anyone had gotten out. The recon pilot answered that one man did, adding "The pilot [also] got out, but the plane fell on him."[37] At this, Forrest asked if the B-17 had exploded on impact. The recon pilot answered that it had blown a hole in the forest.

"No town nearby?"

"No, sir. We lucked out on that one."[38]

Under the circumstances, it *did* feel lucky. An impact on a town could have killed hundreds, maybe even more. Forrest signed off, and then called for Joe Andrecheck and Cornelius Engel to "shag ass," announcing to them that they were the two jump pilots up next.[39]

Among those who heard Forrest's order was Frank Houston, the backup pilot to the four sorties of August 4. As he understood it, *he* should have been slotted in to fly the failed mission targeting Siracourt. Andrecheck's and Engel's B-17s were targeted on two other sites. Houston wasted little time pondering why he'd been passed over, however. Years later, he admitted that the only thing on his mind was how unbelievably lucky he was. He continued listening to the radio traffic but now with the relief of a man whose execution had been cancelled—or at least stayed. Houston was especially concerned about the very thing that had given Pool and Enterline pause: the way the B-17 babies had been made top-heavy by overloading them with nitrostarch. When he first saw the way their plane was loaded, Houston's electronics expert, Willard Smith—called "Smitty"—told Houston that he'd "been involved in some half-ass things in my life, but this is the all-time low. If my worst enemy had designed this system, it couldn't be worse. How can they expect to steer this airplane into a target when it obviously isn't even airworthy?"[40] Much as Pool would resolve to rely on his rudder for flat turns, to avoid banking, Smitty asked Houston to under-control the B-17 by making no sharply banking turns. Houston agreed.

Thankfully, Houston could now look at this exchange with Smitty as moot. They were not flying; Andrecheck and Engel were. But then Forrest's voice sounded out over the ready room.

"Who's the supernumerary?" And when there was no immediate response—for Houston (he later admitted) had sunk down in his chair, as if to hide—the base CO demanded, "Come on, we haven't got all day."[41]

Before Houston could muster the voice to respond, someone else identified him. Forrest gave him the same order he had given Andrecheck: *Shag ass.* Andrecheck, it seemed, had just radioed from the hardstand that his controls where dead. Forrest explained to Houston that, when the nitrostarch was loaded and tied down in Andrecheck's plane, a couple of control cables had gotten bound up and couldn't move. The only thing to do now was to defuse the entire load, take it out, fix the cables, and then reload.

Normally, Houston would not have cared about the explanation. The point—the really awful point—was that *he* was flying and Andrecheck now had the reprieve that had been *his*. And that was the only point that mattered. Except that, this time, the explanation made it all, bad as it was, even worse. Despite Smitty's sensible arguments about the top-heavy load, Houston tried to comfort himself with the notion that the people who put the mission together were very smart people— engineers and scientists. So, yes, it *looked* bad. The load certainly *looked* top-heavy. But they, the planners, must know what they're doing when it comes to loading the plane. Except that Andrecheck had just gotten to live to see another day because his controls had been killed because someone didn't know how to load a plane properly. Smitty's doubt, pessimism, and foreboding had just received an undeniably practical ratification.

Nevertheless, Houston left the officer's ready room, poked his head into the enlisted men's ready room, and called out to Smitty, *Let's go.*

Houston fully expected his electronics man to be even more reluctant than he himself was. Instead, Smith responded with cheery fatalism: "Well, if we gotta go, we gotta go, eh, Lieutenant?" As the two men took their seats in the back of the jeep that carried them to the hardstand, the enlisted man took the liberty of slapping the officer on the knee. "Anyway," he said with a smile, "it's a nice day for flying."[42]

Initially, Houston was shocked by Smitty's display of complete calm. Perhaps he was relieved that he would not have a panic-stricken autopilot specialist on his hands. In some ways, however, the enlisted man's nonchalance must have only added to his own anxiety, as he now feared betraying his own barely suppressed terror. Before long, however, Houston experienced a phenomenon many others experience in combat. Fear of shame—of his subordinate thinking him a coward— overtook the fear of death itself. As Houston strained to control his emotions, it suddenly occurred to him that Smitty had not yet heard about Fisher's fate. Even knowing that it would be ornery as hell to shatter his blissful innocence, Houston could not stop himself from asking, "You heard about Fisher, didn't you?"[43]

"Sure," Smitty answered without emotion. "We all heard it." Then he allowed: "Tough break."[44]

Houston must have been disappointed. If his subordinate's calm was not due to ignorance, was its source a level of courage superior to his own? Maybe. Or maybe it was all about one man not wanting to show his fear to another. Whatever the explanation, Houston understood that his task now was to go through all the preflight routines and get B-17 No. 461 airborne. As for Smitty, unlike Enterline flying with Pool, he did not forget to set 25 percent flaps. As a result, the aircraft cleared the vegetable garden and pine trees at the end of the runway with much less drama than Pool's aircraft had. Once airborne, Smitty at last spoke up: "Now remember, Lieutenant, we won't make any sharp turns, will we?"[45]

Despite having been addressed rather like a misbehaving child, Houston was grateful for the reminder—not because he had forgotten the earlier conversation, in which Willard Smith had stressed the importance of level flight in a hopelessly top-heavy aircraft, but because he was now certain that Smitty was as scared as he was. That knowledge gave him the strength to generate nonchalance of his own: "Don't worry about a thing, Buddy-o. We're in the air now. It's all routine from here on!"[46]

"The worst is over now," Smitty agreed.[47]

No sooner were the words out of Smitty's mouth than No. 461 bumbled into a swarming succession of B-24 Liberators rising to get into formation for a "routine" bombing raid. The wartime airspace over England was crowded and air traffic control primitive. On a rare day of CAVU, various elements of the Eighth U.S. Air Force were mustered to fly and to drop their bombs. Houston had no choice but to execute a sudden 90-degree banking turn—precisely the kind of maneuver Smitty had predicted would result in catastrophe—as the electronics expert, lacking a seat in the stripped-bare B-17, clung on to Houston's seat for dear life.

The maneuver averted a midair collision, which would have been disastrous both for the crew of No. 461 and for any number of Liberators, but, as Smitty had feared, the top-heavy bomber was very difficult to control. It continued to shear away from the rising B-24s, and Houston had to manhandle it back into straight-and-level flight. Smith instantly understood his role in the situation. Clawing his way to the copilot's position—which lacked a seat but still had a functional set of controls, including the yoke—Smith laid hold of the copilot's yoke and, on Houston's command, helped him recover from the evasive turn. From this moment on, as Houston embarked on the rectangular pattern of flight that gave the men time and space to calibrate the autopilot and set the controls, he executed each corner of the rectangle using rudder only. The turns skidded sloppily across the sky, but they kept the aircraft level. He was not about to tempt fate a second time.

Houston sent Smitty below to calibrate the ACE and set the autopilot. As was not the case in Pool's and Enterline's plane, the ACE functioned perfectly. All the warning lights dutifully winked out, and Smitty was able to move on to setting the autopilot in just a few seconds. He shouted up to Houston that the ACE and autopilot were ready, and Houston told him to *go*. After hooking onto the static line, Smitty prepared to jump. Houston repeated his *go* command, and Technical Sergeant Willard Smith dangled his legs through the escape hatch and then shoved himself free of the plane, with its menacing number 2 propeller.

He felt a terrific jolt on exiting, as the nearly 200-mile-per-hour slipstream snapped his body from vertical to horizontal. He saw that his head had narrowly missed the ventral antenna support that protruded from the belly of the fuselage. Then came the second, even more violent jolt as his main chute deployed in a white rush above him.

The jolts were unforgettable, of course, but what he remembered most when he narrated the jump some twenty-five years later was the intoxicating scent of the summer air over the farmlands of England. It was the scent of life itself. Against his own reckoning of the odds, Willard Smith of Doylestown, Pennsylvania, came to a surprisingly gentle landing in the weeds.

As Smith jumped, descended, and landed, Frank Houston reduced his air speed to 175 miles per hour and commenced the gentle dive that would bring the B-17 to the 300-foot altitude at which the ACE would automatically hold it as the bombardier in the mother ship guided it across the Channel. This job completed, he transmitted the "Taxisoldier" code word twice, then rose from his seat, turned, and prepared to drop into the crawlspace. Interviewed years later, he remarked on his own calm, a sensation that surprised even him. Where was the panic, the terrible fear?

Without warning, Houston found himself supine on the deck of the bomber, loudly strangling. The "calm" pilot had left his seat without unfastening his throat mike, which yanked him back like a choke chain around a dog's neck—transmitting, in the process, every death rattle–like gurgle.

With confused, questioning voices sounding in his headphones, Houston returned to his seat and repeated, "Taxisoldier."

Foster Falkenstein, piloting the mother ship, replied with "Roger," punctuated, however, by a verbal question mark rather than the customary period—*Roger?*

"That's right," Houston repeated with testy emphasis. "Taxisoldier!"[48]

Until he told his story to Jack Olsen in the late 1960s, Frank Houston never revealed his rookie mistake. After the mission, asked about the ungodly noises, he denied having heard, let alone produced, anything of the kind. He suggested they might all have been victims of a new type of German radio-jamming signal.

His little accident with the throat mike had cost some time—plus, he estimated, 300 feet of altitude. That put him at 1,500 feet, and he did not want to bail out below 1,000. Before lowering himself into the crawlspace, he set the safety clock for ten minutes. Once in the crawlspace, he pulled the lanyard to arm the fourteen impact fuses linked to the crates of nitrostarch and then inserted the two jacks to arm the redundant electric backup. Figuring that the two minutes spent doing these things had brought him down to 1,300 feet, he put on his emergency chest-pack parachute and connected his seat pack to the static line.

Time to jump—and with precious little time and altitude to spare!

And yet he found that he was unable to force himself to step out into the narrow void that was the navigator's escape hatch. Many a paratrooper trainee has frozen in the door of the C-47 at the moment of truth. Chickening out at the last moment was terrible—humiliating—but not fatal. At least, it was not when flying round-trip in a C-47. But riding a loaded bomb, Houston knew there was no turning back—and no alternative to jumping other than death by horrific explosion.

Still, he could not bring himself to do what Smitty had done: leap. Instead, he sat on his seat pack, inching his way across the deck, like a toddler at play. When his feet reached the lip of the hatch, he dangled them over as he sat on the edge. The fierce slipstream pulled at his pants and boots—pulled harder and harder, until, without any act of will on his part, it sucked him out of the airplane.

Rolling involuntarily on his back, he saw the brilliant blue of the CAVU sky, felt the static line pull at him with a surprising gentleness. He cringed as he awaited the "Mack truck" impact of the opening chute.

It did not come.

He was falling—trailing thirty-five feet of static line behind him. The stout ribbon had torn off at the root. It was attached to his seat pack but not to the airplane. Houston's scant parachute training kicking in, he pulled the red ripcord handle of his emergency backup. The pack cover tore away, as it was supposed to—but the parachute inside remained inert, folded. With frantic hands, he grabbed at the white silken material, manually paying out the emergency chute, which began to catch the wind just as leaves and twigs and branches cracked and flew all around him.

If you are coming in for a hard landing, his parachute instructor had told him, *cover your throat with one hand and your crotch with the other.* This, however, was a set of gestures far from instinctual. Both of Houston's hands instantly flew up over his face.

Later, much later, he reported how the leaves and branches got thicker and thicker until his plunge to certain death suddenly stopped with a shot of searing pain through one shoulder even as his legs went cold dead on him. Everything turned black, until he was violently flung upward, in precisely the opposite direction of his fall, back upward through branches and leaves. He reached a slingshot apogee, then descended again, but just a short distance, and came to rest, hanging, swaying in his harness from a flexible bough, some eight feet off the ground.

The tree had broken his fall, but now it had him in its grip. Houston twisted and turned in an effort to get at the small jackknife he had in his pants pocket. He succeeded, however, only in tangling himself more hopelessly in the parachute risers. Eventually, letting his head fall backward, he saw an old man in overalls standing some ten feet away. The man stared but said nothing.

Houston called out: "Hey!"

The old man's mouth fell open. But no words issued from it, and he made no other motion.

"What the hell are you looking at, you idiot?" Houston screamed.

"Are you a Yank?" the old man asked.

"You're goddamn right I'm a Yank!"

This elicited nothing more from the old man than his continued gaze.

Houston swore again. "Can't you see I'm stuck? Now help me get out of here!"

"Are you quite sure you're a Yank?"

By way of response, Houston delivered his name, rank, and serial number, followed by his hometown, the name and address of his mother, and whatever other useless American information he could dredge up.

But the old man persisted. "If you're a Yank, what are you doing in that tree?"

In an extremity of exasperation, Houston bellowed that he was picking raspberries and then—with singular irrelevance—threatened to summon a "constable" if the man did not help. Bizarrely enough, that threat was sufficient to elicit, at long last, an offer of assistance: "Well, what can I do?"

Houston asked for a knife, which the old man handed him. He cut the risers, landed beside the man, got to his feet, returned the knife along with an icy glare, and then set off—only to collapse at the old man's feet after a few steps.

The farmer, uncomprehending as ever, stood silently.

"I'm still a Yank," Houston said.

With that, the old man promised to fetch help.[49]

* * *

FOR THEIR PART, mother ship pilot Lieutenant Foster Falkenstine and controller Jim Rand were practically as uncomprehending as the East Anglian farmer. Speculating on the weird strangling noises they had heard and having failed to get any report from the recon pilots of his bailing out, the two wondered if Frank Houston might still be in the baby, perhaps disabled or unconscious. It was a puzzle that seemed impossible to unknot—until Rand, like Alexander the Great, applied the blade of a simple, swordlike solution. He declared that Houston had indeed bailed out, based on the fact that, number one, he gave the code word and, number two, if he had *not* bailed out, one of the many planes observing the operation would have said something.

It was hardly impeccable logic, but Falkenstein agreed with it. Accordingly, Rand set about guiding No. 461 against Wizernes, which was a little closer than the alternate target, Mimoyecques. Code-named by the Germans Bauvorhaben 21 (Building Project 21) or Schotterwerk Nordwest (Northwest Gravel Works), the local French called it simply La Coupole (the Dome). Dug into the side of an abandoned chalk quarry, La Coupole was built near the village of Wizernes as a V-2 storage, arming, fueling, and mass launching facility. Truly grand, the installation, as planned, would have required a million tons of concrete to complete. Its enormous concrete dome—nearly 17 feet thick and with a diameter of 233 feet—sheltered the central facility, which accommodated workshops, storage areas, fuel tanks, a liquid oxygen generating plant, electric dynamos, a large barracks, and a small hospital. The facility was served by underground railway tunnels to enable it to receive completed V-2 rockets for storage and launch. While the principal intended target of these launches was London, well within range at just under 120 miles, American analysts noted that La Coupole had been sited within a half degree of the Great Circle bearing on New York City. Therefore, they assumed that it would also serve as a facility to store and launch—perhaps even to build—the so-called America Rocket, which some believed was the V-3.

Construction of La Coupole began in August 1943, and the Allies launched the first air raid against the site on March 11, 1944. This was followed by a dozen more attacks, including, on July 17, the dropping of a dozen Tallboys. Whereas the previous attacks caused minimal damage, the damage inflicted by the Tallboys was major—a fact that was not clearly apparent from aerial photography. As with Watten and Siracourt, the site was abandoned before it became operational; however, the Germans kept up the appearance of activity in order to lure additional Allied bombers to waste munitions, planes, and time and to expose aircraft and crews to defensive fire. Two more conventional bombing raids followed the assault of July 17—though only the first of those, on July 20, was able to drop on La Coupole. A raid on July 21–22 was turned away because of bad weather.

As far as Allied intelligence was concerned, La Coupole remained a major threat on August 4, 1944, and Rand eagerly guided the baby over the final English checkpoint, Orford Ness, on the Suffolk coast. He was distressed by white puffs, which drifted between the mother ship, at 21,000 feet, and the baby, at 300. Puzzled—since flak bursts are black—he asked Falkenstine what they were.

The answer was not what he wanted to hear. They were clouds—suddenly materialized out of cloudless sky.

Falkenstine's navigator affirmed that they and the baby below were on course, and Rand, squinting through his modified bombsight, repeatedly caught glimpses of the bright white wings of the baby through the thickening clouds below. Falkenstine, in the meantime, shouted out his sighting of the great white dome that gave La Coupole its name.

As far as he could tell from decreasingly frequent flashes of the baby's white wings, it was headed straight for that dome. The B-17 was responding with gratifying crispness to the left and right azimuth switches. The ACE was holding the 300-foot altitude. Between the increasing cloud cover and the anticipation of an assault by some 400 German antiaircraft guns, the approach was incredibly tense, however. If visibility could be maintained and the guns held off for just a minute or two more, the baby would be 1,000 feet from its target, the point at which throwing the dump switch would send it directly into the dome.

At very nearly the dump point, the baby entered a cloud and became totally invisible to Rand. He had no choice but to do quick math in his head, calculate the 1,000-foot point, and flip the switch.

A moment later, Falkenstine sighted the baby through a break in the clouds. He reported his hopeful impression that it was descending, and began a steep bank to observe. Rand, bracing himself against the G's, gazed out of the Plexiglas of the bombardier's compartment in the nose of the B-24 mother ship.

There it was! And in perfect alignment with the dome. Another cloud intervened. Again unable to see the baby, Rand waited for the explosion. But then those bright white wings unexpectedly reappeared.

"Get down! Get down, you son of a bitch!" Rand screamed.[50]

Too late. Once again, the dump switch had failed to dive a robot bomb. The B-17 overshot La Coupole by a quarter of a mile before exploding into a massive yellow fireball.

Falkenstine and Rand assumed that it had descended, albeit in a shallow rather than steep dive, making its impact beyond its intended target. A Luftwaffe intelligence document, captured later, reported that it had actually been shot down by flak and had exploded upon the impact of a flak burst, producing fragments that were scattered over a radius between 500 and 1,500 meters (1,640 and 4,920 feet), fragments big enough to create some impressive craters (including one measuring 20 meters [66 feet] across). "No traces of a crew or aerial guns were found," the document stated, concluding that a "great quantity of explosives must have been used, based on the complete destruction of aircraft."[51] The Aphrodite personnel did not know it at the time, of course, but the observations in the Luftwaffe document revealed that German intelligence had guessed that the Allies were attacking their missile fortresses and bunkers with remote-control aircraft bombs.

*   *   *

ALTHOUGH BY THIS TIME Fersfield had some forty war-weary B-17s on base, just one flight-ready baby remained unspent by the late afternoon of August 4. Manned by Lieutenant Cornelius Engel and Tech Sergeant Clifford Parsons, it rolled down the runway at 4:02, just minutes after Rand signaled that the attack on La Coupole at Wizernes had been a failure.

Instead of taking another run at La Coupole, the fourth baby would be guided against Mimoyecques, the fortress under a chalk hill at the Pas-de-Calais, a few miles due north of Wizernes. Unlike Aphrodite's first three targets, Mimoyecques was never officially abandoned, but relentless Allied air raids at first reduced the operational plan for the site and then indefinitely suspended it before the commencement of Operation Aphrodite.

Takeoff was uneventful, but while flying the rectangular checking course over England, Engel saw bursts of "friendly" flak. The Aphrodite pilots had strict orders to abandon their aircraft if they were fired on. Accordingly, Engel shouted to Parsons, who was down in the crawlspace wrestling with the autopilot, on which the warning lights were proving difficult to tune out. Engel barked at him to bail out. Intent on tuning the autopilot, however, Parsons kept turning knobs.

"Goddamn it, Sergeant, they're firing on us. Get out of that hole!"[52]

Reluctantly, Parsons struggled into his chest pack, lowered his legs through the navigator's escape hatch, and began to feel the powerful pull of the slipstream, drawing his legs and then his lower body out the hatch. As the rushing wind pushed his lower torso parallel with the fuselage, he hung on—only to realize that he had forgotten to attach the static line to his seat pack. Exerting all his might, Parsons pulled himself back into the airplane, hooked up, and then dropped through the hole again.

The rest was a textbook jump—up to a point. The static line ripped the pack, the parachute billowed up, there was a sharp jerk of deceleration and then a relatively gentle descent. However, Parsons landed not on the ground but on the steep gable roof of a house, from which he soon slipped, falling two stories and painfully spraining his ankle.

Under fire, pilot Cornelius Engel had standing orders to bail out. Moreover, the aircraft was acting erratically because the balky autopilot had not been fully adjusted when Parsons obeyed his order and jumped. Nevertheless, Parsons radioed his "Taxisoldier," indicating that he had left his seat, hastily performed both the manual and electrical arming procedures, and then bailed out. Like Frank Houston, he suffered both a main parachute failure and the failure of his emergency chest pack. Like Houston, he clawed frantically at the chest pack in an effort to get enough silk into the air to slow his descent. When he landed, he landed very hard. Several of his teeth were pushed back into his throat, and his back was severely sprained.

From the perspective of mother ship pilot Pappy Tooman and bombardier-controller Glen Hargis, the behavior of the baby defied explanation. The aircraft persisted in climbing far above the 300-foot altitude on which all target calculations had been based. After climbing, the baby repeatedly stalled and descended. When Hargis complained that there was no way to control it, Tooman advised him to improvise. After failing to gain any degree of control, however, he told Tooman that he was going to hit the dump switch just long enough to apply full down elevator in an effort to get down to 300 feet.

"It won't work," Tooman replied, "but you might as well try."[53]

Hargis could see the Mimoyecques fortress in the distance. Under the influence of the dump switch, the baby descended. Hargis moved the switch to *off,* hoping that the ACE would level the baby out at 300. Instead, the aircraft continued its descent and augered in at least 1,500 feet short of the target, producing a greenish-yellow fireball that Tooman, for the benefit of his crew, announced over the interphone as "the biggest explosion you'll ever see." Pausing, he then added the obvious: "Too bad it didn't hit something."[54]

At this point both Tooman and Hargis realized that flak was exploding all around them. In the intensity of his effort to help Hargis gain control of the baby, Tooman had let his B-24 mother ship descend to 6,000 feet—well within flak range: *British* flak range. This time, however, the gunners were not actually firing at the Allied aircraft. The voice of Tooman's tail gunner roared over the interphone: "Hey, we're in the goddamn middle of a goddamn buzz bomb attack"![55]

As misfortune would have it, the final Aphrodite sortie of the day crossed paths with an incoming German V-1 attack. The English AAA gunners had not been firing at the baby and were not now firing at the B-24. They were trying to shoot down doodlebugs before they reached London.

Tooman radioed for a cease-fire but received no response. He veered north-northeast, flying out along the coast, in a successful effort to outrun the range of the Dover-based AAA batteries.

*   *   *

EARLY THAT EVENING, Lieutenant Colonel Forrest debriefed the crews of the four failed missions. Their record was valiant but completely void of achievement. True, no one had blown themselves up, and no aircraft had killed any English civilians. But one man had died and others had been injured. The radio controls, the ACE, the autopilot, the arming mechanisms—all were largely improvised, and their unreliability was understandable. The technology was untested. But the injuries, if not the single fatality, were all directly attributable to a piece of technology that was both simple and time-tested: the parachute. For its repeated failures, there was no excuse.

"Ain't that beautiful?" Forrest remarked. "Four up and four down, and nothing near a target. The end of a perfect day."[56]

When the debriefings were completed, Forrest checked in at the officers' club. Seeing Frank Houston at the bar, he slapped him heartily on the back.

Houston involuntarily spat out a mouthful of whisky.

"Colonel!" he exclaimed. "Please don't interrupt me, sir. I will be drunk in a few minutes and ready for action."[57]

When Forrest asked him what he meant by that, Houston answered that he had "to kill a man with my bare hands tonight, and I've never killed a man before, and I'm getting up my courage."[58]

Taking the bait, Forrest asked him who he was going to kill.

"The parachute man."

"You can't kill him . . . I've already shipped him out."[59]

That item of news delivered, Forrest issued another.

"I've asked Major Rand to bring up another baby for you," he told Houston.

Rising from his barstool and assuming the exaggerated brace of a West Point cadet, Houston replied: "Sir, I appreciate your kind offer. Sir, I joined the Army Air Corps because I love my country. Sir, because of my intense love and devotion for my country, I wish to tell you what I think of your kind offer. Sir, kindly take your kind offer and shove it up your ass!"[60]

Houston's response merited a court martial. From Forrest, it received a sustained burst of raucous laughter—and Houston was duly "unvolunteered." Fain Pool, however, rushed up to Forrest at the bar, raised a glass of bourbon to him, and promptly volunteered to jump again.

Nonplussed, Forrest responded, "You're what?"

"With your permission, I'd like to volunteer for another mission."

Forrest grinned broadly at Pool, put his arm around his shoulder, and told Pool he liked him and always had. But, he continued, "there is one very basic reason why I don't drink to that, and why you won't fly another mission."

"What's that, sir?"

"Because you're demented, that's why!" And he went on to explain the basis of his diagnosis: "Any son of a bitch that volunteers to do this twice has got to be crazy."[61]

Having downed several gins, Forrest stopped by the orderly room on his way to his quarters. Finding his G-2 (intelligence officer) laboring away at his typewriter, Forrest asked him why it was taking him so long to write up the report on Mission 515. The G-2 answered that it was tough to get the wording right. "We had a lousy day, and I'm trying not to say so."[62]

Forrest gently pushed the G-2 out of his chair and sat down in front of the keyboard himself. He typed deliberately, pulled the paper out of the carriage, and read aloud from it:

> Mother and robot crews feel that the equipment is good and are satisfied that they can make successful attacks. They derived good experience from the missions and have gained a great deal of confidence in the project.[63]

Handing the G-2 the paper, he told him to put all the stats in front of it and then send it up through channels, culminating with Hap Arnold, commander of the USAAF.

⁂

THE NEXT NIGHT, August 5, German aircraft circled Fersfield and dropped a load of bombs, which went wide by six miles. Frank Houston was glad that the attack hadn't interrupted the resumption of the celebratory bender he had begun the evening before. As he downed a whisky at the officer's club, he greeted Joe Kennedy, Jr. as the young man bellied up to the bar.

"If my Old Man was an ambassador, I'd get my ass transferred out of this outfit," he told him.[64]

By way of reply, Kennedy only smiled.

CHAPTER 8

A BASKETFUL OF
RATTLESNAKES

THE SUNDAY AFTER THE FAILED SORTIES OF MISSION 515, AUGUST 6, was warm and sunny. Joe Kennedy and the pilot and copilot of one of the navy's mother ships bicycled back from Mass, which they had been granted a special pass to attend. They stopped to rest in the shade of a hedgerow.

"Jeez," Joe announced to his companions. "I just wonder about this damn mission . . ."[1] Apparently, United States Army Air Forces commanding general Hap Arnold harbored no similar doubts. His reply to the August 4 mission report Roy Forrest dashed off for his stymied G-2 glowed:

> PRELIMINARY REPORT ON YOUR AUG. FOUR EFFORT VERY ENCOURAG-
> ING. ALL PERSONNEL CONCERNED ARE TO BE COMMENDED.

Arnold's congratulatory tone was a far cry from Forrest's own private assessment of "Four up and four down, and nothing near a target." After reading the cable, Forrest turned to a staff officer, Lloyd "Humpy" Humphries: "Well, well, Humpy, nothing succeeds like failure."[2]

The fact was that few Air Corps officers shared Arnold's optimism. On the evening after Mission 515, following an informal dinner Lieutenant General Carl Spaatz hosted at U.S. Strategic Air Forces in Europe headquarters in Bushy Park, Forrest repeatedly encountered smug grins, snickers, and grimaces whenever Operation Aphrodite was brought up. He finally confronted his patronizing fellow officers, asking them to simply speak their minds. Most quietly backed down, but a few told Forrest bluntly that Aphrodite was almost universally regarded as a joke—at least among those below the level of Arnold and Spaatz. No one, they said, was surprised that the August 4 mission had accomplished nothing tangible.

Stiffening, Forrest nevertheless refused to bristle.

"If the project's a joke," he calmly rejoined, "then how come it's got the top priority in the theater and everybody keeps telling us how important we are?"

When no one offered a response, he invited everyone to "act like honest people. If your feeling is that we're not doing the job, then let's scrub the son of a bitch, and I'll go home and meet my new daughter."[3]

It was a grand rhetorical gesture, but it elicited a response that stunned Forrest. A lieutenant colonel spoke for the group when he told him that "we'd all *love* to scrub this damned fool model-airplane program you're running, but we can't."[4]

Growing hot at last, Forrest asked why not and was told that Aphrodite was "the Old Man's pride and joy and consuming interest."[5]

By "Old Man," Forrest assumed they were talking about Spaatz. But, no, he was corrected. They meant the leader of the entire Air Corps, Hap Arnold. He considered robot- and radio-controlled flight the future of military aviation, and he intended to see Aphrodite succeed. With that information, Forrest suddenly believed that nothing could stop the project he commanded. Moreover, the revelation allowed him to make sense of the sudden arrival of the naval unit—Project Anvil—at Fersfield. Arnold worked, lived, and breathed in the newly built Pentagon, not in Europe. His top-level colleagues were army, air corps, *and* navy leaders. Forrest initially assumed that Arnold had shared the secrets of Aphrodite with the navy and invited them to join the operation. It apparently did not occur to Forrest that the navy top brass may have shared *their* secrets with Arnold. Forrest would soon experience an awakening when he saw how far beyond Rand and Aphrodite the U.S. Navy had developed radio-controlled flight.

But the navy—and Joe Kennedy—were not yet at bat. The Army Air Corps had more missions to fly, and both Forrest and Rand were determined to make improvements before the next mission. First, Rand ordered new designs for loading. This was to address two issues: the impact on flight stability that resulted from loading the explosives too high and preventing any part of the load from fouling aircraft control cables. Forrest and Rand also followed the navy's lead by substituting Torpex for nitrostarch, which meant that the babies could carry a lighter load while still delivering the same explosive punch. This factor alone would solve the stability problem without compromising destructive effect. Rand used his top-priority Ike card to prevail on the Royal Navy to immediately furnish him with 500 tons of the stuff.

Forrest and Rand assigned Pappy Tooman to make test flights to figure out why the dump switch repeatedly failed to dive the baby. Tooman quickly discovered that the switch actually did work, in that the elevators responded to the down command. The problem, however, was that the autopilot and servo motors lacked the mechanical force to *hold* the elevators down. The first solution proposed was installing a heavy spring on the bell-crank arm that actuated the elevators. When the dump switch was applied, the elevator would snap full down—and stay there. Rand objected, however, arguing that the spring was too dangerous. If it somehow took hold while the baby was over England, the aircraft would enter an unrecoverable dive, killing pilot, electronics expert, and very likely blowing up several city blocks in the process. It was decided that controllers would just have to learn to anticipate the down command problem and keep throwing the dump switch in an effort to force and hold the elevators down.

The final problem that needed to be addressed urgently was parachuting. Five of the seven crew members who actually jumped—John Fisher *fell* out of his B-17 at low altitude—experienced parachute trouble and were, to varying degrees, injured. Jumpers were tearing up their fingers by instinctively grabbing for the lip of the navigator's escape hatch as they exited the plane. Reasoning that this was instinctual and reflexive, Rand sought to minimize rather than try to prevent the injury. He directed maintenance crews to smooth off the ridge at the aft end of the hatch, to enlarge the hatch as much as practicable—to afford an easier exit—and to install a wind deflector at the forward end of the hatch opening.

Of course, exiting the hatch was only one problem with bailing out. The other was parachute failure. Jump pilot Glen Barnes (who had not yet jumped) identified the static line as the root of the problem and suggested eliminating it. This, however, raised vehement objections from a senior engineering officer, who protested that an inexperienced jumper could not be expected to remember to pull the rip cord at all, let alone at a prescribed distance from the aircraft. The officer explained that the static line took care of everything for the jumper. All he had to do was *jump*.

Barnes countered with the simple fact that the record of the Aphrodite missions so far showed that the static line often failed. He could have ended there, but he continued, arguing that there was a strong possibility that the static line would not only fail but get fouled, either in the parachute rigging or on the body of the jumper, catching his arm, leg, torso, or even neck.

At this point, another technical officer broke in. He did not have an opinion as to whether the static line was good or bad for the jumper, but he *was* concerned about the effects of thirty-seven feet of heavy, woven nylon line whipping around after it had opened the parachute pack and the jumper was free. Everything about the ability to radio-control the drone, he pointed out, depended finally on the antennas sprouting from the belly of the aircraft. If any of them was damaged by the wildly whipping static line, controlling the baby might well prove impossible. One of the mother ship bombardiers seconded this concern, suggesting that it might have accounted for the malfunctioning of the radio altimeter—the ACE—at least twice.

It was all good, fast thinking. But, in the end, the only changes made were the explosive and the way it was loaded and the slight modification of the escape hatch. The issue of how to hold the elevators down was left mostly unresolved, as was the matter of the static lines. Everyone agreed the static lines left much to be desired, but the consensus was that eliminating them would introduce more problems than it cured. Thus, the lines would be retained for at least a few more missions, pending further developments.

So the two sorties scheduled to fly on August 6 would be flown in aircraft and with procedures little changed from those that had failed two days earlier. The sole significant innovation was tactical. Only the first of the babies, code-named *Franklin Yellow,* would be loaded with Torpex high explosives—9 tons of it. It would be aimed at the concrete bunker near Watten. If all went according to plan, its impact would, at the very least, blast cracks and fissures into the reinforced concrete structure. *Franklin White,* the second baby, was loaded with incendiaries: 9 incendiary bombs in the nose, 35 more in the pilot's compartment (leaving room for the pilot), 116 in the radio operator's compartment, and 20 more in the ball turret. In addition, 830 gallons of napalm were loaded into tanks and placed in the bomb bay. Pursuant to experiments conducted at Eglin Field, Florida, in which rats were suffocated in a scaled-down bunkerlike environment when gasoline was ignited over all exit holes, the idea was to crack open the Watten bunker with the first drone and then, with the second, suffocate (or burn to death) everyone inside it.

In standard USAAF air raids, incendiary attacks often followed the dropping of high explosives. The idea was that the blast debris created by the explosives made better kindling for the fires created by the incendiaries, thereby greatly increasing the net destructive impact of the raid. But, in the case of the attack on Watten, the tactic served only to multiply the chances of failure. For the two-drone raid to work as planned, *both* drones had to function perfectly, and both had to hit the target. The failure of the first would ensure the failure of the second—since incendiary devices would have virtually no effect on a concrete bunker that had not been breached.

If anyone questioned the wisdom of the two-drone tactic, no record of doubt exists. All we know is that Lieutenant Joe Andrecheck took command of the first baby, *Franklin Yellow,* and another pilot, Lieutenant John Sollars, followed ten minutes later in *Franklin White.* Andrecheck was the pilot whose control cables had been fouled by carelessly loaded crates of nitrostarch. The first thing he did when he took his seat in *Franklin Yellow* was to try the yoke and the rudder pedals. Satisfied that all was working well, he took off precisely on schedule, at 10:50 am, and the flight proceeded like a well-oiled machine. Sergeant Raymond Healy lowered himself into the crawlspace and was able to balance the autopilot and ACE within minutes—all warning lights obediently winking off. Healy shouted up the good news, and Andrecheck radioed "Flyball" (the new code word replacing "Taxisoldier") to signal that he was leaving his chair and that the mother ship crew should prepare to take over control. He shouted down to Healy his version of the order to jump: "Go! Have a nice trip!"[6]

Once Healy had jumped, Andrecheck radioed another new code phrase—"Change pictures"—confirming that he was surrendering control. After setting the ten-minute delay on the safety clock, he lowered himself into the crawlspace. All he had to do was pull the lanyard on the arming cables and insert two jacks into the redundant electrical arming system. Per protocol, he first checked the warning lights to make sure that the safety clock was holding the detonator switches open. If the lights were out, all was well. If they glowed, then plugging in the jacks would set off 9 tons of Torpex—instantly.

Things were going swimmingly when, much as Frank Houston found it all but impossible to force himself to jump out the escape hatch, Andrecheck could not take his eyes off the warning lights. They were out, clearly out. Yet the thought nagged at him. *What if they are glowing, ever so slightly—too dimly for me to see?* So he looked closer—and closer, putting his wide-open eye up to each bulb. His imagination flashed to a detonation, and he broke into the iciest of cold sweats. Panic—something he had never before experienced as a pilot—washed over him. Panic drove him to formulate a hasty escape plan. The electrical arming procedure was just a backup. No one would be the wiser if he skipped it, pulled the lanyard, and just slid through the escape hatch. *Now. Right now.*

In the end, he just couldn't do it. He could fool everyone, but he could not fool himself. "Well," he said aloud, "it'll blow up or it won't blow up, one or the other, and it won't take long to find out, that's for sure."[7]

With this, he rammed the jacks home, pulled the lanyard, and then let himself slip out the hatch. The chute opened just as it should, he floated to earth, scraping through the outermost branches of a scrubby pine, hit the ground with his feet, and, as he had been taught, rolled to one side. It was a perfect, painless landing. And things only got better. Finding that he had come to rest in the midst of an all-female antiaircraft gun crew, he answered their challenges with a prepared story about having to bail out of a burning airplane. In response, they invited him to tea—which was interrupted by the all-too-timely arrival of the U.S. military police, who scooped him up for a return ride to Fersfield.

In the meantime, the bombardier in the mother ship piloted by Foster Falkenstine guided the baby left and then flicked the switch to turn it right. In response, however, the baby turned left again. Then, unbidden, it executed a barrel roll onto its back and promptly crashed into English Channel.

* * *

TEN MINUTES AFTER *Franklin Yellow*'s perfect takeoff, *Franklin White* followed. After receiving the "Change pictures" code phrase from pilot Sollars, Glen Hargis, bombardier in Pappy Tooman's B-24 mother ship, took control. It quickly became apparent, however, that the autopilot had not been set up correctly. It failed to respond to either left or right signals.

Mission protocol dictated that the pilot would not bail out until the mother ship confirmed having established control of the baby. When Hargis told Tooman that the autopilot needed adjustment, he radioed *Franklin White* but received no response. The pilot of a recon aircraft listening in on the communications channel broke in: "*Franklin White* is empty."

"Son of a bitch!" Tooman called to Hargis over the interphone. "They both bailed early."[8]

On the off chance that the problem was on the transmission end, Tooman called in the alternate mother ship to take control. Tooman and Hargis watched as *Franklin White* began a 360-degree turn. Hargis assumed that the alternate controller was trying to put the baby on a new heading. What happened next made it clear that he was doing no such thing. *Franklin White* straightened out—and began flying a course straight for London.

Clearly, the alternate had *not* established control. No sooner did Tooman and Hargis realize this than *Franklin White* disappeared into a haze. Tooman ordered everyone on his mother ship to look for the errant baby. After ten minutes without catching sight of it, Tooman radioed the fighters escorting the mission to find and destroy *Franklin*

White. By way of reply, someone—he did not identify himself—radioed back to Tooman: "*You* find it and destroy it!"[9]

This elicited a cascade of curses from Tooman, whose eruption was interrupted by his tail gunner on the interphone reporting a B-17 doing 360s below them. When Tooman asked just where it was, the tail gunner replied that it was to the right, over the outskirts of Ipswich.

Tooman nosed down for a look, saw the white wings, and told Hargis to start controlling again. If *Franklin White* kept circling, it would either descend or run out of gas. Either way, its load of incendiaries and napalm would do untold damage to a major English town.

Tooman flipped his left-turn switch and held it. Then he applied the right-turn switch in an effort to coax the baby out to the Channel. At this point, however, he lost the baby in the haze. The tail gunner piped in with the good news that she was headed out to water. A second later, however, he corrected himself. No! The baby was turning back inland.

Looking on the bright side, Hargis remarked that they had at least gained a few miles' distance from Ipswich, and he once again applied control, gradually nudging the baby toward the coast. Once there, however, *Franklin White* completely disappeared in a fog rolling in from the North Sea.

Everyone on the mother ship strained to catch a glimpse of the white wings. Minutes ticked by. At last, Hargis called out on the interphone that he thought he saw something over Blyth Estuary. Yes—he believed it was the drone.

"Are you sure?" Tooman demanded.

"No, I'm not sure. All I saw was a flash of white."

"How far out?"

"A few miles."

"Clear of the coast?"

"Yes, sir. I think so."

That was enough for Tooman.

"Then dump it," he ordered. "We've got to take the chance."[10]

This time, the dump command worked flawlessly. Through the fog, the mother ship's crew saw a great ball of flame. To Tooman's radio operator, it looked like the whole North Sea was on fire. *That,* Tooman remarked, "is better than Ipswich."[11]

*   *   *

JIMMY DOOLITTLE AND EARLE PARTRIDGE convened a debriefing as soon as everyone was back at Fersfield. Gone completely was the earlier sentiment of *well done!* and *good try!*

Doolittle's particular wrath was reserved for his old friend, Jim Rand. The general demanded to know why Rand was able to fly his drones perfectly in practice, but "The second you take off on an operational mission everything goes blooey! Why? It doesn't make sense, Major!"

Rand responded with the truth: "I don't know, General."

Doolittle agreed: "You're goddamn right you don't know, and until you can find out, you're finished here!"[12]

Then Doolittle turned to the others. *Franklin Yellow* had failed because control had failed. But nobody knew why. And *Franklin White?* The autopilot expert bailed out early, as did the pilot. When Doolittle asked why, he was told that "somebody" said they were fired on. But nobody was sure about this. The uncertainty—the lack of positive answers—left Doolittle not merely dissatisfied but disgusted. Looking to salvage something from the mission, he asked about the parachuting. Was *that* any better, at least?

A project officer was able to respond that the first crew jumped flawlessly but the "second one had a little trouble."[13] The officer elaborated, explaining that the electronics expert had hurt his leg and ankle—sprains or a torn ligament—and the pilot, well, the pilot, Lieutenant John Sollars, had lost an arm.

Doolittle was stunned.

The officer explained that the static line had caught in his arm. "It was mangled so bad they had to take it off."[14]

For Doolittle, this "little trouble" was the last straw. "I've asked you a lot of questions," he told the assembled officers, "and you've given me very few answers. It seems to me that this whole project is put together with baling wire, chicken guts, and ignorance." With that, he told the men of Aphrodite that they were returned to training status indefinitely.[15]

Some hours after the angry debriefing, Doolittle and Partridge announced that Major Rand's double AZON system was washed up. The commanders had reached the conclusion—inescapable, really—that AZON was not designed to do what it was being asked to do and was at best "merely an expedient until the proper control equipment could be brought from the States."[16]

That equipment—that *proper* equipment—it turned out, was the FM television control system developed by the U.S. Navy at its Philadelphia Aircraft Factory and something called the Castor system, which the Army Air Corps had developed at Wright Field in Ohio.

As for Jim Rand, he had no further part to play in Operation Aphrodite or Project Anvil. Doolittle authorized the award of a Bronze Star and put him on a plane bound for 388th Bomb Group Headquarters at RAF Knettishall, near Thetford, Suffolk. At a point, when it seemed things could not possibly get worse for the major, the transport aircraft crash-landed, sliding into a gasoline truck parked on the apron alongside the Knettishall runway. At great risk to his own hide, Rand managed to pull one of the crew to safety and was headed back to the wreck to save another when the whole thing suddenly exploded. Rand and the man he saved both survived—except that the major collapsed in what at the time was called a "total nervous breakdown." His last months in the Air Corps would be spent in a psychiatric hospital. It was now the navy's turn to fly.

*   *   *

FEAR OF THE GERMAN vengeance weapons created panic—less, it seems, among the civilian population the weapons were intended to terrorize and demoralize than among USAAF brass, which had rushed Operation Aphrodite into operational status. Doolittle, Rand, and his men were spurred in part by what they thought was accurate knowledge of the destructive potential of the V weapons, in part by the demands of their own higher command, and in no small part by a burning desire to beat the U.S. Navy at this game of drones. Indeed, for those in the front lines of the operation, interservice rivalry may have been the sharpest spur of all.

Yet, at the end of June—more than a month before the six failed Aphrodite sorties—Doolittle decided that the Air Corps operation needed help, and he reached out to the navy to get it. His request was immediately relayed to Admiral Ernest King, who was, as chief of naval operations, the most senior commander in the U.S. Navy. A veteran of the Spanish-American War, the Mexican Revolution, and World War I, he was sixty-six in the summer of 1944 and steeped in what everyone liked to call "the Old Navy." Yet he had been a forward-looking, even pioneering commander in both the submarine service and in naval aviation. He understood, appreciated, and fostered the advanced work of the Naval Aircraft Factory in Philadelphia and at the naval air station in Traverse City, Michigan, where experiments in robot- and radio-controlled flight had been conducted since World War I. Like most U.S. Navy top brass, King thought of drones as target aircraft to be used for training naval antiaircraft gunners. But when the call from Doolittle reached him, he was quick to assign the group at Traverse City to a new operational mission.

The Naval Air Material Center (NAMC), headquartered at the Naval Aircraft Factory, had been considering using war-weary bombers as assault drones—the very thing the Army Air Corps was doing independently—since 1943. It was not until March 21, 1944, however, that Captain Harry B. Temple, director of the Special Weapons Section of the Office of the Deputy Chief of Naval Operations for Air, called on NAMC to study the feasibility of converting new aircraft—specifically the PB4Y-1—into drones. Meetings were held in Washington, not only with naval officers but with those in the Army Air Corps, yet no cooperative or collaborative program was launched, and, on May 27, Admiral King actually cancelled the PB4Y-1 study.[17]

The activation of Operation Aphrodite by the Army Air Corps late in June 1944 led to Doolittle's call for help and the reactivation, on June 24, of the PB4Y-1 program. Under the direction of Commander Victor H. Soucek, work was put on an urgent footing. Soucek skipped over all theoretical planning and instead ordered the Naval Aircraft Factory to take one PB4Y-1, serial number 32271 (ex USAAF B24J 42-110007—just five months off the Consolidated Aircraft assembly line), and put into it everything NAMC had learned about radio control.

What it had learned went far beyond Jim Rand's cobbled-together double AZON system. In round-the-clock work, No. 32271 was fitted out with an autopilot, television transmitter, TV camera, radio-control transceiver unit, servo control motors, and linkages not just to control elevators and rudder but also ailerons and flaps, including cowl flaps.

Separately, an ordnance control system was put together. Its most visible feature was a crude-looking plywood "breadboard" arming panel, which had just two principal controls: a toggle switch labeled "Destruct" and a toggle switch labeled "Arm." Both were held back with a twist of wire that served as a safety.

As for the radio-control system, two twin-engine PV-1 Lockheed Venturas were to function as the control aircraft. Onboard each was a remote-control unit whose sophistication made a vivid contrast with Rand's primitive system. Double AZON provided just three switches—one to turn left, another to turn right, and a third (the dump switch) to dive. The navy's control panel used a combination of a joystick-like control (called a peter-stick) for direction and a modified standard telephone dialer to input a remarkable catalog of controls, including flaps down, cowl flaps open, carburetor heat on, and more.

Although, in theory, the radio-control system provided a sufficient range of control for remote-controlled, pilotless takeoff, thereby eliminating the need for a live pilot, Soucek recommended the presence of a jump pilot, as in the Air Corps B-17 modification. He did not want to rely on radio control until the aircraft, loaded with 20,000 to 25,000 pounds of Torpex, had cleared the field and was near the coast. Additionally, although the inclusion of a television system made it feasible to control the drone without maintaining continuous visual contact—the navy had been flying target drones and assault drone prototypes this way for years—Soucek and the others felt that the stakes were too high and the four-engine heavy bomber too complex to trust to video alone. Again emulating Operation Aphrodite, Project Anvil would fly with the control Venturas in continual visual contact with the robot PB4Y-1.

On July 1, Special Attack Unit (SAU) 1 was formed at Traverse City under Commander James A. Smith. Just before midnight of that day, Smith phoned naval lieutenant Wilford John "Bud" Willy to tell him that he was going to be his executive officer and that they were leaving for NAMC in Philadelphia for a few days of training prior to being transferred to England. Smith provided no further description of the assignment but warned Willy to keep the details of the transfer secret—even from his wife.

Thirty-five-year-old Bud Willy had been born and raised in blue-collar Newark, New Jersey. He joined the navy during the depths of the

Depression, in 1933, not as an officer but as an able seaman, and earned what service members call a "mustang" promotion—jumped to ensign directly from the ranks of the enlisted. He learned military electronics, and he learned to fly, a combination that inducted him into the tiny fraternity of naval aviation radio-control experts. The transfer to England would be his very first combat assignment.

And he *did* assume he was about to see combat. He knew very well what had been going on at Traverse City, especially the recent work on assault drones. He correctly surmised that he would play a role in transforming radio-controlled flight from the realm of gunnery training to that of "special attack." The prospect thrilled him.

Soucek, Willy, and twenty-five others were selected to bring Project Anvil to England. Lieutenant Joseph P. Kennedy Jr. and others already in the UK would quickly join SAU 1 at RAF Fersfield. First, however, the Traverse City personnel spent three days in Philadelphia attending an intensive indoctrination and conducting both ground and flight tests on the modified PB4Y-1. The aircraft performed flawlessly—except for the ordnance control board, the arming panel. During one test flight, the arming circuit lit up, accidentally energized. (Some sources report *three* instances of accidental arming over Philadelphia.[18]) Had the Torpex load been on board and wired, the aircraft would have exploded spectacularly in midair. Willy and others guessed that the inadvertent arming was the result of FM interference created by an errant signal from some radio transmitter—military or civil—in the densely populated Philadelphia area. But there was no time to track down this guess. Instead, the problem was merely noted, and the aircraft, complete with the arming board as it was, was "ferried" (flown) to RAF Dunkeswell, in England.

* * *

ALTHOUGH NO. 32271—now designated more simply T-11, the number painted on its fuselage—had been modified for radio control in Philadelphia, there was still plenty of work to be done at Dunkeswell. The aircraft had to be stripped bare inside and out and then reinforced with timbers to ensure that the structure would not be compromised by a dozen tons of high explosives. All of its guns and gun turrets were removed at Dunkeswell. In a gesture intended to give the appearance that the plane was not totally defenseless, painted broomsticks were installed in place of the turret and tail guns. The silver aircraft received a coat of white paint on its wing tops to heighten visibility even further.

Very soon after they arrived at Dunkeswell early in July, Smith and Willy met Joe Kennedy. With his commanding officer, Jim "Sunshine" Reedy, present, Smith and Willy at long last explained the mission Joe had volunteered for.

Smith and Willy began by describing just what they had done to the PB4Y-1—how it had been fitted with a system by which it could be radio-controlled to climb, bank, glide, lower its flaps, descend, and dive. It could not, they claimed, take off or land on its own—and wouldn't be allowed to, even if it could. They told Kennedy that the airplane would be loaded with 21,170 pounds of Torpex in 347 pine crates. This, they said, was twelve times the explosive load of a single V-1 buzz bomb, the weapon first used against London about three weeks earlier. The explosives would be carefully tied down and fused. His mission, the pair told Kennedy, would be to take the aircraft up and fly it in a designated pattern during which he and one crew member would prepare it for handoff to a remote-control pilot in a Ventura, who would fly the robot plane into a hardened V-weapon facility on the coast of France. After handing it off and before leaving English airspace, Kennedy and his crew member would bail out. At that point, the mission was over—for them. And, oh yes, before handing off control and before bailing out, they would have to arm the explosive payload.

Even now, Reedy did not actually assign or promise Joe Kennedy the mission. There were alternate pilots available, and Reedy may have been plagued by second thoughts about putting the son of the controversial but still-influential ex-ambassador on top of 12 tons of one of the most powerful explosives in existence. He did, however, invite Joe to select his flight crew. The number one man on his list was Demetrios—Dee—Vilan, who had flown with him as radioman on many antisubmarine patrols.

Reedy was commanding officer of Squadron VB-110, but its operational flying skipper was Commander Page Knight. It was Knight who summoned Vilan to his office. Like Joe Kennedy, Vilan had completed more than his required quota of combat missions and was due at least thirty days' stateside leave. He assumed that Knight was calling him in to authorize it. Instead, Knight announced that something had come up and that he needed a radioman. He told Vilan that the assignment would keep him in England for at least another month, that it was strictly voluntary, but that it was precisely suited to his talents and so he was the very first man to be asked.

"Will it be interesting?" Vilan found himself inquiring.

"Very interesting. And dangerous, you must know that."

"I'll take it."[19]

At this point, Knight told him that he'd be flying with Lieutenant Kennedy. Knight told him that there would be a meeting tomorrow. Pleased as Vilan was about flying with Kennedy, the prospect of the meeting created in him an almost unbearable suspense. He lay awake all that night.

Joe, it turned out, was anxious too. Reedy had not rendered his final decision as to which of the pilots and crews would be assigned to fly the first mission of SAU 1. When, come the morning of the meeting, there was still no word, Joe pitched Reedy shamelessly, reportedly verging on bringing outright political pressure to bear on his commanding officer.[20]

Reedy never admitted to having been pressured politically, and Joe Jr. did not live to recount why Reedy ultimately chose him, apparently without seriously considering any of the alternatives. All that is known, based on information later supplied by Dee Vilan, is that Joe Jr. emerged from Reedy's office, saw Vilan waiting anxiously in the hall, and reached out to vigorously shake his hand, telling him it was "all set."[21]

Vilan, Joe, and a mechanic—Red Bradfield—convened in Reedy's office a half hour after Joe's proffered handshake. Reedy told them they were being transferred to SAU 1 and would be stationed with the Air Corps at RAF Fersfield. On August 2, just three days after they arrived, Joe took T-11 up for a test flight fully loaded with more than 20,000 pounds of sandbags to simulate the Torpex load. Indeed, unlike the USAAF crews of Operation Aphrodite, Joe and his men practiced daily for hours. During this time, Aphrodite flew its sorties of August 4—all failures. On one hand, Joe and his companions felt keen pangs of doubt and fear. On the other hand, Joe enjoyed a kind of relief. The

Air Corps' failures made room for his success. He was being set up for
a breakthrough.

But then the war news became increasingly encouraging. July had
been marked by much frustration in the Allied ground war. D-Day,
June 6, 1944, had been a hard-won success, of course, but progress in
the subsequent weeks was painfully slow. The Allies' inland advance
was hung up in the hedgerow country of Normandy and was also met
by incredibly stiff German resistance. Then, on August 1, Patton's
Third Army became operational in France and commenced a spectacular breakout in three directions, west into Brittany, south and east
toward the Seine, and north, toward Falaise. The speed of these operations, particularly in the south, was breathtaking. Joe began to worry
that the war would end before he had a chance to fly the mission that
would make him. To Dee Vilan, Joe began to seem "angry and edgy."[22]

*   *   *

AFTER THE FAILED APHRODITE MISSIONS of August 4, that incident
back in Philadelphia—the unexpected energizing of the arming circuit—began to prey on the minds of Bud Willy and Commander Smith.
They decided to install a new safety device in the circuit, a simple metal
pin inserted into a plywood panel behind the pilot. In the event that a
spurious FM signal accidentally energized the arming circuit, the pin
would physically hold back a mechanical part called the arming bar,
which would prevent the arming solenoid from moving into the on position that would detonate the payload. On the face of it, this seemed
a welcome precaution, but there were a few dissenting voices among
the technicians. These individuals worried that, if the arming circuit
was unintentionally energized, forcibly restraining the arming solenoid
would keep it from moving into the armed position, but it would also
hold closed a switch that was intended to open immediately after the
radio signal sent battery current to the solenoid. The switch was a safety
device intended to instantly cut off current to the solenoid once it had
moved. The uninterrupted flow of current to the restrained solenoid
would cause its coil to overheat, very possibly becoming hot enough to
ignite the explosives. To the ranking technicians, however, this seemed
unlikely, and the safety pin was installed. A rip cord with a parachute

handle was tied to the pin, and the pilot was instructed to pull it just before bailing out.

As an additional concession to lingering fears about radio interference, special frequency-search flights were launched daily. Flying twelve to fifteen tedious hours a day, these aircraft kept their FM receivers on, searching for stray signals. Not once did they detect a signal in the spectrum of the secret FM arming frequency.

Embittered by the failures of August 4, many of the Army Air Corps personnel at Fersfield made no attempt to hide their resentment of the small naval contingent and its shiny new PB4Y-1. Lieutenant Colonel Ray Forrest, however, had a humbler and more professional attitude. He was intensely interested in the navy's approach, and when he walked up to the navy aircraft and climbed into the cockpit, he was impressed. The equipment was clearly far more sophisticated than anything the army had produced.

But then Forrest's eye lighted on that arming panel breadboard. He turned to Commander Smith, who was showing him the plane.

"Jimmy, this looks like something you'd make with a number two Erector set and Lincoln Logs."[23]

Forrest was not an electronics expert, but he knew a dangerously brittle cold-soldered joint when he saw one, and he knew that screwing a plywood circuit board directly to a steel aircraft bulkhead invited a whole mess of short circuits and voltage spikes. Most of all, he knew what a jerry-built piece of junk looked like. He also appreciated that the success of the mission, the lives of the aircrew—hell, the life and limb of every man on the airbase—depended on that plywood piece of shit.

Forrest grilled, as good-naturedly as he could, Commander Smith on this item of hardware, but all Smith could say was that it came straight from the Naval Aircraft Factory at Philadelphia, which certainly knew what it was doing. Getting no satisfaction from the navy, Forrest brought up his concerns in the officers' club at dinner that evening with a colonel in Third Bomb Division HQ.

The colonel listened. *The* arming *panel?* he replied. *What did* either *of them know about the* navy's *arming panel?* Securing a martini from a proffered tray, he fixed eyes on Forrest: "It's *their* problem."[24]

As an army officer knows, the gulf separating the man who wears the oak leaves of a lieutenant colonel from the man who owns full-colonel eagles is even wider than that dividing a full colonel from a brigadier general. It was time for Forrest to shut up, and he knew it. But he couldn't stop himself.

"It's a matter of conscience with me," he exclaimed, "and goddamn it, they've got it wrong. They're gonna try to blow a load of 10 [actually 12] tons of Torpex with an arming system that's about as safe as a basketful of rattlesnakes."[25]

The colonel could have pulled rank with a warning that the *lieutenant* colonel was out of line. Instead, he did something worse. Raising his fresh martini, he proposed a toast: "To you and your wild imagination," adding, "When the Navy blows up its drone, give me a ring. Nobody wanted the Navy here in the first place."[26]

* * *

NEITHER THE ARMING PANEL nor anything else concerned Dee Vilan and Joe's roommate, Jim Simpson. Both were candidates for the number-two spot in Joe's cockpit, and both worried that they would be passed over for a new man: Bud Willy.

Willy was indeed a formidable contender. He had spent years in Philadelphia and Traverse City as a radio-control designer and technician. He did not merely understand the equipment, he had participated in the design of much of it. Moreover, he was pilot-qualified to fly the demanding PB4Y-1. Simpson was qualified as a copilot and had often flown with Kennedy in that capacity, but he had no radio-control expertise. Vilan was highly qualified in radio communications but not specially qualified in radio control—and he was not a pilot. As for Bradfield, he was a mechanic—intensively if quickly trained in radio control, but hardly a specialist. Nor was he a pilot. Vilan comforted himself that he had a history with Joe, having flown with him on many patrols and having extended his own tour of duty to fly with him some more. Loyalty had to count for something. Deciding that he needed to end his own suspense, Dee Vilan asked Joe directly: Was he flying the mission? Perhaps to his surprise, Joe responded directly: He had chosen to fly with Bud Willy.

Vilan was angry and disappointed, but Joe did not respond in kind, nor did he pull rank. Instead, he sympathized but insisted that the decision had been made. In Bud Willy, he had a backup man who was not only a pilot but who knew everything there was to know about radio control in general and this system in particular.

As for Simpson, Willy did pull rank on *him*. A lowly ensign, Simpson just didn't have a chance.

Joe's own principal anxiety had two sources. Either the army would succeed before he got a chance to fly his mission or the war would end. On August 6, one source was eliminated when the two Air Corps missions of that day failed miserably, and Doolittle himself grounded Operation Aphrodite until such time as the new Castor system was ready to replace the discredited double AZON.

So Joe, Willy, and T-11 were up—whenever the weather permitted. As it turned out, the weather permitted none too soon. There was time for more practice, and there was also time for a major procedural decision to be made. The rationale for including living personnel aboard a robot bomb was twofold: First, radio-control technology was limited. Rand's double AZON system had not been designed to take off on its own. In contrast, the navy had succeeded in taking off—and even in landing—by radio control, but its system was still far from foolproof. There was, in fact, a high possibility of failure. And that brings up the second rationale: No way was anyone in charge going to trust radio remote control to guide a planeload of high explosives off a huge military airfield and then over a portion of England that included several densely populated cities. Even London itself was not far. These two reasons for risking two lives also implied an imperative to terminate the risk as soon as possible. Operation Aphrodite called for the jump pilot and his electronics expert to remain with the baby just long enough to set the autopilot and ACE and to arm the payload. In the interval between the Aphrodite missions of August 6 and the first Anvil mission, navy planners decided that Kennedy and Willy would fly a much longer pattern and would not bail out until they were near Dover, some 150 air miles south of Fersfield.

The reason for the long flight, riding tons of high explosives wired to detonate, was to ensure that control between the mother ships and the drone was well and correctly established. At least some of the Aphrodite failures were clearly attributable to flaws in radio control. But was all that extra time worth it? Control pilot Lieutenant Rosy Lyon objected to it as an unnecessary risk. Willy, however, backed the decision—and may even have instigated it. He wanted the luxury of time to fine-tune the equipment so as to establish perfect control. As for Joe Kennedy, rumor had it that he wanted to parachute in the south, near Dover, to rendezvous with the "Crash-Bang" girl to whom he was supposedly engaged. This, of course, was sheer nonsense, but Joe seems to have let the rumor circulate without opposition or correction from him.

The hours and days crept by. CAVU—ceiling and visibility unlimited—remained elusive. Kennedy used one day for another practice flight and then he turned the T-11 over for loading. In contrast to the B-17 babies of Aphrodite, in which crates of nitrostarch were stacked and secured in ways that allowed for considerable—and unnerving—sway, Lieutenant Tom Martin, a navy armament engineer, closely supervised the securing of the PB4Y-1 load with quarter-inch steel cable. Open spaces between sections of crates were shored up with pine timbers. His objective was to reduce crate movement to zero. After ten hours of labor, all of the Torpex was loaded and secured. In the space between the topmost crates and the overhead of the fuselage, Martin ran the wires of his arming circuit, taking care to insulate all connections to prevent ground faults.

T-11 was loaded and ready by dawn on August 11, but dense fog ruled out any flight, and Joe brooded as he listened to a BBC account of the juggernaut that was General George S. Patton Jr. and the Third United States Army. He took comfort in the fact that Patton was not pushing toward any known V-weapon sites, but he doubted the German coastal troops who defended the sites could hold out all that much longer.

*   *   *

AUGUST 12 DAWNED CLOUDY. Yet another day without CAVU? Well, there was fog—but, Kennedy and the others noted, it was just ground fog, rising less than a foot off the earth. The air felt reasonably dry, and there was a strong likelihood that the clouds would part and the skies would clear.

Joe Kennedy, in company with Simpson and Willy, went to the officers' mess. As they ate their breakfast, they heard the familiar whine of an auxiliary starter followed by the Pratt & Whitney cough of the engines they knew belonged to T-11. The crew chief was starting his preflight check. The conclusion was inescapable: He had been told to prepare for a mission that day.

Holding their own anticipation in check, Joe and his companions finished their breakfast, walked out, and studied the sky. The gray cloud cover was now riven with blue. Looking down, it was apparent that the ground fog had completely burned off. Rosy Lyon pulled up in a jeep to tell Joe that there was a final briefing at 1500—3 pm. That was hours away. In the meantime, Vilan and Bradfield, both bounced from the operational mission, pitched in to perform a thorough preflight, with Vilan focusing on the all-important radio equipment.

At 10:30, Joe was handed the latest weather forecast. It looked promising for CAVU both at Fersfield and at the target, about which Joe had not yet been informed—not that, as jump pilot, he really needed to know.

Joe had last written to his mother and father on August 4, the day of the first four failed Aphrodite sorties. "I am working on something different," he explained at that time. "It is terribly interesting . . . but at this point . . . quite secret. Per usual I have done nothing, but it is far more interesting than patrolling over the bay." Then he wrote a sentence outwardly designed to allay parental anxiety yet clearly meant to provoke reading between the lines: "Don't get worried about it, as there is practically no danger." He apologized for having volunteered beyond his mission quota but assured his mother and father that when "I tell you the whole story I think you will agree" that it was a mission worth staying for. "All the boys who did go home, now wish they had stayed over."[27]

With time on his hands—so much time, it seemed at 10:30 am—Joe phoned Lorelle Hearst, second wife of William Randolph Hearst. A sometime war correspondent and a good friend, she kept an apartment at Claridge's, the exclusive London hotel. Joe asked her to pass a message to his father: "I'm about to go into my act," he told her. "If I don't come back, tell my dad—despite our differences—that I love him very much."[28]

Like so many utterances that end up counting among a person's last, it is both moving and touching. Yet it is also perplexing. *"Despite our differences."* What did Joe Jr. mean by that? It sounds like the statement of a son who had fallen out with his father or whose father had fallen out with him. But nothing of the kind happened. Before he joined the navy, Joe Jr. had been almost slavish in toeing his father's isolationist line. There was no argument over that issue. And while his father wanted to secure him an important but safe staff appointment, he did not protest when Joe Jr. became a naval aviation cadet, although he clearly recognized the dangers. When Joe Jr. earned his wings, it was Joe Sr. who pinned them on his uniform.

Did the phrase betray some unexpressed resentment on the part of the son? Perhaps a feeling, never put into words, that the ex-ambassador's relentlessly public defeatism and what often seemed a cynical contempt for heroism, sacrifice, and even democracy—all sentiments publicly expressed—had forced him into risking his life?

*   *   *

AT 1500, 3 PM, the men assigned to the first mission of SAU 1 gathered in the Nissen hut that served as the briefing shack. The two six-man mother ship crews were present: the primary commanded by Rosy Lyon, with John Anderson serving as control pilot, the secondary flown by Harry Wherry with John Demlein as control pilot. Also present were the personnel of the auxiliary aircraft: a B-17 Flying Fortress navigation plane; a P-38, piloted by Roy Forrest and carrying Commander James A. Smith as an observer; a Mosquito photo plane, flown by FDR's son Colonel Elliott Roosevelt, assigned to document the bailout; and sixteen P-51 Mustangs—"little friends"—assigned to provide security. Seated up front in the briefing were Joe Kennedy and Bud Willy, Joe carefully taking notes on the knee pad he would carry with him into the cockpit.

Roy Forrest personally delivered the mission brief. Joe was already very familiar with its outline. He was to take off and climb to 2,000 feet over the village of Framlingham, which was twenty-three minutes southeast of Fersfield. It was expected that Anderson, in the primary Ventura, would have established radio control by the time T-11 was over Framlingham. Even so, Kennedy and Willy were to remain on board, as passengers, to ensure that control was maintained and fully operational. Anderson would turn T-11 northeast toward Beccles, a twenty-minute flight from Framlingham. During this time, Kennedy and Willy would continue checking all controls before Anderson turned

T-11 south, to the departure point that would take the drone across the English Channel.

As they flew above the Thames estuary, approaching "point X-ray," the designated bailout point, Willy would test the arming circuit with a "safety lamp." When he was satisfied that the circuit was safe, he would remove the wire safety on the "arm" switch and move it to the *arm* position. This would energize the arming solenoids—which, however, would not be actuated until the "safety pin" was removed. The original plan called for the removal to be done by the pilot, just before he bailed out. Presumably, concern over the possibility of overheating the solenoids by restraining them too long prompted an alteration in plan. It was now Willy's responsibility to pull the rip cord that withdrew the safety pin.

By this time, assuming all went as it should, T-11 would be across the Thames and Willy would squeeze through the nose-wheel doorway. This was the only way out of the modified PB4Y-1. Joe would follow immediately, pulling the manual arming wire just before thrusting himself through the same doorway. Both men were to parachute down near Manston Field, a short distance north of Dover.

In the interests of procedural confirmation, Kennedy was ordered to hold the arming wire in his hand as he parachuted to earth and to present it after he landed—as proof that the manual phase of arming had been completed. As with Aphrodite's B-17, an electrical arming procedure was redundant with the manual one; however, in Project Anvil, the final electrical arming would be accomplished by radio control, from the mother ship. Anderson would flip a two-handed *arm* switch, which transmitted an FM signal that completed the final arming circuit.

Having outlined the procedures of a successful mission, Forrest next reviewed what was referred to as the dumping bill. Among the several procedures left loosely improvisational in Operation Aphrodite was what to do if establishing reliable radio control over the drone proved impossible. In Project Anvil, the procedure was meticulously laid out in the dumping bill.

If neither the primary nor the secondary mother ships could establish control during the forty-minute span of the triangular pattern Joe and Willy flew aboard T-11, Joe was to set the autopilot for the North Sea, and he and Willy were to bail out before the aircraft reached water. Once they were out and T-11 was safely over water, either the primary or secondary mother ship controller would throw the "destruct" switch, and the PB4Y-1 would explode in a great yellow fireball. As an extra safety precaution, the drone would not be armed until full radio control had been established and assured. This meant that, even if the destruct signal failed, the unarmed Torpex aboard the T-11 would not detonate even if the bomber crashed on land—assuming, of course, the plane flew until it ran out of gas before it crashed. If fuel remained onboard and a fire resulted on impact, there was every possibility that the explosive would cook off and detonate.

The Anvil control pilots had far more to work with than the Aphrodite bombardiers had. A television camera in the PB4Y-1's nose was linked to a transmitter that conveyed a grainy drone's-eye view to the controller. Although the copilot in the Ventura maintained direct visual contact with T-11 and relayed guidance to the controller, the controller relied most immediately on the video picture and on radar, which was focused on the drone, tracking it continuously.

In Aphrodite, the secondary control aircraft functioned strictly as a backup for the primary. In Anvil, the two control craft worked together far more closely. Anderson, the primary controller, was to dive T-11 to an altitude of 700 feet over the Channel—higher than Aphrodite's 300 feet, but still below the horizon of German defensive radar. Also in contrast to the Aphrodite procedure, in which the mother flew very high above the baby, Anderson's Ventura would be lower and certainly within flak range. Since he was tailing the drone, he would be quite close to the coast by the time the shooting started. At that point, while the primary Ventura drew the Germans' fire, Anderson would transfer control to Demlein in the secondary Ventura. Once the transfer was successfully completed, the primary would shear off, away from the coast and away from the flak.

One more B-17 crew attended the 3 pm briefing: the crew of the aircraft, commanded by Joe's roommate and longtime copilot Jim Simpson, assigned to scout the target area of Mimoyecques. This much-feared V-3 fortress had been the objective of the last sortie of Aphrodite Mission 515 on August 4.

Did the name "Mimoyecques" mean anything to Joe Kennedy? It was a vanishingly tiny hamlet, populated by no more than fifty souls,

ks, sentries, drivers, and GIs of all ranks mingled with of-
ery level, up to and including the top brass. By 1700 hours—
eryone was watching.

T-11 had been taxied to the hardstand. Dee Vilan climbed
to check the VOX (voice) radio and set the pilot frequencies
e designated for the mission. As he left, Jim Simpson climbed
d to give the radio-control equipment a final preflight check. Out-
he aircraft, mechanic Red Bradfield performed a slow, painstaking
k-around. The three men were all expecting to fly this mission and
been bumped by Bud Willy. Whether they resented this or felt the
lief of a reprieve, we cannot know. What is clear, however, is that
one of them surrendered a stake in the mission. Each made himself
responsible for ensuring the readiness of the aircraft. Perhaps no U.S.
military combat plane prior to the mission of the *Enola Gay* against
Hiroshima on August 6, 1945, had been so meticulously, even obsessively preflighted.

When Kennedy and Willy arrived by jeep, it must have struck
them—and the onlookers—as extravagantly superfluous to add *their*
walk-around to those of the others. But it's what a pilot and copilot
(which partly described Willy's role) do, and so they did it, pausing
only to shake hands with Commander Smith, who was present on the
hardstand.

The walk-around completed, Kennedy and Willy shook hands with
Vilan and Bradfield. Holding Kennedy's hand a moment, Bradfield said
something about the magneto on the number three engine. Kennedy
nodded in acknowledgment and followed Willy into the aircraft via the
nose-wheel doorway through which they were also to exit the bomber.
Even though the men carried little with them—both wore their chest-
pack emergency chutes, and Willy also carried a checklist for the radio-
control handoff—it was a tight squeeze. Their seat packs, containing
their primary parachutes, were already on board, Joe's on the pilot's
seat, and Willy's secured near the nose-wheel doorway. As in the modified B-17, only the pilot had a seat. Simpson was still in T-11 when Kennedy and Willy climbed aboard.

Joe took his seat, and Willy, standing behind him, began reading
aloud the standard prestart checklist. Outside, Red Bradfield confirmed
that all personnel, vehicles, and other objects were clear of the big

and quite easy to overlook. Ye⸺
pany with his sister Kick, had⸺
convertible his father had given h⸺
which passed within two miles of M⸺
the briefing focused on the work of t⸺
of the jumpers, Kennedy and Willy. Th⸺
survival—were quite straightforward. An⸺
trast, had to locate Mimoyecques, and Dem⸺
the bunker's main doorway—whether its mass⸺
or not. This target, fifteen by sixteen feet, was t⸺
the structure was most vulnerable. Assuming the ⸺
cated and the doorway identified, Demlein had to use ⸺
thread the needle. Everything, moreover, had to be tim⸺
precision. The object was to contact the target at 1900—⸺
the sun, low in the western sky, would be behind the drone⸺
ing the bunker while blinding the flak gunners.

Demlein, who likely felt so much of the burden of success o⸺
on his shoulders, was intensely keyed up when he, Joe, and the ⸺
filed out of the briefing shack.

"You got your insurance all paid up?" he asked Joe.

He must have regretted the quip instantly. If it bothered Joe, however, he didn't let on. Grinning broadly, he delivered an answer worthy
of a rich man's son: "I've got twice as much as I need. I don't need it and
nobody *connected* with me needs it."

Was the comeback intended ironically, or was it simply the truth?
However he meant it, Joe gave Demlein a warm handshake. "I won't say
I'll see you, but so long."[29]

* * *

THE EIGHTH U.S. AIR FORCE LAUNCHED bombing missions almost
daily from England—often several a day. They were as routine as any
highly dangerous enterprise ever was in a time of war. But the launch
of an Aphrodite/Anvil mission was no everyday occurrence, and that
of August 12, 1944, drew practically everyone at Fersfield away from
whatever they were doing to watch the takeoff of all involved aircraft.
In a military organization fighting in the defense of democracy, the occasion gave the appearance of democracy itself. Mechanics, technicians,

loaders, co⸺
ficers at ev⸺
5 pm—e⸺
The ⸺
aboard ⸺
to tho⸺
aboa⸺
side ⸺
wa⸺
ha⸺
r⸺

bomber's four propellers. He then positioned himself on the port side of the plane, locked eyes with Joe, and flipped his right thumb up.

Joe began the start-up sequence in the normal manner, with the number three—starboard inboard—engine. The engine turned over just as it should. For a 1,200 horsepower R-1830-35 Pratt & Whitney, "just as it should" was pretty dramatic. There was an initial throaty growl as the electric starter motor fought inertia. The pitch slowly rose from growl to whine to banshee scream, and the propeller began to rotate. As soon as he saw that, Joe engaged the engine, which coughed loudly, shot a single bolt of flame aft, blew a dense black cloud of smoke, and, dragonlike, roared into life. Satisfied, Joe switched on number four, next to it, followed by number two—the inboard port engine—and number one. After pausing a second or two to read his instruments and listen to the engines, Joe raised his fists up to the windscreen, put both thumbs up, and jerked them to port and starboard. Instantly, two ground crewmen pulled free the lanyards trailing from the wheel chocks on both sides of the plane and dragged them away.

Red Bradfield stepped into Joe's view, extended his right clenched fist and, with the forefinger of his left hand, beckoned the hulking bomber, loaded to its 65,000-pound maximum takeoff weight, as an impatient parent would summon a toddler. In response, Joe revved the number four engine to pivot the aircraft in the direction of the taxiway. With that rapidly turning engine now putting the starboard outboard prop out of sync with the others, there began the deep, visceral, drumbeat of a low-frequency interference wave. The slow, insistent beat was punctuated by the groan of metal and the alto squeal of brakes intermittently applied and released.

Joe knew very well where to go. Bradfield pointed out the taxiway nevertheless. Then, straightening, he snapped a textbook navy salute. T-11 rolled to the end of the runway, joining the other aircraft of the armada. First off were the two Ventura mother ships, one after the other. They circled over the field at 1,000 feet. In the primary Ventura, control pilot Anderson put the radio-control equipment through its paces while T-11 stood idling. Simpson, who had not yet exited the drone, stood behind Kennedy to observe the results. When Anderson moved his peterstick forward, Joe radioed back, "Down elevator." When he moved the stick to the right, Joe reported "Right aileron." In this manner, each control command was checked. Joe and Willy were cleared to take off, confident that radio control would be established and that they would not be riding on 12 tons of Torpex in vain, let alone putting untold numbers of English civilians at risk.

Satisfied with the test, Simpson reached out first to Bud Willy, who was squatting next to him. The men shook hands. Then, to Joe, he said simply: "I wish I were going along with you."

"You'll make the next one," Joe assured him. "And if I don't come back, you can have the rest of my eggs," referring to the stash secreted in his "treasure chest."[30]

With that, Simpson slipped out the nose-wheel doorway and trotted out to the B-17 assigned to cross the Channel and observe the execution of the mission's final stages. Along with another B-17, designated as the navigation plane, several P-38 Lightning fighters (among them Roy Forrest's personal aircraft) functioning as observation craft, and Elliott Roosevelt's photo-recon Mosquito, Simpson's observation B-17 would take off after the departure of T-11. Most of the Mustang fighter escorts preceded T-11 into the air, taking off in groups of three. Then it was finally Joe's turn.

While Dee Vilan and Red Bradfield stood up in their jeep, looking on from the perimeter of the runway, Joe locked his brakes and throttled up each engine in turn while Vilan and Bradfield listened. To an aviator in the era of piston engines, no instrument was more sensitive, accurate, or important than the trained human ear. Number one engine roared up and then was throttled back; number two was next, number three, and four.

Bradfield insisted that number three did not sound right. Vilan disagreed, and seeing how agitated Bradfield seemed, he shouted over the engine noise: "It's a good thing you're not in that plane."[31] But he made no attempt to dissuade, let alone restrain the mechanic from jumping out of the jeep and running out to the aircraft. Bradfield signaled to Joe, who throttled back all engines and waved him up into the cockpit. The mechanic shinnied up through the nose-wheel doorway, and Vilan, still in the jeep, listened as Joe again throttled each engine successively up and down. Vilan could see Bradfield standing next to the seated Kennedy. He saw the mechanic nod, indicating that—this time at least—number three sounded just fine. Less than a minute later, Bradfield rejoined Vilan in the jeep.

By now it was approaching 1800—6 pm. Time to take off, if the drone was to approach its target within an hour, when the sun would be positioned just right. Joe wasted no time slamming the T-11 into takeoff position, but he did not rush the takeoff itself. Never a "natural" pilot and no seat-of-the-pants flier, Joe was always methodical in the cockpit. Setting his brakes, he ran each engine up and down for a third time, a procedure that consumed seven minutes. Then he pushed all the throttles forward for full power. T-11 strained against its brakes. Joe released them. The aircraft rolled forward, accelerating slowly but steadily.

To Vilan, it seemed as if Joe would never "rotate"—take off. He watched anxiously as the PB4Y-1 ate up more and more of the field. In the last few yards of the runway, the nose finally lifted off the ground and the main wheels reluctantly followed. Vilan and Bradfield watched as they spun in the air before Joe, tapping his brakes, stopped them and retracted the gear. As the roar of four big engines diminished with distance, the radioman and the mechanic became aware of cheers rising from the throat of every man gathered along the runway.

The rest of the auxiliary aircraft, in turn, now followed T-11 into the blue, but Vilan and Bradfield focused exclusively on Kennedy and Willy's plane, straining after it until they could see it no more. The time was 1752, eight minutes to six. There was nothing to do now but go to the mess hut and get dinner. The two men were relieved, at least, that the aircraft had neither exploded nor crashed on takeoff and that it had left with plenty of time to get to its target. For once, the gods of war were smiling, it seemed, and the mission was off to an excellent start.

* * *

IT WAS AT PRECISELY EIGHTEEN MINUTES into the mission, as T-11 approached Framlingham, the initial checkpoint, that Joe radioed the code phrase "Spade Flush," signaling that the aircraft was trimmed, the autopilot was set and engaged, and T-11 was therefore ready for handoff to the mother ship.

Anderson acknowledged the radio call, switched on his equipment, and began controlling the PB4Y-1. Relying on a combination of radar and direct visual reports from Rosy Lyon's copilot in addition to the video fed to him from the camera in T-11's nose, Anderson steered the rest of the way to Framlingham and then turned left, toward the next checkpoint, Beccles, north-northeast. Anderson and Kennedy used the time and the miles to check each of the controls, essentially running the same radio-control check they had run on the ground.

So far, it was textbook—had there been a textbook for something no one had ever done before. But, five minutes north of Framlingham, Anderson's radar showed T-11 twelve miles off its course for Beccles. The plane was veering too far east, too soon flying toward the Channel coast. At this point, T-11 was closing in on the River Blyth, passing over the Westwood Marshes. Elliott Roosevelt maneuvered his Mosquito to within a few hundred feet of the drone and began taking pictures. Roy Forrest approached in his P-38, giving Commander Smith, huddled in the plane's Plexiglas nose, a clear and close view of the drone. Both Roosevelt and Smith could distinctly see Joe Kennedy and Bud Willy through the PB4Y-1 cockpit windows.

Blyth River empties lazily into an estuary that is one of the gems of the Suffolk coast, its salt marshes home to a wide variety of water birds, its gentle, flat landscape conducive to solitary walks and quiet contemplation. At the very margin of the marsh is Newdelight Wood. At 1820—twenty minutes past six—as the T-11 began to pass over Newdelight, Anderson went to work, seeking to put the drone back on course. A twelve-mile error was unacceptable, especially when the objective was to hit a target measured in feet.

Anderson nudged the peter-stick left, and T-11 exploded. One blast was followed a second later by another.

Elliott Roosevelt was closest to T-11 when it blew apart, but he did not see very much, since it was all he could do to fly his mostly wooden plane clear of the debris. Pulling at his controls, he sheared away from the fireball. That's mostly what riveted the attention of Rosy Lyon, in the primary Ventura—how Roosevelt's Mosquito stood on its wing in a sharp turn away from the blast. Lyon did not look to his right, but he distinctly heard his copilot emit a low animal grunt, and, just then, the Ventura rode rough over the blast wave, rising and falling hard, like a fast-moving old truck encountering an unseen rise and dip on a road gone suddenly bad.

In the secondary Ventura, control pilot John Demlein saw nothing but the sudden disappearance of the radar blip that had represented an airplane carrying two human beings. Glancing at his round video monitor, he saw nothing but what early video technicians called "grass"—the video chaos of a lost signal.

It was Commander James Smith who had the clearest view, from the Plexiglas nose of Forrest's P-38. But all that came to him at the time was the strange insight that nothing larger than a basketball could have survived the blast.[32]

Demlein moved away from his control console to pilot Harry Wherry's shoulder. With him, he stared through the windscreen. By this time the blast had resolved into a pair of vivid orange columns, one appearing to rise into the sky, the other to sink in counterpoint toward the estuary and the woods below. Demlein later described the image as the "biggest explosion I ever saw until the pictures of the atom bomb," and Wherry spoke of "a terrific flame and many, many pieces."[33]

Less than a thousand feet outside of Newdelight Wood, situated between that tranquil place and the little town of Blytheburgh, was Shepherd's Cottage, home to Miss Ada Westgate, unmarried at forty-four, a woman who enjoyed Newdelight and conversing with her few neighbors. Standing in the doorway of the tile-roofed cottage she shared with her niece, passing the time of day is just what she was doing when the sky suddenly cracked open. Something like lightning flashed, and so she would have thought it—had the war not taught her to think first of rockets.

Ada Westgate turned from her neighbor in midsentence and dashed into her house. She did not immediately notice that its door had been blown off its hinges. Her first thought was of her cousin inside. He had come to live with her at Shepherd's Cottage after a V-1 had destroyed his flat in London. But there he was—*under* her front door, stunned, to be sure, but unhurt. Thankful for that, Miss Westgate's inventory of loved ones turned next to her aunt and uncle, who lived nearby, on the Fen, which, as she figured it, was even closer than Shepherd's Cottage to the source of the explosion. She took hold of her niece and asked her, please, to run upstairs to fetch her coat. She needed to check the house on the Fen.

The girl bolted up the stairs.

"Oh, Aunty," she called from above, "the ceiling's all down."[34]

CHAPTER 9

"I DON'T WANT TO HAVE TO TELL HIM THE TRUTH"

THE "KENNEDY COMPOUND" IN HYANNIS PORT WAS INTENDED AS a place of escape and seclusion, a place to experience, in private, a family's joy and grief, as each might come in its time. Of the two emotions, none is more private than grief, and yet we know a great deal about how the news of the death of Joseph Patrick Kennedy Jr. came to Hyannis Port and how it was received there.

We know that the news arrived about two o'clock on the afternoon of August 13, 1944. We know that Jack was present in the compound, recently released from the naval hospital but still in agony, both with regard to his back and his stomach. We know that he was on the broad porch of the big house with his sisters Jean and Eunice and his twelve-year-old brother Teddy. Their mother, Rose, was reading the Sunday paper in the living room. The senior Kennedy was in the bedroom upstairs, taking his customary afternoon nap. Everyone had partaken in a picnic lunch. The strains of Bing Crosby crooning "I'll Be Seeing You" emanated from the phonograph in the living room and wafted out, through the screen door, to those on the porch.

From recollections Ted Kennedy delivered many years later, we know that a large dark sedan drove up the driveway, that a pair of "naval chaplains got out, walked up the steps to the porch, and knocked on the screen door." Rose greeted them. Assuming that their visit concerned "some charity or other matter," she invited them into the living room to wait with her for her husband to rise from his nap. "One of the priests," Rose wrote in her memoirs, "said no, that the reason for calling was urgent. That there was a message both Joe and I must hear." But he didn't wait for the arrival of Joe Sr. to deliver it: Their "son was missing in action and presumed lost."[1]

The children, who either followed the chaplains and their mother into the living room or listened through the screen door, heard (according to Ted Kennedy) "a few words: 'missing—lost.' All of us froze."[2]

But not Rose Kennedy. She rushed upstairs to wake her husband. Within moments, the two came downstairs and ushered the chaplains into another room. "When they emerged," Ted Kennedy recalled, "Dad's face was twisted. . . . Suddenly the sunroom was awash in tears . . . everybody was crying; some wailed. Dad turned himself around and stumbled back up the stairs; he did not want us to witness his own dissolution into sobs." Jean, sixteen at the time, quietly left, riding her bicycle to church—alone. Jack turned to Teddy: "Joe wouldn't want us sitting here crying. He would want us to go sailing. Let's go sailing." And they did.[3]

Kick, who was perhaps closer to Joe Jr. than even Jack was, flew home from London in a military transport plane on August 16. William Cavendish, Marquess of Hartington, her husband of four months (though they had lived together for no more than one) was "somewhere in France" (as the wartime phrase went), with the elite Coldstream Guards, unreachable. She had not had a single letter from him in weeks.

It was a very large and very terrible war. Kick would never again see her brother or, as it turned out, her husband. On September 9, 1944, the twenty-six-year old major fell to a sniper's bullet in Heppen, Belgium, which his regiment was attempting to capture. Word did not reach Kick until September 16—and then, not directly, but via her father, who had received a telegram in his suite at New York's Waldorf Astoria. Eunice was with him when the telegram came, and she went to fetch Kick, who, she knew, was shopping at Bonwit Teller's. She told her only that Dad wanted to see her.

The senior Kennedy did not really know his son-in-law and had not attended his wedding to his daughter. But he knew that Joe had been fond of him. And with this latest tragedy, coming so soon after Joe's death, it sank in yet more deeply that this war had done precisely what he feared it would do. It hurt his second son, it killed his first, and it did not even spare the husband of his dear, rebellious daughter. Long a public man, impeccably attired, handsome, smiling, Joseph Kennedy Sr. now cut off contact with almost everyone outside of the family. He looked suddenly very old. Always a voluminous letter writer, he now wrote almost none. He rarely took phone calls—and there were many—and almost never returned any. Invitations to deliver this or that speech the inveterate politician now ignored.

The world hardly noted Joe Jr.'s passing. A lot of handsome young men, many of them wealthy and prominent, fell in the war. But exactly eight months after Joe was killed, on April 12, 1945, the whole world reverberated with news of the sudden death of Franklin Delano Roosevelt, victim of a cerebral hemorrhage. A great portion of that world was instantly plunged into grief and mourning.

Not so the former ambassador to the Court of St. James's. On May 1, Joe Sr. wrote to Kick, who had returned to London and her war work, mentioning how "Roosevelt's death . . . was a great shock to the masses," but declaring that now "you rarely, if ever, hear his name mentioned." He proclaimed to his daughter that "there is also no doubt that it [FDR's death] was a great thing for the country," because the president "had stirred up a hatred in the minds of at least half the country." Kennedy conceded that he could "easily understand England's feeling sorry for [FDR] because he did everything that a man could do for that country," but he claimed that the spectacle of Churchill's eulogizing him "in Parliament with tears in his eyes," calling him "a great friend . . . to England" and mentioning "some of the nice things he had done" did not make "any great impression on America." As for the war into which Roosevelt had dragged the United States and with reference to the United Nations conference under way at the time in San Francisco, Kennedy bluntly told his widowed daughter that it was "a horrible thing to contemplate, with the death of all these boys and with the world economically and socially in chaos, that we haven't anything to look forward to in the line of peace for the world as the pay-off for everyone's sacrifices."[4] *Pay-off.* Even in grief, the senior Kennedy expressed himself in the language of business.

As the war marched toward victory, Kennedy spoke privately against the Allies' demand for *unconditional* surrender in Europe. On August 8, two days after an atomic bomb was dropped on Hiroshima and one day before another was dropped on Nagasaki, he and publisher Henry Luce called on Francis Spellman, cardinal archbishop of New York, asking him to intercede with President Harry S. Truman for a truce with Japan to give its government's leaders an opportunity to surrender. And when Emperor Hirohito finally did surrender, on August 14, Kennedy found neither joy nor relief. On November 26, 1945, he wrote to Cissy Patterson, owner of the *Washington Times-Herald,* with his customary egocentric focus. It seemed, he wrote, "ironical that somebody who opposed the war as bitterly as I did should lose his oldest son, his son-in-law, and have his second son badly banged up." He continued: "it does seem that it is rather too much to hope for that the world will be any better as a result of the sacrifices of all these fine young men."[5]

*   *   *

WE KNOW HOW THE KENNEDYS received the news of Joe Jr.'s death, but they were told almost nothing of what had happened to their son and brother. Essentially, the information they were given came down to the two words Ted and his sisters had heard—*missing* and *lost*— and there is no record of the father, the mother, or their children ever making an attempt to find out just what had killed Joe Jr. Secretary of the Navy James Forrestal wrote a personal letter of condolence to Joe Sr., but he provided no explanations, and the most thorough historian of Operation Aphrodite and Project Anvil, Jack Olsen, who had access to many of the principals in both programs, reported that "those involved . . . were walking on eggshells lest the irascible Joseph P. Kennedy, Sr., find out the true circumstances of his son's death."[6] Very soon after August 12, plans were made to name a destroyer after Joe Jr. In itself, this was hardly unheard of. Destroyers during this period were traditionally named after naval heroes, especially those who gave their lives in service to the nation. Yet, even after USS *Joseph P. Kennedy*

Jr. (DD-850) was launched on July 26, 1945, ceremonially christened by Jean Kennedy—Joe's sister *and* godchild—the circumstances of the death of the destroyer's namesake were still largely a mystery.

Samuel Eliot Morison, not only a distinguished academic American historian but the official historian of the U.S. Navy and holder of the rank of rear admiral, U.S. Naval Reserve, was unable to secure access to documents relating to the loss of Kennedy and his airplane when he wrote *The Invasion of France and Germany,* an authorized fifteen-volume naval history published between 1947 and 1962. In 1962, the year volume 15 was published, Morison penned "The Death of a Kennedy" for *Look* magazine, explaining that he had finally been granted access to the official records. Yet it was not Newdelight Wood that was identified to him as the site of T-11's loss, but rather St. Margaret, a village along the route T-11 would have taken, had it not drifted twelve miles off course. What is more, Morison affirmed that Kennedy's aircraft had essentially vaporized, leaving no debris, "not even a button."[7]

Of course, Miss Ada Westgate and some fifty-eight other residents living in or near Newdelight Wood, whose houses were damaged by a dense shower of debris, could have furnished any number of large pieces of T-11. A short distance from Miss Westgate's cottage, three of the airplane's four engines fell near Hinton Lodge, home of Sir R. B. M. Blois, and the fourth, also reasonably intact, landed about a mile away, near the Blythburgh water tower, where it reportedly lay undisturbed for years after the war.[8]

Being a quiet place—except for the time some of its few residents bore witness to the biggest military explosion prior to Hiroshima—Newdelight rarely generated anything newsworthy. The local newspaperman, Christopher Elliott, therefore had plenty of time to investigate the events of August 12, 1944. After poking into the story for twenty-five years, he was able to reveal, for the first time outside of the group involved with Aphrodite and Anvil, that Joe Kennedy Jr. was the pilot of the plane that had been blasted into so many pieces.[9]

Was it a cover-up, an embarrassment, or an oversight?

Earl Paul Olsen held the naval rank of lieutenant (jg) when he served on the technical staff of SAU 1 during Project Anvil. With Lieutenant Colonel Roy Forrest, he had been among the very few who voiced concern over the crude arming panel installed in Kennedy's PB4Y-1. In the 1960s, now a civilian, he worked as an electronics engineer in the Systems Integration Laboratory of the Navy Missile Center at Point Mugu, California. When President John F. Kennedy was about to pay a visit to that installation, Olsen was notified to prepare himself for a long talk with the president. Taken aback, he asked why *he* should prepare. JFK, he was told, would be keenly interested in his involvement in Operation Aphrodite and Project Anvil—"that secret mission with Joe in World War II." Flabbergasted, Olsen protested that he did not want to talk to the president about it.

"Why not?"

"I don't want to have to tell him the truth."[10] In fact, the nature of this "truth" remains a mystery as well as a subject of speculation.

*   *   *

THE ENLISTED CREW OF THE TWO Ventura control planes shared quarters with Dee Vilan and Red Bradfield. As soon as the crew of one of the planes walked into the Nissen hut, Vilan asked them how everything went.

The question was in some measure disingenuous. The men walked into the hut at 7 pm, and Vilan well knew that their return was premature. That fact and the expression on the crewmen's faces spoke loudly. The news could not be good.

How did it go?

"It didn't. The plane blew up."

"*After* Kennedy and Willy bailed out?" Vilan asked.

"No. They didn't bail out."[11]

Hearing this, Bradfield had no doubt as to the cause. "It was the number-three engine! I shouldn't have let them take off!"[12]

Of course, it was not the engine. Everyone knew trouble in one of four engines was no great catastrophe and certainly could not cause a plane to explode. But, like Bradfield, everyone connected with the mission felt a profound responsibility and groped frantically for some instant explanation.

Commander James A. Smith approached control pilot John Anderson as soon as he emerged from the primary Ventura mother ship.

"Did you hit the destruct button?" Smith demanded.

Anderson struggled to control himself. "Of course, I didn't touch the destruct button," he said as calmly as he could. "We'd barely started the control procedures."

Smith grabbed Anderson's arm: "Are you sure?"

"Skipper, I just finished telling you I didn't touch the destruct button. You must think I'm some kind of lunatic." Then, as if realizing that there was nothing to debate, he invited Smith to go inside the Ventura and look at the control panel. Smith sent a man inside. The wire safeties on both the *arm* and *destruct* buttons were intact. John Demlein, the secondary control pilot, was similarly questioned and, on the same evidence, cleared. Neither the number three engine nor the *destruct* button could have caused the explosion.[13]

Other theories quickly emerged: The Torpex load had somehow shifted. German radio-jamming equipment triggered the detonation.

Smith was anxious to nip the loose talk and wild speculation in the bud. He gathered all the returned crew members together informally and began to grope for words: "This accident was," he said, "very unfortunate. In Mr. Kennedy and Mr. Willy we have lost two valiant gentlemen. But we are not beaten. We are not giving up." He looked down, bit his lip, and concluded: "That's all I have to say now."[14]

Besides putting an end to ill-informed speculation and guesswork, Smith had two compelling reasons to launch an immediate investigation to determine the cause of the accident. The first was that, although he had one more PB4Y-1 drone on hand, he could not in good conscience authorize another mission until the cause of the detonation was determined. The second was that Secretary of the Navy Forrestal was known to be a close friend of former ambassador Joseph P. Kennedy Sr., who, Smith well knew, had been opposed to U.S. entry into the war and would not only be grief stricken over the death of his firstborn son but very likely charged with a bitter, possibly vengeful rage. Smith feared that a hunt for scapegoats in this incident would begin quickly if he did not preempt it.

But before he had time to start the wheels rolling, Smith himself was summoned to Plymouth, home of the Fleet Air Wing, on August 13, less than twenty-four hours after the explosion. His orders were to explain the accident to the Air Wing's commander, Captain Tom Hamilton. No sooner did Smith leave Fersfield than Rosy Lyon used his authority as ranking officer and acting commanding officer of SAU 1 to convene a kind of drumhead court, an ad hoc inquiry, the major finding of which was a recommendation to discontinue the remote arming of drones and instead emulate the Air Corps practice of arming from within the drones themselves.

When he returned to Fersfield, Smith was appalled that Lyon had held any kind of inquiry and was even more upset by its recommendation, which implied that the arming system had killed Kennedy and Willy. In Plymouth, Hamilton ordered Smith to prepare a report for the Judge Advocate General's Office of the Secretary of the Navy, and he now rushed to do just that.

He began by dutifully enumerating the possible causes for the explosion:

> Static electric discharge
> Sabotage
> Friendly fire—flak
> Fuel leakage into the bomb bay
> Torpex instability
> Heating of electric fuses
> "Unknown and undetermined"

He addressed each:

> Static discharge was unlikely because the aircraft was thoroughly grounded.
> Sabotage was unlikely because the aircraft had been well guarded 24/7.
> Friendly fire was unlikely because no flak bursts had been seen by any observer.
> Gasoline leakage was unlikely because no one reported telltale fumes.
> As to instability of the Torpex and the heating of fuses, Smith reserved judgment.[15]

This left "unknown and undetermined" as the most likely cause of the accident. It was, Smith knew, an honest answer, but he also realized it would satisfy no one.[16] Certainly it did not satisfy him, and he asked Rosy Lyon to head a committee of officers to add to it. They ended up replacing the "unknown and undetermined" conclusion with two possibilities that could not be ruled out: jamming of the arming circuits either by stray FM signals or by deliberate German radio interference, and the possible instability of the Torpex. The conclusions of the so-called Lyon committee were put into Smith's secret report, which he sent up the chain of command on August 14, 1944.[17]

In the meantime, Tom Killefer, a navy flier who had been Joe Jr.'s friend at Harvard Law School, having received orders to transfer from the Pacific theater and report to the British Empire Central Flying School, stopped on the way to visit the Kennedys at Hyannis Port. There he was shocked to hear about Joe's death, and he assured his friend's father that he would try his best to find out what had happened to Joe. En route to the flying school, Killefer stopped at Fersfield. Not surprisingly, his inquiries there and in the vicinity yielded nothing of value. One eyewitness, Kenneth Williams, a local vicar, even swore up and down that the airplane had exploded while coming in for a landing. In the end, all Killefer could do was to tell Kathleen Kennedy that Joe's commanding officer was putting his name up for a Medal of Honor.[18] Did she convey this news to her father? We do not know, but it is doubtful that she did, since it would hardly have consoled a man who blamed those who had authority to award the medal, the president and Congress, for his son's death.

Manifestly unsatisfied with Smith's report, Captain Hamilton sent Lieutenant Clayton W. Bailey, an electronics expert from the navy's drone program, to arrive at more definitive conclusions. Coming from outside SAU 1, Bailey possessed the virtue of objectivity, and was also an expert in the field of radio-controlled flight. After visiting Fersfield and asking many question, he delivered on September 19, 1944, a "Top Secret Memorandum to Headquarters Training Task Force," in which he identified the "safety pin" added to the arming unit as the most likely source of the detonation. Bailey theorized that, in the first place, the radio receiver in the arming unit was too sensitive and therefore vulnerable to activation by stray FM signals, especially since it was open to not one but two frequencies. He concluded that a signal had reached the receiver, which would have armed (but not detonated) the Torpex load;

however, because the safety pin prevented the solenoid from actuating to open the arming circuit, the circuit overheated, thereby detonating the fuse.[19]

William F. Trimble, author of a detailed history of the Naval Aircraft Factory in Philadelphia, believes Bailey identified the most likely cause of the explosion. Moreover, a Bureau of Aeronautics report to the Chief of Naval Operations, signed by Admiral D. C. Ramsey and dated September 26, 1944, categorically disavows any bureau responsibility for the explosion, thereby possibly lending weight to Bailey's theory by implying that the cause of the accident must have been something done *after* the aircraft and its arming system had left the factory. A day later, however, on September 27, the Chief of Bureau of Ordnance sent a top-secret letter to the Chief of Naval Operations (signed for Admiral G. F. Hussey Jr.), stating, "It is positively concluded that [overheating due to leaving the arming current on too long] will not result in fuse detonation." Two weeks later, on October 10, 1944, Admiral Hussey wrote a top-secret letter reversing himself and conceding as "conceivable" that an overheated solenoid could cause a "cook-off"—that is, become sufficiently hot to detonate the fuse and cause an explosion.[20]

We do know that on August 12 U.S. Army Air Forces lieutenant colonel Joe Pomykata monitored the video transmission from T-11 in the Fersfield radio shack and saw the screen go from a clear image to "grass" when the aircraft exploded. His immediate assumption was that the remote-control arming system, of which he always disapproved, was to blame.[21] And we also know that Fersfield commanding officer Lieutenant Colonel Roy Forrest was appalled by the jury-rigged appearance and evidently poor workmanship of the arming breadboard installed in T-11. In the opinion of Kennedy's Dunkeswell roommate and sometime copilot Jim Simpson, "There's a twelve-year-old girl at the pub down the road that could have done a better job of designing this system." Lieutenant (jg) Earl P. Olsen agreed: "It's the worst piece of junk I've ever seen."[22] Yet none of these assessments appeared in any of the "secret" reports, including the one Smith issued on August 14, in which Earl Olsen had a hand as a member of the Lyon committee.

Was the criticism of the arming system—particularly the breadboard—suppressed in the official reports? Was there a cover-up? Naval Aircraft Factory historian Trimble does not believe so—or at least concludes that the official explanation, which exonerates the Naval Air Material Center (NAMC) design and blames the safety pin, a field modification, is the more plausible. Almost certainly, the cause of the accident will never be determined definitively. It is, however, a fact that on the next and final Anvil mission, flown on September 3, not only was the remote arming system abandoned and an internal fusing system used instead, the possibly unstable Torpex was replaced by tried-and-true (but far less potent) TNT. In that mission, the jump pilot safely parachuted, and the PB4Y-1 drone flew on to its designated target—no longer a V-weapon site but the German U-boat pens on Heligoland Island in the North Sea. At the very last minute, however, the robot veered off course and missed its target.

* * *

THAT SEPTEMBER 3 MISSION was the last for SAU 1. Arguably, it had come close to demonstrating the feasibility of Project Anvil, but the U.S. Navy ordered the termination of the program and the unit. The reason was less a matter of performance and reliability than a shrinking supply of targets. By the end of summer 1944, Allied ground forces had overrun the major V-weapons sites within range of England, only to discover that almost all had been abandoned weeks earlier. Although the very last V-1 launch site would not be overrun until March 29, 1945, the last one in range of England was captured in October 1944. As for the V-2 attacks, the last two rockets hit English soil on March 27, 1945. These were fired from mobile sites rather than massive bunkers. Like the V-1 bunkers, the V-2 fixed installations within range of England had been abandoned by late summer 1944. As for the much-dreaded V-3, it never became operational in any form. The bunker at Mimoyecques—the target that cost Joe Kennedy and Bud Willy their lives—had never become operational and had been effectively abandoned by the Germans in July 1944.

The failure of Allied reconnaissance and intelligence was staggering. Analysts had been unable to recognize that, by the end of July, the targets of Aphrodite and Anvil had been or were in the process of being abandoned. The blunder was in part a testament to the awe German *Wunderwaffen* (wonder weapons) inspired among Allied politicians and military planners. In part, too, the failure was the result of highly effective German efforts at deception; sufficient activity was maintained in and around the major V-weapon sites to suggest that they were operational. Mostly, however, the failure of intelligence was due to the outward appearance of the structures themselves. Although badly damaged, the bunkers all looked viable from the air. Besides, the V-2s, launched from hidden mobile sites, kept coming, leading the Allies to believe that some of the fixed sites were still active.

The navy abandoned Anvil when its only other drone had been used up. The Army Air Corps, however, flew several more missions after the navy's unsuccessful attack on the Heligoland U-boat pens. The Air Corps would launch repeatedly against Heligoland, but its other targets were of no great strategic importance. As it turned out, the Air Corps kept the drone program active less to destroy top-priority targets than to finally prove the potential of drones, so that they could be deployed in the Pacific theater.

By this time in World War II, it was clear that both Germany and Japan had been defeated militarily. The surrender of Germany, it was felt, was just a matter of time—and very little time at that. Japan, however, was a different matter. Very few military commanders knew anything about the top-secret work under way on the Manhattan Project, the program to create an atomic bomb. Even those with ultra-secret clearance, such as President Roosevelt and Secretary of War Henry Stimson, had good reason to doubt whether the crash program to transform arcane theoretical physics into a war-winning weapon would actually work. For this reason, plans to invade Japan were being drawn up. They were accompanied by the grim prediction that a "defeated" Japan would resist invasion so fiercely that anywhere from 500,000 to a million American military personnel would be killed or wounded in Operation Downfall—the projected invasion's code name. As Jimmy Doolittle, Hap Arnold, and Tooey Spaatz saw it, unmanned drone bombers, used against a fanatical Japan, might well save the lives of many American fliers.

* * *

SCARCELY DOCUMENTED BY THE USAAF, Project Castor had been under way for five or six years by the time Jimmy Doolittle brought it to Fersfield as a replacement for Jim Rand and his discredited double

AZON system.[23] That Rand's bold improvisations had been totally un-
informed by the navy's far more advanced work on Project Anvil is flab-
bergasting, especially since Doolittle consulted the navy as early as June.
Yet it is at least explicable, if not excusable, by the often-intractable
interservice rivalry that prevailed in the U.S. military during the World
War II era. That neither Doolittle nor anyone else tapped into the work
of the Army Air Corps' own Castor team, however, seems appallingly
irresponsible and just plain stupid.

At the very least, it is difficult to account for. Ever since the 1942
B-25 raid on Tokyo, Jimmy Doolittle had a reputation for seat-of-the-
pants improvisation. The Tokyo raid was as close as the Air Corps ever
got to flying a suicide mission, at least until Doolittle sponsored Operation Aphrodite. But in contrast to Aphrodite, the Tokyo raid succeeded.
One reason was that, appearances to the contrary notwithstanding,
Doolittle was by no means a casual planner. The popular belief that he
favored improvisation over methodical preparation is belied by the fact
that he was no mere barnstormer. Among other things, James Doolittle
held a PhD in aeronautics.

Whatever the reason for having excluded Castor from Operation
Aphrodite, it arrived in August, led by its technical chief, Lieutenant
Colonel Dale Anderson. In experiments at Muroc Army Air Field, near
Rogers Dry Lake, California, Anderson's team had successfully taken
off by remote radio control and staged a demonstration in which the
drone was successfully flown into *another* radio-controlled aircraft, a
target drone, which it destroyed.

Although Aphrodite had ignored Castor—or was perhaps ignorant
of it—the Castor system actually borrowed much that had gone into
both AZON and double AZON as well as the work of the navy. To
these elements, Castor personnel added their own improvements. The
Castor drones not only had sophisticated radio-control units, which
included complete remote control of the throttle and a "repeat-back"
compass that allowed the remote pilot to view the drone's onboard compass via video, they also had an elaborate forward television imaging
system and innovative electronic navigation gear. Both of these would
supplement—though not entirely replace—a remote-control system that
relied wholly on maintaining uninterrupted visual contact between the
mother ship and the baby. To improve direct visual control, the Castor

system equipped each drone with a sophisticated smoke system that could be turned on and off by remote control to create a highly visible tracer effect.

The Castor technicians closely studied Aphrodite's and Anvil's failures and made improvements in distributing the explosive load to maintain a lower center of gravity, understood and accommodated the limitations of the temperamental ACE radio altimeter, and definitively abandoned remote-control arming. Castor also modified the use of the static line for the jump crew, so that it would separate entirely from the drone after it had ripped open a jumper's parachute pack. In this way, there would be nothing left attached to the aircraft, flapping around in the slipstream and potentially damaging the drone's delicate underbelly antennas.

In short, Castor was what neither Aphrodite nor Anvil had been: a synthesis of all U.S. military remote-control experimentation and experience accumulated since World War I.

For his part, Roy Forrest welcomed the arrival of the Castor team and wanted to make a profound impression by launching the first Castor mission against a spectacular target—the infamous German battleship *Tirpitz*. Commissioned on February 25, 1941, *Tirpitz* displaced more than 52,000 tons under full load. The heaviest battleship built by any European navy, *Tirpitz* could nevertheless make a swift 30 knots. It mounted fifteen-inch main guns as well as torpedoes and four catapult-launched aircraft. Although *Tirpitz* actually saw little combat, it was perceived as such a threat that the British Royal Navy felt compelled to maintain a significant force in waters off Norway just to contain the battleship. In effect, *Tirpitz* served as what naval strategists call a "fleet in being," a force—in this case consisting of a single ship—that exerts major tactical and strategic influence without ever leaving port.

When Forrest learned that the British had developed so-called hydrostatic bombs capable of detonating at a predetermined underwater depth, he proposed loading a B-17 drone with 25,000 pounds of hydrostatic munitions and flying it against *Tirpitz,* so that the entire load would detonate under its hull with such force that it would break the ship in two. Told that the main problem would be loading the required number of bombs into a drone, Forrest, an engineering aide—Major Ralph Hayes—and a team of Boeing technicians stationed at Fersfield concluded that parts of the top of the B-17 fuselage, including the top of the cockpit canopy, could be removed without creating any structural compromise. The result was what Forrest dubbed a "roadster," the only four-engine heavy bomber in World War II with an open cockpit. Every pilot wanted to fly it.

Forrest succeeded in persuading the British to ship him the hydro-static bombs, which were lowered into the B-17 roadster from above, using a cherry-picker crane. By the time this delicate process was complete, however, both the Royal Air Force and the Royal Navy Fleet Air Arm intervened, complained, and killed the mission, protesting that they and they alone would sink the *Tirpitz*. This was in fact accomplished on November 12, 1944, by RAF bombers dropping 4,000-pound Tall-boys—the same munitions that had wreaked havoc on the V-weapon bunkers at the Pas-de-Calais.

Undaunted, Forrest proceeded with Castor, and on September 11, 1944, launched B-17 30180 against the Heligoland U-boat pens. The baby was flown by Richard "Lindy" Lindahl, with Donald Salles serving as the electronics specialist. Takeoff proceeded perfectly—except that Lindy took it into his head to buzz the Fersfield control tower, even while packed with explosives. Doubtless, this stunt would have cost him disciplinary action, perhaps even a court martial, had he returned to face the music.

But Richard Lindahl did not return.

Radio control was established with the mother ship, the payload was armed, and Salles bailed out while Lindahl made final adjustments on the autopilot, the controls for which, in the Castor system, had been moved from the crawlspace below the flight deck up into the cockpit itself. Lindahl made the adjustments and was seen by observer aircraft emerging from the navigator's escape hatch. His body, however, looked suddenly stiff, and neither his primary nor secondary parachutes ever opened as he fell to earth.

As for the drone, it headed straight for the U-boat pens—only to be shot down at the last minute by German flak. Having been thoroughly spooked by the September 3 Anvil Heligoland mission, the gunners, it seemed, were intent on destroying any incoming aircraft.

Aphrodite had one fatality and one amputation. Anvil, two fatalities. Castor now had one as well. Four brave and highly skilled men killed and one maimed, with nothing to show for their sacrifice. Forrest pressed on. On September 14, two Castor B-17 drones were launched against an oil refinery complex at Hemmingstedt, in the German state of Schleswig-Holstein. Despite the electronic refinements Castor introduced, weather conditions so reduced visibility that both drones missed the refinery.

After the September 14 mission, Lieutenant Colonel Roy Forrest was rotated back to the United States. A new Fersfield commander launched a pair of drones against Heligoland again on October 15. While low visibility shielded them from German antiaircraft defenses, the weather also made it impossible for control pilots to fly them into their target. Two weeks later, on October 30, another pair of B-17s were hurled against Heligoland and were again foiled by bad weather.

At this point, General Spaatz intervened, banning further attempts against military "hard targets." Instead, he ordered Castor drone attacks against "industrial" objectives. Accordingly, on December 5, 1944, two more B-17s were sent against the railroad marshaling yards at Herford, Westphalia. Although this was a large target, cloud cover made it impossible to locate, and the control pilots were directed instead to Edermünde, an industrial town at the junction of the Eder and Fulda Rivers southwest of Kassel. Both drones ran out of gas and crashed on the outskirts of the town, inflicting damage of no strategic or tactical importance. On January 1, 1945, the B-17 babies *Darlin' Dolly* and *Stump Jumper* were sent to destroy the Oldenburg power station but were downed by antiaircraft fire en route.

No further missions were launched in January and, on the 27th, Spaatz cabled Doolittle:

APHRODITE BABIES MUST NOT BE LAUNCHED AGAINST THE ENEMY UNTIL FURTHER ORDERS.[24]

The urgency of the cable was the result of a high-level decision by the British Chiefs of Staff and the British Defence Committee that drone attacks, successful or not, might well provoke "similar attacks by German war-weary bombers."[25] Arnold, Spaatz, and Doolittle still wanted to use the European theater as a proving ground to perfect the drone program for use against Japan. They therefore prevailed on President

Roosevelt to intercede directly with Prime Minister Churchill at the Yalta Conference during February 4 to 11, 1945, and in a telegram of March 29, Churchill promised that he would reconsider the Chiefs' and committee decision. He delayed, however, and the death of FDR on April 12, 1945, prompted him to next communicate directly with Harry S. Truman, on April 14. In what was only his second letter to the new president, Churchill told Truman, "If the United States military authorities really consider this practice [the use of 'pilotless bombers'] necessary to bring about the end of the German war, we [Churchill and the British Chiefs of Staff] will not dissent."[26]

Even today, Harry Truman is rarely given the credit he deserves for the nuanced decision making his record as president demonstrates. His response to Churchill's letter is an example of the subtlety of his political, diplomatic, and strategic thought. He could have stopped with Churchill's opening concession and authorized the continuation of Aphrodite/Castor. Instead, he went on to ponder Churchill's further observations: that "the war situation has turned so much in our favour that the making of these great explosions in German cities is no longer of its former importance" and "that if the Germans have a number of war-weary bombers that could make the distance, London is the obvious and indeed the only target." Such attacks "would be a very great disappointment to the people at this time when they had hoped that their prolonged ordeal was over." Churchill went on to calculate "losses to the Greater London area in killed by enemy action as one in 131 . . . the highest losses sustained by any similar locality on the Allied side in the Second Great War." He concluded his letter: "having put these facts before you I leave the decision entirely in the hands of your military advisers, and we shall make no complaint if misfortune comes to us in consequence."[27] Responding to the tone of dissent rather than the assertion of agreement, Truman ordered Aphrodite/Castor suspended. It was, in fact, the end of the program.

*   *   *

"FOUR UP AND FOUR DOWN, and nothing near a target," Roy Forrest had complained after the failed missions of August 4, 1944. By January 1, 1945, the record stood at eighteen up and eighteen down—with the same result.

Beyond question, Aphrodite/Anvil/Castor was a tactical and strategic bust. It could be reasonably argued that it was nevertheless a major step in the evolution of guided munitions of all kinds, from smart bombs, to cruise missiles, to the Predator and Reaper drones of today. The three main U.S. service branches—army, navy, and air force (which became an independent branch in 1947)—have all developed and deployed a variety of guided cruise missiles, smart bombs, and unmanned aerial vehicles (UAVs), making the evolution of U.S. radio-controlled military aircraft continuous from Aphrodite to the present. Nevertheless, few military or aviation historians assert that the World War II program in any way "led to" modern remotely controlled aircraft.[28]

Why the reluctance to credit Aphrodite/Anvil/Castor? It is undeniable that Germany made the most extensive strategic use of pilotless aerial weapons in World War II. The V-1 cruise missile was deployed in more than 8,000 sorties during the war and the V-2 ballistic missile in more than 3,000. While the propulsion systems of both weapons—especially the V-2—were more advanced than anything the Allies fielded, and while some aspects of the internal guidance systems of both weapons were also more advanced or, at least, more practical, neither the V-1 nor V-2 was radio-controlled. Some V-1 prototypes were produced with radio control systems, it is true, but these were soon abandoned as too expensive and unreliable. In any case, they were unnecessary in a weapon intended for the strategic purpose of terrorizing civilians by hitting anywhere in a large city as opposed to the tactical purpose of precisely targeting a particular structure of military importance. That German non-radio-controlled pilotless weapons have substantially overshadowed the Allies' radio-controlled combat aircraft in the history of the UAV is both unfortunate and ironic. This historical distortion, however, is not exclusively due to the extensive and dramatic use of the V-1 and V-2 in combat. We must also consider the effect of Operation Paperclip, the late-war and postwar U.S. intelligence operation that rounded up German military scientists, especially those involved in V-1 and V-2 development, and brought them to the United States.[29] Through these scientists, the postwar development of radio-controlled and unmanned flight in America was largely influenced by German technology.

And what place in history should be accorded Joseph P. Kennedy Jr.? He never did receive the Medal of Honor, but he was awarded, posthumously, the Navy Cross (as was Bud Willy), a higher distinction than brother Jack's Navy-Marine Corps Medal. He was further memorialized by the naming of the destroyer *Joseph P. Kennedy, Jr.* (DD-850). Christened by his sister and godchild, Jean, on July 26, 1945, it was the ship on which his brother Robert sailed as a U.S. Naval Reserve apprentice seaman in 1946, and it was part of the fleet that enforced President John F. Kennedy's "quarantine" of Cuba during the Cuban Missile Crisis of October 14 to 28, 1962.

If German dominance of World War II missile weapons technology denied Aphrodite/Anvil/Castor its rightful place in history, Anvil itself robbed Joseph P. Kennedy Jr. of both his life and the role in history his father imagined for him. Killed in action, he would never be president of the United States. And yet this, in its way, made possible the elevation of the *second* Kennedy son to that office. The martial heroism of John F. Kennedy, the story of PT-109, surely facilitated his political ambitions, just as both Joe Jr. and his father had hoped an admirable war record would enable the *first* son to build a political career for himself. The death of Joe Jr. did not merely create a vacancy for Jack, however. PT-109 helped the American public see candidate John F. Kennedy more as a war hero than as the son of a defeatist appeaser. That Joe Jr. was killed in action, fighting for the very democracy his father seemed to never quite believe in, defined Jack Kennedy as both the hero of PT-109 *and* the brother of another hero in that same war. In the resulting national, personal, and family portrait, the gravely flawed image of the father—a man remarkable but far, far from greatness—receded into the background.

NOTES

PROLOGUE: TWO VIEWS FROM LONDON

1. Max Arthur, *Forgotten Voices of World War II* (Guilford, CT: Lyons Press, 2004), 106.
2. Arthur, 102–103.
3. "The London Blitz, 1940," EyeWitness to History, 2001, http://www.eye witnesstohistory.com/blitz.htm.
4. "The London Blitz, 1940," EyeWitness to History.
5. Arthur, 111.
6. Hugh Sidey, "The Dynasty: The Kennedys," *Time,* June 14, 1999, http://content.time.com/time/subscriber/article/0,33009,991275,00.html.
7. James Roosevelt with Bill Libby, *My Parents: A Differing View* (Chicago: Playboy Press, 1976), 208–209.
8. James Roosevelt, 208–209.
9. Arthur Krock, *Memoirs: Sixty Years on the Firing Line* (New York: Funk & Wagnalls, 1968), 333.
10. Henry Morgenthau, diary, December 8, 1937, quoted in David Nasaw, *The Patriarch: The Remarkable Life and Turbulent Times of Joseph P. Kennedy* (New York: Penguin, 2012), 274.
11. Henry Morgenthau, diary, quoted in Nasaw, 274.
12. Boake Carter, letter to Joseph P. Kennedy, December 28, 1937, quoted in Nasaw, 275–276.
13. Amanda Smith, ed., *Hostage to Fortune: The Letters of Joseph P. Kennedy* (New York: Viking, 2001), 219–220.
14. "Ambassador Kennedy Visits Chamberlain," *New York Times,* March 5, 1938.
15. Joseph P. Kennedy, Pilgrims Society Speech, March 18, 1938, quoted in Nasaw, 294–295.
16. Smith, ed., 248.
17. Nasaw, 305–06.
18. Harold L. Ickes, *The Secret Diary of Harold L. Ickes,* vol. 2, *The Inside Struggle, 1936–1939* (New York: Simon and Schuster, 1954), 415–416.
19. Sumner Welles and Joseph P. Kennedy, transcript of telephone conversation, September 26, 1938, quoted in Nasaw, 342.

20. Harold George Nicholson, *Diaries and Letters* (New York: Atheneum, 1966–1968), 1:370–371.
21. Nasaw, 346.
22. Joseph P. Kennedy, Trafalgar Day address, October 19, 1938, quoted in Nasaw, 353–354.
23. "Kennedy for Amity with Fascist Bloc," *New York Times*, October 20, 1938.
24. Jay Pierrepont Moffat, diary, November 4, 1938, quoted in Nasaw, 355.
25. Smith, ed., 299–300.
26. Joseph P. Kennedy, unpublished "Diplomatic Memoir," quoted in Nasaw, 356.
27. John F. Kennedy, letter to Joseph P. Kennedy, undated, quoted in Nasaw, 357.
28. Joseph P. Kennedy, letter to Robert Fisher, November 25, 1938, quoted in Nasaw, 366.
29. Kennedy, letter to Fisher, quoted in Nasaw, 366.
30. *Chicago Daily Tribune*, December 5, 1938, quoted in Nasaw, 367.
31. Joseph P. Kennedy, cable to Franklin D. Roosevelt, March 3, 1939, quoted in Nasaw, 373.
32. Nasaw, 373.
33. Smith, ed., 354–355.
34. Smith, ed., 356–360.
35. Cordell Hull, *The Memoirs of Cordell Hull*, 2 vols. (New York: Macmillan, 1948), 1:662.
36. Joseph P. Kennedy, unpublished "Diplomatic Memoir," quoted in Nasaw, 401–402.
37. Smith, ed., 374.
38. Joseph P. Kennedy, diary, September 17, 1939, in Smith, ed., 378–379.
39. Neville Chamberlain, transcript of declaration of war, September 3, 1939, http://www.bbc.co.uk/archive/ww2outbreak/7957.shtml?page=txt.
40. Joseph P. Kennedy, diary, September 3, 1939, in Smith, ed., 366.
41. Michael R. Beschloss, *Kennedy and Roosevelt: The Uneasy Alliance* (New York: Norton, 1980), 190.
42. Breckinridge Long, diary, September 7, 1939, quoted in Nasaw, 410.
43. Smith, ed., 374–376.
44. The description of Joseph Sr. as "frantic" is from James Farley, *James Farley's Story* (New York: McGraw-Hill, 1948), 198–199.
45. Joseph P. Kennedy, diary, October 5, 1939, in Smith, ed., 393.
46. Smith, ed., 385–386.
47. Harold L. Ickes, *The Secret Diary of Harold L. Ickes*, vol. 3 (New York: Simon and Schuster, 1954), 15.
48. Joseph Alsop and Robert Kintner, "The Capital Parade: Kennedy, the Pessimist," *The Atlanta Constitution*, December 19, 1939, 8.
49. Smith, ed., 410–411.
50. Winston Churchill, letter to Franklin D. Roosevelt, May 15, 1940, in Warren F. Kimball, ed., *Churchill and Roosevelt: The Complete Correspondence*, vol. 1, *Alliance Emerging* (Princeton, NJ: Princeton University Press, 1984), 37–38.
51. Smith, ed., 432–433.
52. Joseph P. Kennedy, cable to Cordell Hull, May 27, 1940, quoted in Nasaw, 448.

53. Winston Churchill, "We Shall Fight on the Beaches," speech to the House of Commons, June 4, 1940, http://www.winstonchurchill.org /learn/speeches/speeches-of-winston-churchill/1940-finest-hour/128-we -shall-fight-on-the-beaches.

54. Smith, ed., 436–437.

55. Joseph P. Kennedy, cable to Cordell Hull, July 20, 1940, quoted in Nasaw, 460.

56. Joseph P. Kennedy, cable to Cordell Hull, August 2, 1940, quoted in Nasaw, 461.

57. Joseph P. Kennedy, diary, August 1, 1940, in Smith, ed., 452–453.

58. Joseph P. Kennedy, diary, in Smith, ed., 453.

59. Joseph P. Kennedy, diary, August 15, 1940, quoted in Nasaw, 468.

60. Smith, ed., 463.

61. Franklin D. Roosevelt, cable to Joseph P. Kennedy, August 28, 1940, quoted in Nasaw, 471.

62. Harvey Klemmer, quoted in Nasaw, 474.

63. Joseph P. Kennedy, diary, August 1, 1940, quoted in Smith, ed., 452–453.

64. Joseph P. Kennedy, cable to Cordell Hull, September 27, 1940, quoted in Nasaw, 479.

65. Joseph Alsop and Robert Kintner, "The Capital Parade," *The Atlanta Constitution,* October 8, 1940, 6.

66. Smith, ed., 475.

67. Breckinridge Long, diaries, November 6, 1940, quoted in Nasaw, 497.

68. Louis Lyons, "Kennedy Says Democracy All Done in Britain, Maybe Here," *Boston Sunday Globe,* November 10, 1940, C1–C2.

69. Joseph Patterson, *Daily News,* quoted in Nasaw, 503.

70. Joseph P. Kennedy, WEAF radio address, January 18, 1941, http://fdr4 freedoms.org/resources/sources/joseph-p-kennedy-radio-broadcast-janu ary-18-1941.

CHAPTER 1: CHOSEN SON

1. Amanda Smith, ed., *Hostage to Fortune: The Letters of Joseph P. Kennedy* (New York: Viking, 2001), 237–239.

2. Rose Kennedy, interview in the files of *Time* magazine, 1960-1961, quoted in Lawrence Leamer, *The Kennedy Men, 1901–1963* (New York: Harper Perennial, 2002), 46.

3. John F. Kennedy, interview, quoted in Leamer, 46.

4. Leamer, 39.

5. Rose Kennedy, interview, quoted in Leamer, 47.

6. Rose Kennedy, diary, quoted in Leamer, 47.

7. Hank Searls, *The Lost Prince: Young Joe, the Forgotten Kennedy* (New York: NAL, 1969), 44.

8. Edward M. Kennedy, *True Compass* (New York: Twelve, 2009), 31.

9. Joe McCarthy, *The Remarkable Kennedys* (New York: Popular Library, 1960), 42.

10. Joseph P. Kennedy Jr., Choate application, quoted in Leamer, 75.

11. Smith, ed., 84.

12. Searls, 64.

13. Smith, ed., 86.

14. Smith, ed., 94–95.

15. Smith, ed., 95–96. Smith includes young JFK's letter (undated, except for "Dec 9") with correspondence from 1931. Clearly, however, the letter was written on December 9, 1929, in reference to Joe Jr.'s holiday home visit during his first year (1929) at Choate.
16. Smith, ed., 95–96.
17. John F. Kennedy, ed. *As We Remember Joe* (Cambridge, MA: Privately printed, 1945), 59.
18. Rose Kennedy, *Times to Remember* (Garden City, NY: Doubleday, 1974), 143.
19. John F. Kennedy, letter to Joseph P. Kennedy, undated, quoted in Leamer, 80.
20. Leamer, 80.
21. Smith, ed., 126–127.
22. Smith, ed., 126-127.
23. Smith, ed., 130–131.
24. Cari Beauchamp, "Two Sons, One Destiny," *Vanity Fair,* December 2004, http://www.vanityfair.com/politics/features/2004/12/kennedy-200412.
25. Beauchamp, "Two Sons, One Destiny."
26. Smith, ed., 145–146.
27. Smith, ed., 133–135.
28. David Nasaw, *The Patriarch: The Remarkable Life and Turbulent Times of Joseph P. Kennedy* (New York: Penguin, 2012), 203.
29. Smith, ed., 133–135.
30. John F. Kennedy, letter to Lem Billings, July 25, 1934, quoted in Leamer, 83.
31. Nasaw, 220.
32. Smith, ed., 142.
33. Smith, ed., 147.
34. U.S. Bureau of Labor Statistics, "1934–36," *100 Years of U.S. Consumer Spending,* http://www.bls.gov/opub/uscs/1934-36.pdf.
35. Nasaw, 221.
36. Robert Purdy, interview, in Leamer, 96.
37. Leamer, 95–96.
38. Leamer, 94.
39. Smith, ed., 143–144.
40. Leamer, 98.
41. Payton S. Wild, quoted in Leamer, 102.
42. Rip Horton, interview, in Leamer, 103.
43. Searls, 99.
44. Will Swift, *The Kennedys Amidst the Gathering Storm: A Thousand Days in London, 1938–1940* (Washington, D.C.: Smithsonian Books, 2008), 61.
45. Swift, 61.
46. Joseph P. Kennedy, letter to Arthur Krock, October 10, 1941, quoted in Nasaw, 326.
47. Leamer, 122.
48. Searls, 123.
49. Leamer, 128
50. Smith, ed., 410.
51. Smith, ed., 410.
52. Smith, ed., 433–435.

53. Henry Raymont, "Recordings Reveal JFK's Lively Debate with Publisher," *Eugene Register-Guard*, August 20, 1970, 5, http://news.google.com/news papers?nid=1310&dat=19700820&id=6JpQAAAAIBAJ&sjid=NuEDAA AAIBAJ&pg=6515,4271658.
54. Beauchamp, "Two Sons, One Destiny."
55. Swift, 149.
56. Beauchamp, "Two Sons, One Destiny."
57. Swift, 214.
58. Swift, 266.
59. Nasaw, 528.
60. Edward J. Renehan Jr., *The Kennedys at War 1937–1945* (New York: Doubleday, 2002), Kindle edition, chapter 17.
61. Joseph P. Kennedy, letter to Joseph P. Kennedy Jr., September 10, 1940, quoted in Nasaw, 476–477.
62. Swift, 295.
63. Joseph P. Kennedy, letter to Joseph P. Kennedy Jr., September 10, 1940, quoted in Nasaw, 477.
64. Swift, 296.
65. Beauchamp, "Two Sons, One Destiny."
66. Leamer, 167–168.

CHAPTER 2: MOST DANGEROUS

1. Euripides, *Phrixius*, 970.
2. Louis Lyons, "Kennedy Says Democracy All Done in Britain, Maybe Here," *Boston Sunday Globe*, November 10, 1940, C1-C2.
3. Lyons, November 10, 1940.
4. Edward J. Renehan Jr., *The Kennedys at War 1937–1945* (New York: Doubleday, 2002), Kindle edition, chapter 17.
5. Renehan, Kindle edition, chapter 18.
6. Renehan, Kindle edition, chapter 18.
7. Renehan, Kindle edition, chapter 22.
8. Renehan, Kindle edition, chapter 22.
9. Renehan, Kindle edition, chapter 23.
10. Renehan, Kindle edition, chapter 24.
11. Renehan, Kindle edition, chapter 27.
12. John F. Kennedy, "Joseph P. Kennedy Jr," John F. Kennedy Presidential Library and Museum, http://www.jfklibrary.org/JFK/The-Kennedy-Fam ily/Joseph-P-Kennedy-Jr.aspx.
13. Hank Searls, *The Lost Prince: Young Joe, the Forgotten Kennedy* (New York: NAL, 1969), 220.
14. Searls, 212.
15. Searls, 230.
16. Patricia Wilson is identified as the mistress of "Crash-Bang" in Edward Klein, *The Kennedy Curse: International Edition* (New York: St. Martin's Press), 148.

CHAPTER 3: THE BITTER FRUIT OF PEENEMÜNDE

1. Amanda Smith, ed., *Hostage to Fortune: The Letters of Joseph P. Kennedy* (New York: Viking, 2001), 395.

2. Smith, ed., 395.
3. Smith, ed., 395.
4. Smith, ed., 395.
5. R. V. Jones, *Most Secret War: British Scientific Intelligence 1939–1945* (London: Hamish Hamilton, 1978), 333.
6. Basil Collier, *The Battle of the V-Weapons, 1944–1945* (Enfield, UK: The Enfield Press, 1976), 68, 82, 84, 103.
7. Jones, 340.
8. Jones, 338.
9. "The V2 Rocket: A Romance with the Future," Making the Modern World, http://www.makingthemodernworld.org.uk/stories/defiant_modernism/01.ST.03/?scene=9&tv=true.
10. Franklin D'Olier et al., "The Secondary Campaigns," *United States Strategic Bombing Survey, Summary Report (European War)*, cited in "Operation Crossbow," http://www.anesi.com/ussbs02.htm.
11. Steven J. Zaloga, *German V-Weapon Sites 1943–45* (Oxford, UK: Osprey, 2008), Kindle edition, "The Sites at War."
12. "V1 and V2 Statistics: Totals by Week," Flying Bombs and Rockets, http://www.flyingbombsandrockets.com/statsbyweek.html.

CHAPTER 4: NEVER SO LUCKY AGAIN

1. Jack Olsen, *Aphrodite: Desperate Mission* (New York: G. P. Putnam's Sons, 1970), 17.
2. James H. Doolittle, with Carroll V. Glines, *I Could Never Be So Lucky Again* (New York: Bantam, 1992), 24.
3. Doolittle, 24.
4. Doolittle, 24–25.
5. Doolittle, 25.
6. Doolittle, 26.
7. Doolittle, 36.
8. Doolittle, 218.
9. Doolittle, 172.
10. Olsen, 18.
11. Olsen, 18–19.
12. Olsen, 19.
13. Olsen, 20.
14. Olsen, 21.
15. Carlo Kopp, "The Dawn of the Smart Bomb," *Air Power Australia,* http://www.ausairpower.net/WW2-PGMs.html; Friis, "Guided German Air to Ground Weapons in WW2," 1.jma, http://www.1jma.dk/articles/1jmaluftwaffegroundweapons.htm; Brian J. Ford, *Secret Weapons: Death Rays, Doodlebugs, and Churchill's Golden Goose* (Oxford, UK: Osprey Publishing, 2013), Kindle edition, chapter 3.
16. Greg Goebel, "World War II Glide Bombs," Vectors, http://www.vectorsite.net/twbomb_04.html.
17. Olsen, 22–23.
18. Olsen, 23.
19. Bjørn Westergaard, quoted in "Inga Arvad," Wikipedia, http://en.wikipedia.org/wiki/Inga_Arvad.

20. "Kennedy Affair with Spy Suspect Reported," *Los Angeles Times,* January 19, 1976, B8.

21. FBI wiretap Freedom of Information Act, quoted in Lawrence Leamer, *The Kennedy Men, 1901–1963* (New York: Harper Perennial, 2002), 181.

22. Robert J. Donovan, *PT 109: John F. Kennedy in WW II* (1962; reprint ed., Camden, ME: International Marine/Ragged Mountain Press, 2001), 106–107, 119.

23. Amanda Smith, ed., *Hostage to Fortune: The Letters of Joseph P. Kennedy* (New York: Viking, 2001), 569.

24. Leamer, 195.

25. Edward J. Renehan, Jr., *The Kennedys at War 1937–1945* (New York: Doubleday, 2002), Kindle edition, chapter 23.

CHAPTER 5: WAR-WEARY

1. Nigel Hamilton, *JFK: Reckless Youth* (New York: Random House, 1992).

2. United States Army Air Forces Office of Flying Safety, Safety Education Division, *Jungle, Desert, Arctic, Ocean Survival* (Washington, D.C.: US-AAF, n.d.), http://cbi-theater-3.home.comcast.net/~cbi-theater-3/survival/survival.html.

3. Hank Searls, *The Lost Prince: Young Joe, the Forgotten Kennedy* (New York: NAL, 1969), 262.

4. "The AZON Project," 458th Bombardment Group (H) website, http://www.458bg.com/azonproject.htm.

5. "The AZON Project."

6. "The AZON Project."

7. Ralph Earle, "The F. B. Development to Date," U.S. Navy Report, November 1, 1918, 1.

8. Earle, 2.

9. A. M. Low, "The First Guided Missile," *Flight,* October 3, 1952, 438; Delmar S. Fahrney, *The History of Pilotless Aircraft and Guided Missiles,* n.d., 103, 104, 998–1001; Rhodi Williams, "The First Guided Missile," *Royal Air Force Flying Review,* May 1958, 26, 27.

10. Fahrney, 112.

11. Earle, 4.

12. Kenneth P. Werrell, *The Evolution of the Cruise Missile* (Maxwell AFB, AL: Air University Press, 1985), 13.

13. Werrell, 13.

14. Werrell, 15.

15. "Kettering Aerial Torpedo 'Bug,'" National Museum of the U.S. Air Force, March 25, 2014, http://www.nationalmuseum.af.mil/factsheets/factsheet.asp?id=320.

16. H. F. "Red" Smith, "The World's First Cruise Missile," *Air Force Magazine,* October 1977, 43.

17. Werrell, 14.

18. Werrell, 15.

19. Werrell, 16, note 43.

20. Werrell, 17.

21. Werrell, 18.

22. The photo description reads: "The RAE Larynx (*Long Range Gun with Lynx Engine*) missile on cordite-fired catapult of destroyer HMS Stronghold, July 1927. The man on the box is Dr. George Gardner; later Director of RAE." *The Evolution of the Cruise Missile*, July 1927, http://en.wikipedia.org/wiki/File:Larynx.png.

23. G. W. Gardner, "Automatic Flight," *Flight*, May 16, 1958, https://www.flightglobal.com/FlightPDFArchive/1958/1958%20-%200642.PDF.

24. Werrell, 18–19.

25. Gardner; Peter G. Cooksley, *Flying Bomb* (New York: Scribner, 1979), 18.

26. Werrell, 22–23.

27. On the origin of the term *drone,* see "Unmanned Systems Branch Honors WWII UAV Pioneer," *Space and Naval Warfare Systems Center Robotics Update* 7, no. 2 (Winter 2007), http://www.public.navy.mil/spawar/Pacific/Robotics/Documents/Publications/Newsletter/RoboticsUpdate_7_2.pdf.

28. Carlo Kopp, "The Dawn of the Smart Bomb," *Air Power Australia,* http://www.ausairpower.net/WW2-PGMs.html; "Guided German Air to Ground Weapons in WW2," 1.jma, http://www.1jma.dk/articles/1jmaluftwaffegroundweapons.htm.

29. Werrell, 24.

30. Werrell, 24–25.

31. The small U.S. Navy drone community took what it was given and ran combat tests in the summer of 1944, beginning with a demonstration attack against a Japanese merchant vessel that had run aground off Cape Esperance in the Solomon Islands. Of four drones deployed against this static target, two scored direct hits and two made near misses. It was not until autumn that forty-six assault drones were used, sparingly, in actual combat, in operations from Sterling and Green Islands. Twenty-nine of the forty-six reached their targets. Japanese antiaircraft fire shot down three, mechanical failure downed nine, and television difficulties prevented five others from reaching their targets. In all, it was a success so limited that it could just as easily be interpreted as a failure, and on September 8, well before the last drone was launched on October 26, Admiral King ordered an end to the program and offered the Army Air Forces its remaining drones, control equipment, and even its program personnel. With Operation Aphrodite/Project Anvil having already run twelve disappointing missions (three of which, including that flown by Joe Kennedy Jr., resulted in fatalities), Hap Arnold politely declined the offer on October 25. See Werrell, 26–27.

32. USAAF, "Engineering Section Memorandum Report," April 25, 1939, quoted in Werrell, 26–27.

33. USAAF, April 25, 1939, quoted in Werrell, 27.

34. Werrell, 28.

35. USAAF, "Controllable Bomb, Power Driven, General Motors, Type A-1," August 24, 1943, quoted in Werrell, 28.

36. "World War II Glide Bombs," Vectors, http://www.vectorsite.net/twbomb_04.html.

37. Jack Olsen, *Aphrodite: Desperate Mission* (New York: G. P. Putnam's Sons, 1970), 26.

CHAPTER 6: FOGGED IN

1. Carl von Clausewitz, *On War,* translated by Colonel J. J. Graham (1874 London edition digitized by Project Gutenberg, 2001), Book 1, chapter 3, 62.

2. Jack Olsen, *Aphrodite: Desperate Mission* (New York: G. P. Putnam's Sons, 1970), 84–85.

3. Eike Frenzel, "Operation Pastorius: Hitler's Unfulfilled Dream of a New York in Flames," *Spiegel Online International,* September 16, 2010, http://www.spiegel.de/international/zeitgeist/operation-pastorius-hitler-s -unfulfilled-dream-of-a-new-york-in-flames-a-716753.html.

4. "Horten Ho 18 A," Luft '46, http://www.luft46.com/horten/ho18a.html; "Arado Ar E.555 series," Luft '46, http://www.luft46.com/arado/are555s .html. The Amerika-Bomber and other transatlantic weapon concepts are discussed in James P. Duffy, *Target America: Hitler's Plan to Attack the United States* (Guilford, CT: The Lyon's Press, 2006).

5. "Eugen Sänger," Luft '46, http://www.luft46.com/misc/sanger.html.

6. Steven J. Zaloga, "The Tausenfüssler supergun site," *German V-Weapon Sites 1943–45* (Oxford, UK: Osprey, 2008), Kindle edition, "The Sites at War."

7. Zaloga, "The V-3 and V-4 in Action."

8. Winston Churchill, "Forward, Till the Whole Task Is Done," broadcast by the BBC, May 13, 1945, http://www.churchill-society-london.org.uk /13May45.html.

9. Zaloga, "The V-3 and V-4 in Action."

10. Zaloga, "Design and Development"; Philip Henshall, *Hitler's Rocket Sites* (New York: St. Martin's Press, 1985), 41.

11. Zaloga, "Design and Development."

12. Zaloga, "The V-3 and V-4 in Action."

13. Zaloga, "Design and Development."

14. F. H. Hinsley, *British Intelligence in the Second World War* (London: Her Majesty's Stationery Office, 1993), 435.

15. Kit C. Carter and Robert Mueller, comps., *U.S. Army Air Forces in World War II: Combat Chronology, 1941–1945* (Washington, D.C.: Center for Air Force History, 1991), http://books.google.com/books?id=RjzLqxg6K lAC&pg=PT530#v=onepage&q&f=false.

16. "Fortress of Mimoyecques," Wikipedia, http://en.wikipedia.org/wiki /Fortress_of_Mimoyecques.

17. Eric Hammel, *Air War Europa: Chronology* (Pacifica, CA: Pacifica Military History, 2006), 204–353.

18. John Ellis, *One Day in a Very Long War* (London: Jonathan Cape, 1998), 297.

19. Ian V. Hogg, *German Secret Weapons of the Second World War* (London: Greenhill, 1999), 48.

20. Henshall, 176.

21. Raymond Victor Jones, *The Wizard War: British Scientific Intelligence, 1939–1945* (New York: Coward, McCann & Geoghegan, 1978), 463.

22. Biographical material on Fain Pool from Olsen, 27–31.

23. Olsen, 30.

24. Olsen, 36.

25. Olsen, 36.
26. Partridge's questions are discussed in Olsen, 40–41.
27. Olsen, 92.
28. Bender's efforts to answer Partridge's questions are detailed in Olsen, 38–46.
29. Olsen, 46.
30. Olsen, 48.
31. Olsen, 55.
32. Olsen, 56–57.
33. Olsen, 57.
34. Olsen, 68.
35. Olsen, 68.
36. Olsen, 68.
37. Olsen, 69–71.
38. William L. Barney, *The Oxford Encyclopedia of the Civil War* (New York: Oxford University Press, 2011), 128.
39. Olsen, 74; "Operation Aphrodite," 12 O'Clock High!, http://forum.12 oclockhigh.net/showthread.php?t=3888&page=2.
40. Hank Searls, *The Lost Prince: Young Joe, the Forgotten Kennedy* (New York: NAL, 1969), 74.
41. Olsen, 77.
42. Olsen, 82.
43. Olsen, 83.
44. Harry C. Butcher, *My Three Years with Eisenhower* (New York: Simon & Schuster, 1946), 35.
45. Olsen, 84.
46. Olsen, 85.
47. David Kirkpatrick Este Bruce, *OSS Against the Reich: The World War II Diaries of Colonel David K. E. Bruce* (Kent, Ohio: Kent State University Press, 1991), 127.
48. Olsen, 89
49. Searls, 252.
50. Searls, 252.
51. Searls, 253–254.
52. Searls, 257.
53. Olsen, 216.
54. Olsen, 216.
55. Searls, 216.
56. Searls, 256.

CHAPTER 7: THE DRONES OF AUGUST

1. Jack Olsen, *Aphrodite: Desperate Mission* (New York: G. P. Putnam's Sons, 1970), 97.
2. Steven J. Zaloga, *German V-Weapon Sites 1943–45* (Oxford, UK: Osprey, 2008), Kindle edition, "The Tausenfüssler Supergun Site."
3. Zaloga, "Design and Development."
4. Olsen, 97.
5. Olsen, 97.
6. Olsen, 97.
7. Olsen, 98.

8. Olsen, 99.
9. Olsen, 100.
10. Olsen, 100.
11. Olsen, 100.
12. Olsen, 101.
13. Olsen, 101.
14. Olsen, 102.
15. Olsen, 103.
16. Olsen, 103.
17. Olsen, 104.
18. Olsen, 105.
19. Olsen, 106.
20. Olsen, 107.
21. Olsen, 111.
22. Olsen, 113.
23. Olsen, 113.
24. Olsen, 114.
25. Olsen, 114.
26. Olsen, 114.
27. Olsen, 115.
28. Olsen, 115.
29. Olsen, 109.
30. The information on the Siracourt V-1 bunker is drawn from Zaloga, "The V-1 Waterworks."
31. Olsen, 110.
32. Olsen, 111.
33. "[A]fter service with 351st BG as *Wantta Spa,* converted to Aphrodite flying bomb and launched against V-site at Siracourt Aug 4, 1944. Control problems led to aircraft crashing in woods at Sudbourne, pilot killed when he abandoned aircraft too soon before impact," in "1942 US-AAF Serial Numbers (42-30032 to 42-39757)," https://web.archive.org /web/20090916173927/http://home.att.net/~jbaugher/1942_2.html.
34. Olsen, 109.
35. Olsen, 145.
36. Olsen, 111.
37. Olsen, 117.
38. Olscn, 117.
39. Olsen, 117.
40. Olsen, 120.
41. Olsen, 122.
42. Olsen, 122-123.
43. Olsen, 123.
44. Olsen, 123.
45. Olsen, 125.
46. Olsen, 125.
47. Olsen, 125.
48. Olsen, 131.
49. Olsen, 133–135.
50. Olsen, 139.
51. Olsen, 140.
52. Olsen, 144.

53. Olsen, 141.
54. Olsen, 141.
55. Olsen, 141.
56. Olsen, 146.
57. Olsen, 147.
58. Olsen, 147.
59. Olsen, 148.
60. Olsen, 148.
61. Olsen, 149.
62. Olsen, 149.
63. Olsen, 149.
64. Hank Searls, *The Lost Prince: Young Joe, the Forgotten Kennedy* (New York: NAL, 1969), 261.

CHAPTER 8: A BASKETFUL OF RATTLESNAKES

1. Hank Searls, *The Lost Prince: Young Joe, the Forgotten Kennedy* (New York: NAL, 1969), 261.
2. Jack Olsen, *Aphrodite: Desperate Mission* (New York: G. P. Putnam's Sons, 1970), 150.
3. Olsen, 151.
4. Olsen, 151.
5. Olsen, 151.
6. Olsen, 161.
7. Olsen, 162.
8. Olsen, 164.
9. Olsen, 165.
10. Olsen, 167.
11. Olsen, 167.
12. Olsen, 169.
13. Olsen, 169.
14. Olsen, 169.
15. Olsen, 170.
16. Olsen, 170.
17. William F. Trimble, *Wings for the Navy: A History of the Naval Aircraft Factory, 1917–1956* (Annapolis, MD: Naval Institute Press, 1990), 299.
18. Searls, 261; Olsen, 186–187.
19. Searls, 250.
20. Searls, 251.
21. Searls, 251.
22. Searls, 257.
23. Olsen, 180.
24. Olsen, 181.
25. Olsen, 182.
26. Olsen, 182.
27. Amanda Smith, ed., *Hostage to Fortune: The Letters of Joseph P. Kennedy* (New York: Viking, 2001), 598–599.
28. Searls, 270–271.
29. Searls, 278.
30. Searls, 280–281.
31. Searls, 281.

32. Searls, 283.
33. Searls, 285.
34. Searls, 284.

CHAPTER 9: "I DON'T WANT TO HAVE TO TELL HIM THE TRUTH"

1. David Nasaw, *The Patriarch: The Remarkable Life and Turbulent Times of Joseph P. Kennedy* (New York: Penguin, 2012), 571.
2. Nasaw, 571.
3. Nasaw, 571.
4. Amanda Smith, ed., *Hostage to Fortune: The Letters of Joseph P. Kennedy* (New York: Viking, 2001), ed., 615–616.
5. Smith, ed., 622.
6. Jack Olsen, *Aphrodite: Desperate Mission* (New York: G. P. Putnam's Sons, 1970), 274.
7. Samuel Elliott Morison, "Death of a Kennedy," *Look,* February 27, 1962, 105–112.
8. Hank Searls, *The Lost Prince: Young Joe, the Forgotten Kennedy* (New York: NAL, 1969), 285.
9. Searls, 285–286.
10. Earl P. Olsen's reluctance to speak with President Kennedy is noted in Olsen, unnumbered preface. For background, see "Earl P. Olsen," Obituary, *Ashland Daily Tidings,* http://www.dailytidings.com/apps/pbcs.dll /article?AID=/20110419/NEWS14/304199998/0/NEWSMAP.
11. Searls, 287.
12. Searls, 287.
13. Olsen, 241; Searls describes the *arm* and *destruct* switches as buttons protected by sealed red plastic covers. Olsen, who describes the equipment in greater detail and bases his description on several interviews, calls them toggle switches crudely "safetied" with twisted wire.
14. Searls, 287–288.
15. William F. Trimble, *Wings for the Navy: A History of the Naval Aircraft Factory, 1917–1956* (Annapolis, MD: Naval Institute Press, 1990), 301.
16. Searls, 295.
17. Trimble, 301.
18. Searls, 295–296.
19. Trimble, 302.
20. Quoted in Searls, 319–320.
21. Searls, 286.
22. Olsen, 199.
23. Donald J. Hanle, *Near Miss: The Army Air Forces' Guided Bomb Program in World War II* (Lanham, MD: Scarecrow Press, 2007), 35–37.
24. Olsen, 308.
25. Olsen, 308.
26. G. W. Sand, ed., *The Truman-Churchill Correspondence, 1945–1960* (Westport, CT: Greenwood, 2004), 22.
27. Sand, ed., 22.
28. See Kenneth P. Werrell, *The Evolution of the Cruise Missile* (Maxwell AFB, AL: Air University Press, 1985), 32–40.
29. Annie Jacobsen, *Operation Paperclip: The Secret Intelligence Program that Brought Nazi Scientists to America* (New York: Little, Brown, 2014).

INDEX

617 Squadron (RAF), 150–51

A-4 missile, 93–94
  see also V-2 missile
ACE (automatic control electronics),
    154–55, 162, 181, 190, 194, 203,
    207, 212, 215, 222, 224, 237, 264
  see also drones
Aeronca Aircraft Company, 140
African-American soldiers, 58, 177
Air Reserve Corps, 107
Alsop, Joseph, 23, 29
Amagiri (Japanese destroyer), 119–20
American Civil Liberties Union (ACLU),
    50
Amerika-Bomber Project, 146–47
Amerika-Rakete (America Rocket), 147
Anderson, Dale, 263
Anderson, John, 176, 240–45, 247–48,
    256–57
Andrecheck, Joseph, 178, 204–5, 223–24
Anschluss, 8
appeasement, 8–10, 13–18, 21–23, 28,
    31–32, 53, 63, 65, 69, 71, 84, 269
Armed Forces Radio (AFR), 172
Arnold, Bion J., 130
Arnold, Henry Harley "Hap," 108–10,
    130, 132, 139, 144, 158, 172, 217,
    219–20, 262, 266
Arvad, Inga, 117–18
Astor, Lady, 10, 84
Atlantic Monthly, 64
Austria, 8, 21
autopilot
  ACE and, 155, 162, 190, 194, 215,
    224, 237
  AZON and, 194, 229, 237
  Castor and, 265
  development of, 86, 139, 221

Franklin Yellow/Franklin White and,
    225, 227
GM and, 139
Houston and, 205, 207
La Coupole attack and, 213–15
Larynx and, 133
Mimoyecques fortress attack and, 152
Operation Aphrodite and, 160, 162,
    181, 190–91, 194
Oslo Report and, 86
PB4Y-1 and, 241, 247
Rand and, 154–55, 162
Smith, Willard and, 205, 207
Sperry and, 127, 135
V-1 missiles and, 96
AZON (azimuth only) system, 115–16,
    124–26, 141–44, 155–56, 173, 176,
    194, 196–97, 227–30, 237, 263
Azores, 146–47

B-17 bomber, 76, 116, 124, 141–43,
    152–61, 163–65, 168–69, 172, 174–
    75, 177, 182–91, 194–98, 200–4,
    206–7, 212–13, 221, 226, 230, 238,
    240–42, 244, 246, 264–66
  see also Flying Fortress
B-24 bomber, 75–76, 125–26, 172, 174,
    196, 199, 201, 206, 212, 215, 225
B-25 bomber, 108–11 170, 263
B-26 Martin Marauder, 150
Battle of Britain, 28
Battle of France, 24
Battle of Midway, 112, 138
Bauvorhaben 21 (Building Project 21),
    211
  see also La Coupole
Bay of Biscay, 75, 78
Bellamann, Henry, 178
Bender, Carroll J. "Joe," 157–59, 199

BG (bomb glider) bombs, 138, 140–41
Billings, Lem, 58, 67
Bilodeau, Tom, 60
Bolshevik Revolution, 63
Boyes, Hector, 85
Bradfield, Red, 233, 236, 239, 244–47, 256
Bryant, Louise, 63
Buck Rogers Boys, 126
Bullitt, William C., 18, 26, 62–63
Burns, John, 67, 77
Burtonwood, 116, 142, 154
Butcher, Harry C., 171

C-47, 192, 208
Calder, James, 52
Cannes, 16, 61–62, 65
Carr, C. W., 70
Carter, Boake, 7
Castor system, 228, 237, 262–69
 see also Project Castor
Catholic Church, 54, 62, 64, 80
Cavendish, William, 80, 252
CAVU (ceiling and visibility unlimited)
 conditions, explained, 163
Chamberlain, Neville, 8–23, 27, 32, 83–84
Cherwell, Lord, 90–91
Churchill, Winston, 8–9, 21–23, 25–28, 83–84, 86, 89–91, 132, 148, 166, 253, 267
Clausewitz, Carl von, 145
concentration camps, 86–87, 91, 100
Convoy, Kikoo, 38
CQ-17, 143–44
Crash-Bang farm, 80–81, 238
Crüwell, Ludwig, 88
Curtiss, Glenn, 129–30
Curtiss N-9 seaplanes, 127–28
Czechoslovakia, 8–12, 16, 21

D-Day, 78–79, 81, 100, 151, 169, 192, 234
dam busters, 150–51
Daniels, Josephus, 128
Danzig, 17–18
de Havilland Mosquito, 88–89, 182, 240, 246, 248
Demlein, John, 240, 249, 257
Donovan, William J. "Wild Bill," 25–26, 64
Doolittle, Jimmy, 103–13, 116–17, 119, 123–24, 130, 144, 170–71, 179, 182, 202, 227–29, 237, 262–63, 266
Drinker, Aimee Ernesta, 63

drones, 95, 132–33, 135–40, 170, 174, 197, 222–23, 227–31, 236–37, 241–43, 245, 247–48, 257–68
 see also ACE
Dulles, Allen, 88, 92
Duncan, Donald, 108–9

Earle, Ralph, 128–29
"earthquake" bomb
 see Tallboy bomb
Eisenhower, Dwight D., 113, 169, 171
Emmons, Delos Carleton, 69
Enterline, Philip, 152, 178–79, 181, 184–96, 200, 203–4, 206–7

Fahrney, Delmar, 135
Fairley Queen (cruise missile), 134
Falkenstine, Foster, 208, 210–13, 225
Farley, James, 68
Fisher, John, 178, 200–3, 205, 221
Fisher, Robert, 14
Fitzgerald, John Francis "Honey Fitz," 4, 36
Fleissiges Lieschen (Busy Lizzie)
 see Hochdruckpumpe
Floods of Spring (Bellamann), 178
Flying Fortress, 76, 142, 152, 155, 160, 172, 187, 240
 see also B-17
"fog of war," 145–46
Folland, H. P., 128
Ford Motor Company, 129–30
Forrest, Roy, 168–70, 172, 174, 203–4, 215–17, 219–21, 235–36, 240–41, 246, 248–49, 254–55, 260, 264–66, 267
Forrestal, James, 257
Franco, Francisco, 62, 64
Frankfurter, Felix, 50–51, 58, 61
Franklin White, 223, 225–27
Franklin Yellow, 223, 225, 227
Friedrich, Carl J., 66
Fritz X, 115, 125, 137, 141

GB (glider bomb) weapons, 140–41
General Motors (GM) Corporation, 139
George, David Lloyd, 132
Ghormley, Robert, 69
Göring, Hermann, 117, 146
Gosslau, Fritz, 95

Halifax, Lord, 8–9, 23
Hamilton, Nigel, 123
Hamilton, Tom, 257–59
Hands Off Spain Committee, 62
Hargis, Glen, 196–200, 214–15, 225–26

Hartington, Billy (Marquess of
Hartington)
see Cavendish, William
Harvard, 3–4, 13–14, 32, 36, 41–42, 45,
48–51, 54, 56–62, 65, 67–68, 154,
178, 259
Hewitt, Peter Cooper, 127–28, 130
Hitler, Adolf
annexation of European countries, 8,
16–17, 20, 71
appeasement and, 8, 10–12, 15–18,
22, 83–84
Arvad, Inga and, 117
Atlantic Wall, 151
Austria and, 8
bombing of Britain, 3, 24, 26, 28, 30,
33, 99, 153
FDR and, 6, 20–21
HDPs and, 151
Kennedy, Joseph P. and, 52–55, 63
Jews and, 13–14, 52
Poland and, 17, 20
propaganda, 53
Molotov-Ribbentrop Pact and, 65
Sudetenland and, 16–17
Tallboy bombs and, 151, 185
V-weapons and, 94–96, 99, 142, 146,
153, 171, 185, 200
HMS *Stronghold* (British destroyer), 133
HMS *Thanet* (British destroyer), 133
Hochdruckpumpe (HDP: high-pressure
pump), 147–49, 151
Hollywood, 38, 44–45, 67
Honington airbase, 142, 153–54, 160,
164
Hornet (U.S. aircraft carrier), 108–11,
170
Horton, Rip, 58–59
Houghton, Arthur, 18
Houston, Frank, 156–58, 166, 178,
204–11, 214, 216–17, 224
Huckepack Projekt (Piggyback Project),
147
Hull, Cordell, 12, 15, 20–21, 25–26, 30,
37, 85
Hunter, Seymour A. D., 118
Hussey, G. F. Jr., 260
Hyannis Port, 43–45, 54, 61, 77, 251,
259

I Could Never Be So Lucky Again
(Doolittle), 104
IBM, 113
Ickes, Harold, 10, 23
intercontinental ballistic missile (ICBM),
147

jamming signals, 183, 208, 257, 259
see also drones
Japan, 6, 30, 75, 108–12, 117, 119–20,
124, 130, 136, 138, 170, 172, 254,
262, 266, 278n31
Jews, 10, 13–14, 28, 41, 44–45, 50, 52,
54–55, 83–84
JFK: Reckless Youth (Hamilton), 123
Jones, John Clark III, 41
Jones, R.V., 85–86, 89–91
Ju 88 fighters, 78, 167–68

Kennedy, Edward (Teddy), 9, 20, 43,
47–48, 55, 64, 251–52, 254
Kennedy, Eunice, 20, 251–52
Kennedy, John F. (JFK, Jack)
appeasement policy and, 32–33
childhood/education, 9, 38–49
Germany and, 53
health, 59, 70, 72
Joe Jr. and, 38–39, 55, 59–62, 65–69,
75, 78, 82, 177, 251–52
Joe Sr. and, 13–14, 19, 31–32, 37, 83,
252
London bombings and, 20, 28
military service, 74–75, 77–78, 117–19,
121, 123, 269
personality, 58–59
Trafalgar Square speech and, 13–14
World War II and, 9, 20
Kennedy, Joseph P. Sr.
ambassadorship, 35, 53, 60–63,
65–71, 77, 80, 83–85
early career, 4
family history, 3–4
FDR and, 4–8, 10–11, 15–23, 27–29,
31, 51, 68–69
Hitler and, 52–55, 63
JFK and, 13–14, 19, 31–32, 37, 83,
252
Joe Jr.'s death and, 252–54
marriage, 4
political ties, 5
Kennedy, Kathleen (Kick), 20, 40, 80–81,
243, 252–53, 259
Kennedy, Robert F. (Bobby), 9, 20, 43,
64, 75, 269
Kennedy, Rose, 4, 19–20, 24, 36–41,
43–44, 46, 48, 55–56, 58, 65,
251–52
Kettering, Charles F., 129–30, 139
Kettering Bug, 130–32, 135, 139
Killefer, Tom, 259
King, Ernest J., 108, 138, 228–29,
278n31
King George VI, 9, 20

Kintner, Robert, 23, 29
Kirk, Alan, 69–70
Klingman, Howard, 118
Knight, Page, 232–33
Knox, Frank, 25
Kolbe, Fritz, 92
    see also Wood, George
Kramer, Max, 115

La Coupole (the Dome), 211–13
Larynx, 133–34
Laski, Harold, 50–52, 54–55, 59, 63, 66
Leamer Lawrence, 65
Lenard, Philipp, 86
Lindbergh, Charles, 26, 32, 106
Lindahl, Richard "Lindy," 265
Lindemann, Frederick, 90
Low, Archibald M., 127–28, 133
Low, Francis S., 108–9
Luce, Henry, 38, 66, 254
Lusser, Robert, 95
Lynx engine, 133
Lyon, Louis, 30
Lyon, Rosy, 237, 239–40, 248, 257–60

MI6, 85, 88–90
Manhattan Project, 262
Marshall, George C., 108
McAllister, Nilus, 55, 58
Messershmitt Me 264, 146
Messersmith, George, 62
Meyer, Hans Ferdinand, 86
Milch, Erhard, 97, 100, 200
Mimoyecques fortress, 148–52, 211, 213,
    215, 242–43, 261
Mission 515, 152, 181, 184–85, 198,
    200–1, 203, 217, 219–20, 242
    see also Operation Aphrodite
Mittelbau-Dora slave labor camp, 95, 100
Moffat, J. P., 13
Molotov, Vyacheslav, 65
Molyneux, Edward, 19, 65
Montgomery, Bernard Law, 88
Morgenthau, Henry, 5, 7, 11, 61–62
Morison, Samuel Eliot, 255
Morrison, Herbert, 172
Most, Elmer, 178, 200–1, 203
Motor Torpedo Boat Squadron Training
    Center, 74–75, 118
Mudville Heights, 79
Mussolini, Benito, 6, 10, 12–13, 51

napalm, 154, 158, 160, 163–65, 167,
    223, 226
NASA, 73

Naval Air Material Center (NAMC),
    229–30, 261
Naval Aviation Cadet Program, 69
Naval Reserve Officers Training School,
    74, 118
Newdelight Wood, 248–49, 255
Niesen, Gertrude, 59–60
Nimitz, Chester W., 138
Normandy, 97, 100, 151, 169, 172, 192,
    234
    see also D-Day
North Sea, 164, 183, 198, 226, 241, 261
Northwestern University, 74

O'Donnell, Thomas J., 124
Olsen, Earl Paul, 255–56, 260
Olsen, Jack, 160–61, 208, 254
Olympic Games, 117
On War (Clausewitz), 145
Operation Aphrodite, 100, 116, 125–26,
    130, 139, 141–42, 145, 157,
    159–60, 163–64, 168–69, 185, 193,
    220, 228–30, 233, 237, 241, 254,
    256, 263
Operation Cork, 78
Operation Crossbow, 91–92, 97, 99–100,
    150
Operation Hydra, 91
Operation Paperclip, 86, 268
Oslo Report, 85–87

P-38 fighter, 170, 182, 202, 240, 246,
    248–49
Panama, 74, 119
Parsons, Clifford, 178, 213–14
Partridge, Earle, 157–59, 179, 182, 199,
    202, 227
Patton, George, 234, 238
PB4Y-1/B-24 Liberator, 75–78, 82, 121,
    174–75, 177–78, 229–32, 235–36,
    238, 241–42, 247–48, 256–57, 261
PBM Mariner, 73–74, 76–77
Pearl Harbor, 32, 72, 108, 111, 114,119,
    136, 171
Peenemünde, 87–91, 93, 100
Plum Pudding Island, 120
Poland, 16–18, 20, 71, 83–84, 149, 172
Pomykata, Joe, 260
Ponsell, Athalia, 61
Pool, Fain, 152–53, 157, 160–63, 171,
    178–79, 181, 184–91, 194–97, 200,
    202–4, 206–7, 216
Popular Mechanics, 104–5
Portugal, 114, 147
Primacord, 186–87

Project Anvil, 92–94, 100, 141, 145, 174,
    220, 228, 230–31, 241, 254–56,
    261, 263
Project Castor, 262–69
Purdy, Robert, 56–57

radar technology, 86, 136, 140, 242,
    247–49
Radio-Controlled Aircraft Project, 135
Ramsey, D. C., 260
Rand, Jim, 103–4, 107, 112–16, 124–25,
    136, 140–44, 154–57, 162, 173–74,
    183, 190, 197, 201–3, 210–13, 216,
    221, 227–30, 237, 239, 262–63
RAZON (range and azimuth only),
    115–16, 124–25, 156
    see also AZON
RCA, 136
RDX, 178, 186
Reardon, Ted, 57
Red Cross, 80
Reed, John, 63
Reedy, Jim "Sunshine," 75–77, 232–33
Remington Rand, 113–14
Ribbentrop, Joachim von, 65
Rogers, Pleas B., 172
Rogers, Will, 62
Roosevelt, Elliott, 240, 246, 248
Roosevelt, Franklin D. (FDR)
    appeasement policy and, 15–18
    Bullitt and, 63
    Chamberlain and, 17, 19
    Churchill and, 26
    death, 253, 267
    Donovan and, 25–26
    Frankfurter and, 51
    Ickes and, 17
    Japan and, 108
    JFK and, 32
    Kennedy, Joseph Sr. and, 4–8, 10–11,
        15–23, 27–29, 31, 51, 68–69
    Marshall and, 108
    military strategy and, 25, 108–9
    Morgenthau and, 11
    New Deal, 51
    neutrality and, 11, 16, 24, 32
    political opponents, 31, 68
    Republican Party and, 31
    Selective Service and Training Act, 68
Roth, Leon Henri, 89
Ruhrstahl AG SD-1400X, 115, 137
    see also Fritz X
Ruston Proctor AT biplane, 128, 133

Salazar, António de Oliveira, 147

Sandys, Duncan, 87, 90
Santayana, George, 178
Schotterwerk Nordwest (Northwest
    Gravel Works), 211
    see also La Coupole
Secret Intelligence Service (SIS), 85
Sherman, William Tecumseh, 84, 168
Siemens Research Laboratory, 86
Silver Queen (plane), 159
Simon, Sir John, 14
Simpson, Jim, 175–78, 236–38, 242,
    244–46, 260
Singer, Allen Grant, 87
Siracourt V-1 bunker, 200–1, 204, 211
    see also Wasserwerk St. Pol
Smith, James A., 230, 232, 234–35, 240,
    244, 248–49, 256–60
Smith, Willard, 158, 178, 204–7
snowbirds, 156
Soden, Mark, 79–80
Sollars, John, 223, 225, 227
Sonnemann, Emmy, 117
Soucek, Victor, H., 229–31
Spaatz, Carl "Tooey," 119, 144, 155, 159,
    166, 172, 220, 262, 266
"spade flush," (code word), 176, 247
Spalding, Charles, 67
Spanish Civil War, 62, 65, 123
Sperry, Elmer A., 127–30, 135
Squadron VP-110, 77, 232
Squadron VP-203, 74
Squier, George O., 129, 131
St. Aidan's Church, 41
St. John, George, 46
St. Margaret (village), 255
St. Moritz, 63–64
St. Paul's Cathedral, 2–3
Stabilizing Automatic Bomb Sight, 151
    see also ACE; drones
Stagg, James, 169
Stalin, Joseph, 65
Stellungsysteme, 97, 200
sterilization law, 53
Steventon, Donald Wilfred, 86–87
Stimson, Henry, 50, 262
Strong, George Veazey, 69
Sudetenland, 8, 11, 16–17
Swanson, Gloria, 4, 44

T4, 178, 186
Taft, William Howard, 50
Tallboy bomb, 150–51, 185, 198, 211,
    265
"taxisoldier" (code word), 181, 194, 196,
    201, 207–8, 214, 224

Taylor, George, 58
Taylor, Megan, 63
television technology, 114–15, 135–36,
    143, 156, 173–74, 197, 201,
    228–30, 242, 263, 278n31
Temple, Harry B., 229
Test Stand 7, 87–88
They Were Expendable (film), 119
Thoma, Wilhelm Josef Ritter von, 87–88,
    90
Tiger Moth (plane), 134
Timilty, Joseph, 77
Tooman, Wilfred Ferguson, 189–90, 194,
    196–200, 202, 214–15, 221, 225–26
torpedo-carrying drone (TG-2), 137
Torpex, 150, 164, 175–76, 178, 221,
    223–24, 230–33, 236, 238, 242,
    246, 257–61
Towers, John H., 138
Trafalgar Day speech (Kennedy), 12–13
Treaty of Versailles, 8
Trimble, William F., 260
Truman, Harry, 7, 254, 267

Udet, Ernst, 114
underground mortars, giant, 149–50
unmanned flight
    see ACE; drones
U.S. Army Air Forces (USAAF), 123,
    140–41, 158–59, 168, 172, 175,
    202, 217, 223, 228–29, 233
U.S. Office of Strategic Services (OSS), 88

V-1 missile, 33, 81, 86, 89, 92, 95–101,
    136, 140, 144–45, 153, 176, 200–1,
    215, 230, 232, 249, 261, 268
V-2 missile, 33, 86–89, 91–101, 140,
    145–47, 150, 171–72, 184–85, 211,
    261–62, 268
V-3 missile, 146–48, 151, 211, 242, 261
VB (vertical bomb) weapons, 141, 232
Vega, 139
Verbunkerung technique, 201

Vergeltungswaffen (V weapons), 33, 86
    see also V-1 missile; V-2 missile; V-3
    missile
video technology
    see television technology
Vilan, Dee, 178, 232–34, 236, 239, 244,
    246–47, 256
von Braun, Wernher, 86, 94
von Richthofen, Manfred (Red Baron),
    114
Votey, S. F., 129

Wallis, Barnes, 150
    see also dambusters
Wasserwerk St. Pol (St. Pol Waterworks),
    200
Watten, 89, 100, 152, 184–85, 197,
    200–1, 211, 223
Wayne, John, 119
Wehrmacht, 89, 92
Welles, Sumner, 17, 29
Western Front, 83, 127
White, Tom, 13
White, William L., 119
Why England Slept (Kennedy), 32, 66
Wiese (German military site), 148
Wild, Payton S., 59
Willis, C. H., 129–30
Willy, Wilford John "Bud," 176, 230–32,
    234, 236–38, 240–41, 243–44,
    246–48, 256–58, 261, 269
Wilson, Patricia, 80–82
Wilson, Woodrow, 50, 63
Wizernes, 100, 185, 211, 213
Women's Land Army, 194
Wood, George, 92
    see also Kolbe, Fritz
Woodbridge, 164–68, 170, 191
Wright brothers 129–30

Yale University, 50, 63, 69
Yalta Conference, 267
Yeomans, Henry A., 66